CHANGIN
POLICY IN

Planning, Adminis
and the Environment

Edited by Nigel Curry and Stephen Owen

CHANGING RURAL POLICY IN BRITAIN

Planning, Administration, Agriculture and the Environment

Edited by Nigel Curry and Stephen Owen

CCP

The Countryside &
Community Press

CCP
The Countryside &
Community Press

The Publishing Imprint of the
Countryside and Community Research Unit
Cheltenham and Gloucester College of Higher Education
Francis Close Hall, Swindon Road
Cheltenham, Glos., GL50 4AZ

Telephone: (01242) 543553

ISBN 0951942794

British Library Cataloging in Publication Data

A CIP catalogue record for this book is available from the British Library.

Countryside and Community Press publications are available from the above address.

Produced by the Design Unit, Cheltenham and Gloucester College of Higher Education, printed in Great Britain by WJL Print.

CONTENTS

	Page
Acknowledgements	vii
Contributors	iv

1. Introduction: Changing Rural Policy in Britain,
   Nigel Curry and Stephen Owen ... 1

Planning

2. The Potential for Landscape Ecological Planning in Britain, *Paul Selman* ... 28

3. New Housing Development and Local Planning Policy in Pressurised
   Rural Areas: The Case of South Lakeland, *Gywndaf Williams* ... 44

4. Rethinking Village Planning and Design: Articulating the Connections
   between Social, Economic and Design Issues in Village Planning,
   Stephen Owen ... 69

Administration

5. Rural Land Use in Britain: Agency Re-Structuring and Policy
   Adaptation, *Alexander Mather* ... 87

6. Rural Training & Enterprise Councils - Local People Influencing Local
   Decisions? *Trevor Hart* ... 107

7. Conservation, Amenity and Recreation Trusts: A Private - Public
   Continuum, *Ian Hodge* ... 127

8. Farmers, Planners and Councillors: An Insider's View of Their
   Interaction, *Andrew Gilg and Mike Kelly* ... 145

Agriculture and the Environment

9. Environmental Reform of the CAP: An Analysis of the Short and Long
   Range Opportunities, *Clive Potter* ... 165

10. Farm Diversification and the Environment, *Bill Slee* ... 184

11. Environment Friendly Farming in South West England: An
Exploration and Analysis, *Martin Battershill and Andrew Gilg*   200

12. Understanding Farmers' Perceptions of Changing Agriculture: Some
Implications for Agri-environmental Schemes, *Helen McHenry*   225

13. Farmers' Attitudes to Woodland Planting Grants and the Potential
Effects of New Forestry Incentives, *Tim Lloyd , Charles Watkins
and Daniel Williams*   244

14. Environmentally Sensitive Areas and the Conservation of the Built
Environment in England and Wales, *Peter Gaskell and Michael Tanner*   262

ACKNOWLEDGEMENTS

We thank members of the Rural Economy and Society Study Group for their support in the development of this volume, and the Economic and Social Research Council for its financial support of the Study Group. In particular, we wish to thank the contributors to this volume for their efforts in providing the results of their research.

CONTRIBUTORS

Martin Battershill was a postgraduate student at the University of Exeter between 1991 and 1995. He was funded by the ESRC and was awarded his PhD in 1995. He is to continue his work on environmentally friendly farming by carrying out a comparative study in France.

Nigel Curry is Professor of Countryside Planning and Head of the Countryside and Community Research Unit at the Cheltenham and Gloucester College of Higher Education. His recent books include *Countryside Recreation, Access and Land Use Planning* (Chapman Hall), published in 1994.

Peter Gaskell is Research Fellow in the Countryside and Community Research Unit at the Cheltenham and Gloucester College of Higher Education. His particular research interests lie in rural landscape change.

Andrew Gilg is Senior Lecturer in Geography at the University of Exeter and has written widely on rural planning issues, most recently in *Countryside Planning Policies for the 1990s* (CAB International). He is as at present working on a totally new edition of the book *Countryside Planning* first published in 1978.

Trevor Hart is Senior Lecturer at Leeds School of the Environment at Leeds Metropolitan University. Prior to teaching he worked in consultancy and was involved in rural planning and economic development as a practitioner.

Ian Hodge is Gilbey Lecturer in the Department of Land Economy, University of Cambridge. He has previously lectured at the Universities of Queensland and Newcastle Upon Tyne.

Mike Kelly is a Chartered Town Planner with several years experience in forward planning and development control. Initially qualified as a geographer he has recently completed his Ph.D. thesis at the University of Exeter. The research examined the implementation of planning policy. His academic and professional interests reflect a continuing concern with the policy implementation process.

Tim Lloyd is Lecturer in Economics at the University of Nottingham. He specialises in the economic and econometric modelling of agricultural land values, commodity prices and farm woodland.

Helen McHenry has just completed her Ph.D. thesis at Aberdeen University. In this she examined the background to farmers' reactions to agri-environmental policies. She is now doing a short research project in Germany comparing German interpretations of conservation with those in Scotland.

Alexander Mather is Professor of Geography in the University of Aberdeen. His academic interests centre on rural land use and environmental resources, both within Britain (and especially Scotland) and at the global scale. Publications include *Land Use* (Longman, 1986), *Global Forest Resources* (Belhaven, 1990) and *Environmental Resources* (with K Chapman; Longman, 1995).

Stephen Owen is Dean of the Faculty of Environment and Leisure at the Cheltenham and Gloucester College of Higher Education, and Honorary Professor of Planning at the University of Pècs, Hungary. Recent books include *Planning Settlements Naturally* (Packard Publishing, 1991).

Clive Potter is Lecturer in Environmental Management at Wye College, University of London. He has written widely on the reform of agricultural and conservation policy. He published the *Diversion of Land: Conservation in a Period of Farming Contraction* (Routledge) in 1991.

Paul Selman is Professor of Environmental Planning in the Countryside and Community Research Unit at the Cheltenham and Gloucester College of Higher Education. He published *Environmental Planning: the Conservation and Development of Biophysical Resources* (Paul Chapman Publishing) in 1992.

Bill Slee is Senior Lecturer in Rural Economics at the University of Aberdeen. His main research interests include diversification of farms and the rural economy, agri-environmental policy and rural tourism. He published the second edition of *Alternative Farm Enterprises* (the Farming Press) in 1989.

Michael Tanner is Lecturer in Geography at the University of Birmingham. His research interests include the impact of agricultural policy on environmental management, and recreation and amenity aspects of water planning and management.

Charles Watkins is Lecturer in Geography at the University of Nottingham. He specialises in rural and cultural geography. His books include *Woodland Management and Conservation* (David and Charles, 1990) and the *Ecological Effects of Afforestation* (CAB International, 1993).

Daniel Williams is Research Assistant in the Urban and Community Forestry Group at the University of Central England at Birmingham.

Gwyndaf Williams, is Senior Lecturer in the Department of Planning and Landscape, Manchester University. His main focus of teaching is concerned with urban development and management, housing policy, and local economic development. He has recently completed research for the Department of the Environment on rural affordable housing issues.

CHAPTER 1

Introduction: Changing Rural Policy in Britain
Nigel Curry and Stephen Owen

 F ew books on rural policy, planning and development claim that their time is anything other than the period of unprecedented change in rural areas. The mid-1990s is no exception. Given that much of this change is driven by national and European policies, many policy reforms for rural areas, instigated from the early 1990s, are now susceptible to evaluation. This book, a collection of edited papers originally presented at the Rural Economy and Society Study Group Annual Conference in Cheltenham in September 1994, provides a number of such evaluations, not only of policies *per se*, but also of the processes through which they operate and the institutions that steer them.

The tradition of planning for rural areas in Britain has been that of two distinct planning systems. From the Scott and Barlow Reports onwards, the control of development and the maintenance and enhancement of the environment have been entrusted to a town and country planning system operating through mechanisms of statutory development plans and development control. Partly as a response to the view of Scott and Barlow that the exploitation of the resources of the countryside, food and timber, was of paramount importance to post war reconstruction, a 'no development ethic' in the countryside emerged which has remained largely unchallenged ever since. In reinforcing and implementing this culture of no development, the town and country planning system has evolved with a narrowly-focused role in the countryside. As a result, its important, and broader, objectives of both maintaining and enhancing the environment in rural areas have not been fully embraced.

Exceptions to this have been a series of 'planning' conservation designations (see figure 1.1 below). The principal power of the town and country planning system has been to resist development in these designated areas. But the principal environmental damage to these areas has not been development *per se* but rather agriculture and forestry operations that have been largely exempted from development control. Even within these 'planning' designations, a planning system different from the statutory planning system has had a significant role to play.

Scott and Barlow proposed and imposed an almost entirely distinct and dominant system of planning for rural areas: resource planning. With food and timber expansion the imperative, they proposed that agriculture and forestry should remain largely unfettered by the *controls* of a town and country planning system but, instead, should be planned with recourse to much more powerful economic *incentives*. This power was manifest not only in the success of increasing food and timber outputs dramatically, but also in power in the political arena. The rural, and particularly farming, vote became linked with resource sector financial support and such support became extremely difficult to dismantle once the imperatives for food and timber expansion became at first less urgent and, subsequently, a European wide problem.

Perhaps most importantly for the mid-1990s, the resource planning sector in post-war reconstruction, unlike town and country planning, had no brief for environmental considerations. Where agriculture and forestry interests interfered with 'planning' conservation designations, the town and country planning system could not refuse development, as it could for all other sectors, but simply had to be *notified* of farm and forestry operations, at which point the principles of the resource planning sector came into play. Farmers and foresters could be offered *financial* compensations for desisting from potentially damaging operations in these areas.

Planning for rural areas in much of the last 50 years, therefore, has been characterised by the town and country planning system with responsibility for the environment having a largely ineffectual role in rural areas other than resisting development, and the dominant resource planning system in rural areas having no long-standing environmental objectives. This situation remained unaltered until the mid 1980s.

Two enduring consequences have followed from this. The first is that an *environmental* crisis in the countryside was bound to ensue. The second is that the 'no development ethic' in the countryside has concentrated economic activity in rural areas into the agriculture and forestry sectors, providing a precariously narrow economic base in the countryside. Once such a base falls into economic decline, as it has done for agriculture and forestry since the mid-1980s, then the whole of the rural economy suffers, with concomitant impacts on the infrastructure of those areas from housing to transport, from services to a sense of community.

It is perhaps easier to see the impacts of such decline where it is concentrated. Few would dispute the devastating impacts of the decline in coal mining amongst those communities that were dependent upon that single sector. Dennison, in his minority report to Scott, used this example of the folly of creating dependence on single sector economies, vehemently to disagree with the prevailing Scott view of single sector agricultural autonomy in post war reconstruction. But for rural areas as a whole, the dominance in the economy of a now declining agriculture and, in places, forestry is having a similar but more widespread impact to the more concentrated decline in coal mining. Discouraging a broader economic base for rural areas and failing to stimulate economic development have led to a *human* crisis in rural areas.

It could be contended that both the environmental and the human crises in the countryside can be attributed in large part not just to misdirected polices *per se*, but to the maintenance of two distinct and unrelated planning systems. The town and country planning system has been successful in not allowing development in the countryside and the resource planning sector has been able to procure more food than we need.

Bringing the policy objectives of these two planning systems into a common focus is an imperative, and some might hold a sense of optimism in this regard with the production of the rural White Paper as a joint venture between the Ministry of Agriculture, Fisheries and Food and the Department of the Environment, the sponsoring bodies of the two planning systems. At the time of writing, the White Paper is still at consultation stage and so the means by which, or indeed the extent to which, the objectives and processes of the two planning systems might be more fully integrated is awaited with interest. Some suggestions are offered in this regard, later in this chapter.

Policies for the Rural Environment under Two Planning Systems

An obvious means of overcoming the environmental crisis in the countryside and securing environmental objectives for agriculture and forestry is to empower further the planning system that was conceived as having responsibility for the environment. But is the extension of full planning controls over agriculture and forestry a realistic proposition? Recent agricultural policy reforms would suggest not. Rather than empowering the town and country planning system with environmental *controls* over agriculture and forestry, both European and domestic agricultural policies have adopted their own environmental objectives for rural areas. This is no surprise given the inherent political tendency for any department of government to seek to protect and enhance its power base, but inevitably it leads to confusion rather than consolidation over roles and responsibilities in policy making: a confusion commonly starkly displayed by many on whom the policies impact (Curry, 1995).

Most important is that many such policies continue to use the traditional *mechanisms* of policy implementation within agriculture and forestry: financial *incentives*. In some instances, therefore, these sectors can actually be *paid* to pursue environmental goals, particularly in the contexts of nature and landscape conservation, whilst all other sectors, through the town and country planning system, are *constrained* to pursue them through the statutory provisions of development plans and development control. Importantly, too, environmental policy mechanisms in agriculture are invariably voluntary, and for all other sectors, compulsory.

The principal impetus for the adoption of environmental concerns in agriculture and forestry planning came with the Agriculture Act 1986, which either introduced, or laid the foundation for, a number of 'agri-environment' measures. These have been consolidated since this time, given renewed impetus in the wake of the McSharry reforms to the Common Agricultural Policy in 1992, and they provide the principal focus for the third part of this volume. The salient among these measures are presented in figure 1.1 below, and are set alongside a number of the more long-standing conservation

Figure 1.1 -Environmental Controls and Incentives for the Countryside Under Two Planning Systems

Resource Planning	Town and Country Planning
Environmentally Sensitive Areas	Tree Preservation Orders (1947)
Nitrate Sensitive Areas	National Parks (1949)
Nitrate Vulnerable Zones	Areas of Outstanding Natural Beauty (1949)
Setaside and Setaside Topup	National Nature Reserves (1949)
Countryside Stewardship Scheme	Sites of Special Scientific Interest (1949)
Countryside Premium Scheme	Management Agreements (1949)
Habitat Improvement Scheme	Purchasing and Leasing (1949)
Wildlife Enhancement Scheme	Local Nature Reserves (1949)
Moorland Scheme	Green Belts (1951)
Organic Aid Scheme	Limestone Pavement Orders (1981)
Hedgerow Improvement Scheme	Nature Conservation Orders (1981)
Farm and Conservation Grant Scheme	Marine Nature Reserves (1981)
FC Woodland Grant Scheme	Areas of Special Protection for Birds (1981)
Farm Woodland Scheme	
Tir Caymen (Wales only)	

1947 Town and Country Planning Act
1949 National Parks and Access to the Countryside Act
1951 Town and Country Planning Act
1981 Wildlife and Countryside Act.

measures and designations that have been traditionally within the remit of the town and country planning system.

Even in the development of these measures, there has been some inter-agency reshuffling. The development of the Countryside Stewardship Scheme, for example, was undertaken within the Department of the Environment, through the Countryside Commission. Now that the more risky experimental phase has passed, and the Scheme has been widely perceived as being successful in its own terms, it is being transferred to the Ministry of Agriculture.

These controls are not exhaustive of the influence of environmental policy in rural areas, particularly over agriculture. Indeed, regulations outside the direct control of either town and country planning or resource planning are having an increasingly important role to play. A wide range of measures has grown up in respect of pollution control: slurry, silage effluent, dirty water systems, sheep dips, artificial fertilisers, pesticides, sewage sludge, fuel oil and so on. These measures are both regulatory, through environmental health and more general pollution control legislation, and advisory, for example through the Ministry of Agriculture's Codes of Good Agricultural Practice, under the general banner 'environment matters' (MAFF, 1991, 1992, 1993). The conservation of resources in the food production process, too, has exercised the minds of government (Curry, 1994).

In addition, broader European and global environmental imperatives have impacted on rural areas. The Ramsar Convention on the conservation of wetlands of international importance in 1971, the Bern Convention on the conservation of European wildlife and natural habitats in 1979, the EC Wild Birds Directive, also of 1979, the Council of Europe programme for the conservation of heathlands and dry grasslands in 1983 and the 1991 EC Directive on the conservation of natural and semi-natural habitats, which introduced the new designation Special Areas of Conservation (SACs), for example, all have been adopted in Britain. But importantly in the context of the two planning systems, they are now manifest entirely through the designation or redesignation of either Sites of Special Scientific Interest or National Nature Reserves, regulatory mechanisms that are the traditional preserve of the town and country planning system. Clearly, even with an emerging common environmental concern, the two planning systems are operating in a less than fully orchestrated way.

Agricultural Policy Reforms

Despite this increasing interest in issues relating to the environment on the part of the resource planning sector , the 1992 McSharry Reforms to the Common Agricultural Policy contained wide-ranging proposals of which agri-environment measures were only a small part. They currently account for only 2% of the CAP budget. Introduced in response to increasing political pressures for change arising from significant food overproduction throughout the European Union, and the overall costs of the CAP, these overall reforms had three principal elements (Lowe and Murdoch, 1994). First, there was to be a general reduction in the prices guaranteed to farmers for individual products.

Second, there was to be compensation paid to farmers to protect them against price reductions. These compensatory payments were now no longer to be tied to agricultural output, but rather to factors of production such as land area or units of livestock. All but the smallest *crop producers* would be required to enter into Setaside agreements in order to receive increasing levels of compensation payments as support prices fell under the Arable Area Payments Scheme.

For *livestock producers*, compensation was to be paid against numbers of livestock (with a maximum per hectare allowed), through a variety of premium schemes. For the *milk sector*, quotas were to be retained but reduced by 1% in the years 1994/95 and 1995/96.

As a third element in the McSharry reforms, there were to be a series of other measures: for early retirement, to allow farms to restructure in a more profitable way (which has not been adopted in Britain); for the encouragement of the growth of timber and amenity woodland on farms; and for more extensive and environmentally friendly farming methods.

Much has been written about these reforms, in terms of their measures, their economic consequences and their environmental effects (see, for example, The Country Landowners' Association [1994], Marshall and Miller [1995], Harvey [1994], Dalton [1993], Saunders [1994] and Winter *et al* [1995]) but it is appropriate here to note some of their principal emerging consequences.

Perhaps inevitably, one of the aspects of the McSharry reforms that has excited greatest interest, is the compensation payments now payable to farmers, not for food production *per se*, but more squarely in relation to their capital stock. However transitional these payments are intended to be, there will always be the concern that, politically, they will be too difficult to remove. Price support measures were seen as long ago as 1958, in the Treaty of Rome, to be short term measures, in place only long enough to allow structural adjustments to agriculture to take place through the Guidance fund. Once the structure of agriculture was rendered efficient, it was argued at that time, the short term protection of price support (Guarantee) payments could be done away with. Compensation payments have an ominously parallel purpose - to allow short term protection for an industry moving towards, this time, world food prices. The longevity and unacceptable cost of price supports, must remain a concern also, now, for compensation payments.

Further, CAP budgetary studies have suggested that the McSharry reforms, far from reducing the cost of the CAP, are likely to cost even more than the pre-reform measures, principally as a result of compensation payments. Copus and Thompson (1993) have estimated that the reforms are likely to increase EU agricultural expenditure by approximately 30% in the United Kingdom, from around £1.4 billion, to £1.9 billion. Direct subsidies to farmers (including compensation payments) are likely to increase from 45% to more than 80% of the CAP budget, and it may prove more difficult to defend such a level of direct income aids, particularly to the public, than more 'hidden' price support. Worse still, there is no clear evidence that a reduction in price support is leading to any significant reduction in food outputs (Lowe and Murdoch, 1994).

Further, for Britain, increasing incomes to farmers from compensation payments have been accentuated by the consequences of 'Black Wednesday'. Both the pound and the green pound were devalued against the ECU providing significant windfall gains for farmers as the value of sterling declined. By the dismantling of the green money system in 1993, many British farmers were enjoying the highest real incomes yet recorded, compensation payments more than offsetting any reduction in price supports.

It is still to be seen what the longer term consequences of the CAP reforms will be. But as one central plank to the operation of resource planning in Britain, the current situation in the transition of CAP does highlight a number of vulnerabilities in a non-mandatory planning system based on the delivery of economic incentives (of whatever type); it remains very expensive, it is difficult to police, and it is exceedingly difficult to understand in operational terms. In the context of the reforms attempting to reduce the overall budgetary costs of the CAP and significantly reduce food surpluses, it also appears to be failing to meet its objectives. And where such large levels of expenditure are involved, it is difficult to divorce a 'rational' approach to planning, from the inevitable process of political horse trading.

Reforms to the resource planning system, therefore, appear still to be preoccupied with the economic cost and productive output of agriculture. Except for a number of agri-environment measures there seems to be little evidence of a planning system moving towards concerns with the environment and the development of the *rural* economy more widely. But have recent developments in the town and country planning system moved any more closely towards the stimulation and development of rural economies and the enhancement of the environment of the countryside?

Changes in the Town and Country Planning System

Despite the blaze of attention afforded agricultural policy reforms, the town and country planning system also has been undergoing an, albeit quieter, revolution in the 1990s. The 1980s was an era of planning deregulation, from Circular 22/80 (Department of the Environment, 1980) which moved the whole of the planning system away from plan-led decision-making to one of negotiation between planner and developer, to the 1989 White Paper *The Future of Development Plans* (Department of the Environment, 1989) which considered the abolition of structure plans altogether.

The quiet revolution has lain in the rekindling of a plan-led planning system. The 1990 Town and Country Planning Act, and Planning Policy Guidance Note *Regional Policy Guidance, Structure Plans and the Content of Development Plans* (Department of the Environment 1990a) reprieved structure plans as the principal plank of strategic planning at the county level, and the 1991 Planning and Compensation Act strengthened their powers. Planning decisions must now accord with structure plans unless material considerations dictate otherwise.

For rural areas in particular, though, it has been the requirement that district and national park authorities, under the 1991 Act, produce district-wide local plans, that is providing for the first time, a comprehensive development plan for all rural areas. The tradition of designating much of rural area 'white land' has now been firmly buried.

Thus, at the county and district levels, a plan-led planning system in the countryside has been reasserted for strategic planning and has, effectively, been introduced for the first time for much of the countryside at the local plan level. But central government, too, has given focused attention to development in the countryside through Planning Policy Guidance Note 7, *The Countryside and the Rural Economy* (Department of the Environment, 1992). Originally introduced in 1988, as *Rural Enterprise and Development*, PPG 7 now seeks to procure a balance between conservation and development, rather than no development at all in the countryside, by allowing a greater degree of flexibility to be exercised within settlements in undesignated areas. Concomitantly, the PPG seeks to see tighter controls in designated areas.

The extent to which the principles of PPG 7 are being implemented within the development plan system currently is being researched. Results of work by Land Use Consultants who are reviewing permitted development rights in agriculture and the use of redundant farm buildings, and Oxford Brookes University's review of the rural development aspects of PPG7, are still awaited at the time of writing. But this work will certainly provide the opportunity to further revisions to PPG 7, possibly in the wake of the publication of the rural White Paper.

Research commissioned by the Rural Development Commission (Rural Development Commission, 1993a), however, does give some indication of how the development plan system is responding to the principle of dismantling the 'no development ethic' contained in PPG 7, although a number of plans considered in the research predated the 1990 and 1991 Acts. Development plans rarely make explicit the objectives of PPG 7, and do not cover topics such as farm diversification, rural services, community facilities and transport issues well. Whilst there is generally a positive approach to small firms in rural areas, policies for the re-use of rural buildings generally are poorly developed. Overall, the picture from this research is one of great variability in the way in which development in rural areas is considered, with some plans being over zealous in the use of even local designations as a means of restricting development, but others having quite liberal policies for development within village and small town boundaries.

This diversity of attitudes extends beyond just development plans. Lord Shuttleworth, Chairman of the Rural Development Commission, reported in Planning (23 September 1994, p.6), suggests that:

"thanks to the nature of modern industries and modern communications particularly telecommunications, the prospects for generating new jobs in the countryside are excellent. However, it is my fear that the planning system will succumb to Nimbyism and block the necessary development".

The Council for the Protection of England (1995) holds the contrary view:

"The planning system is not restricting economic development and diversification in rural areas. The countryside - and business itself - needs the protection of the planning system now more than ever".

Despite this variable picture in attitudes towards the success of the town and country planning system in facilitating development in the countryside, the Rural Development Commission (1993b) provides some impressive figures for rural economic growth. There has been a 20% growth in manufacturing in rural areas since the 1960s compared to a decline in urban areas. Unemployment rates in 1989 were 33% below the English average in the 'accessible' countryside and 12% below in 'remote rural areas'. Employment growth in rural areas during the 1980s exceeded that in urban areas. But, of course, these figures can be interpreted in a number of different ways.

Given the enduring 'no development ethic' in the countryside since World War II, all *percentage* growth figures are from a very low base and are therefore not necessarily representative of any significant growth in absolute terms. Further, low unemployment rates in rural areas are as likely, if not more likely, to be due to the rural unemployed leaving rural areas in search of work in urban areas (and thus distorting urban unemployment statistics) as to the availability of any specifically rural job opportunities.

A central aspect of all of the current discussion of a diversifying rural economy, and the role that the town and country planning system might or might not be playing in bringing this about, is the quality not just of the natural environment, but of the *built* environment in rural areas. There is still an underlying assumption in both PPG7 and in development plans, that built development in some way detracts from the quality of the rural environment. The central tenet of PPG7, a balance between conservation and development, suggests that these two characteristics are in some way opposed, but this is a false dichotomy (Owen, 1994). Development needs to take place in order that rural settlements can be sustained socially and economically, but creative thought needs to be given to the notion of development actually *enhancing* rather than detracting from the rural environment.

The Countryside Commission (1993, 1994) has paid particular attention to this issue, but the fact that much development that has taken place in rural areas since World War II has had an undeniably urban or suburban form has provided an understandable apprehension on the part of many for further development of this type in the countryside. The requirement that development in rural areas should be well-designed and sympathetic needs to be further exploited through town and country planning.

If resource planning, then, is still grappling with issues of budgetary cost and food overproduction, any move on the part of the town and country planning system to dismantle the 'no development' ethic is a matter of controversy and hot debate. Certainly by the mid-1990s there is little evidence of the two planning systems reaching any significant common ground. Their continued separation cannot be divorced from the emergence of a new phenomenon in policy and planning for the countryside in the 1990s: the growth in informal planning.

The Growth in Informal Planning in the Countryside

Countryside strategies, rural development strategies, economic development strategies, nature conservation strategies and so on have burgeoned during the 1990s. Some would say they have had a degree of success, at least in part, in overcoming a shortfall in responses to rural needs from the two formal planning systems. These strategies have a number of antecedents. The Countryside Commission (Stansfield, 1990) sees their origins lying in a proposal of the Countryside Policy Review Panel (1987) which recommended that "each county council should prepare a rural/countryside strategy for its area embracing economic and social development objectives, environmental and recreational objectives and policies for the use of rural land". But the Local Government and Housing Act 1989 also provides a general power for all local authorities to promote the economic development of their area. Under this Act, there is a duty for all local authorities intending to undertake economic activities to produce a strategy document setting out proposals. These are to be non-statutory documents (Rural Development Commission, 1993a).

Others, however, see these informal strategies as part of a more general trend in the production of non-statutory strategic statements. In Hampshire, for example, the strategy was conceived in 1987 (Hazel and Savage, 1990) as a natural successor to the county's Countryside Heritage Policy, produced in 1984, as a means of arresting further destruction of woodland areas through agricultural use. In fact, the pace of agricultural change generally has been cited by planning officers as the most common spur to the initiation of a strategy (Stansfield, 1990).

The Rural Development Commission (1991) also sees these informal strategies as a natural evolution from Tourism Development Action Programme (TDAPs) and Rural Development Programmes (RDPs) which they have initiated as a requirement for grant bids specifically for Rural Development Areas (RDAs) since 1984. Countryside strategies provide a counterpart for co-ordinated and integrated development in non-RDA rural areas. In addition, English Nature (1991) sees the environmental White Paper

(Department of the Environment, 1990b) and its call for the implementation of the principles and practices of sustainable development, as a principal spur to their growth. It is, for example, this White Paper that provides the trigger to the West Sussex Nature Conservation Strategy (West Sussex County Council, 1991).

Specifically for nature conservation, the Department of the Environment Circular *Nature Conservation* (27/87) endorses the development of countryside strategies as a supplement to structure planning. It considers that useful measures to conserve nature include "the preparation of local nature conservation strategies as an aid to integrating conservation into the authority's forward planning".

Strategies also may have developed for less positive reasons. Their growth cannot be disassociated from the threatened abolition of structure plans in the White Paper, *The Future of Development Plans* (Department of the Environment, 1989). The possible loss of such a planning function at the county level provided an significant stimulus to the development of a non-statutory surrogate, and the reprieve of structure plans has done little to weaken this impetus.

The popularity of strategies also might reflect the requirement prior to the 1991 Planning and Compensation Act for central government approval of structure plans and their ineffectual role in relation to much rural activity, particularly agriculture and forestry, which many strategies are now attempting to embrace. Undoubtedly, strategies can be produced much more quickly and with less bureaucracy than structure plans.

The Countryside Policy Review Panel's (1987) proposal suggested that strategies should be produced only after the issue of Department of the Environment advice. This has not been forthcoming, a reflection, perhaps, of central government's view of their real importance. A great variability in both the process and the product associated with countryside strategies has arisen as a result and such strategies remain essentially uncoordinated. Partly in response to this, a guidance document has been produced by the Countryside Commission, English Nature and the Rural Development Commission jointly (1992), since all agree that a co-ordinated local approach is the best way of tackling competing countryside demands. It became available, however, only after over 40 identifiable strategies had been produced (Curry, 1992).

Perhaps, then, the resistance to adapting the two planning systems in the countryside has done much to spawn a diverse and independent informal planning sector that, although not statutorily accountable, is working very much at the interface between planning and agriculture, where the two existing planning systems are at their weakest.

Reconciling the Processes of the Two Planning Systems

Just as town and country planning and resource planning *policies* have an uneasy relationship in respect of the rural environment, the two kinds of planning also diverge significantly in their respective *processes*. There is worth in considering the relative merits of their processes to see if, by selecting or even synthesising the more effective characteristics of each, they have particular merit for guiding rural change.

Town and country planning, for example, is based on strong development planning (structure and local plans) within a clear *strategic framework* extending up to 10 or 15 years into the future. Resource planning, on the other hand, works to a less clear strategic planning framework (with the possible exception of forestry planting) being more strongly committed to annual price negotiations and annual compensation payment levels. Whilst the resource planning sector in many respects has to operate within annual planning cycles, a clearer vision of the development of rural resources over a longer planning horizon might be a characteristic of town and country planning that usefully could be adopted and adapted.

Town and country planning can, to a degree, deal with *local distinctiveness*, since its operation occurs at county, district and even parish level, where local variations are capable of being taken into account. Resource planning is dominated by national and European imperatives, that take regional variation into account only by virtue of the predominance of different farming systems in different types of rural area. As agriculture becomes more driven by environmental imperatives, local distinctiveness will take on a greater significance in the implementation of policy. Interestingly, in recognition of the need to embrace regional differentiation in forestry planning, the Forestry Commission has sanctioned the production of Indicative Forestry Strategies at the county level, and has charged county councils with this task. They are to be informal, non-statutory plans. Will indicative agriculture strategies follow, and who will be charged with their production? Already, a number of county councils have addressed local agricultural issues through their informal countryside strategies.

Public accountability is another of the hallmarks of town and country planning, that is not apparent to the same degree in resource planning. Development plans are subject to full public consultation, and development control decisions are made by publicly elected representatives. To what extent could resource planning become more publicly accountable? Certainly, as agriculture becomes more centrally concerned with environmental imperatives, and support for farmers is more dominantly through direct transfer payments, there will be increased pressure for a greater public say in the disposal of such resources.

Town and country planning, however, has *no direct powers to bring forward development*. Its powers might be construed as being negative to the extent that development control decisions can refuse development, but cannot ensure that the right development (relative to the development plan) comes forward in the right place at the right time. Resource planning, in contrast, has the direct power to influence change, and has therefore powers for positive action. This power would seem to be desirable in any deliberate process of intervention to steer change.

The town and country planning process is, to a large degree, a statutory process that has *mandatory regulatory powers*. Resource planning operates through many powers, certainly outside price support, that are discretionary and voluntary. The ability to exercise powers more fully than just in response to voluntary uptake might also be considered important in any process of steering rural change. Indeed, agricultural policy is now developing more fully the 'middle ground' in planning policy control, through the development of *cross-compliance* (Parrison, Hanley and Spash, 1994).

Such a policy approach combines both incentives and controls to achieve an appropriate balance in the pursuit of policy objectives (you *may* receive Arable Area Payments but to do this you *must* set a proportion of your land aside from agricultural use). Indeed cross-compliance is finding favour, albeit with some reservations, within town and country planning, through the rationalisation of the use of planning obligations under the 1991 Planning and Compensation Act (you *may* receive planning permission, but you *must* agree to provide some community benefit in return). It would seem that any planning process that can combine *controls* to resist undesirable developments (or ensure desirable ones) together with *incentives* to bring forward desirable developments, has advantages over processes that are restricted to the use of only one of these types of mechanism.

There are differences, too, between these two planning systems, in terms of the direct impacts of the *costs and gains* of policy (indirect effects are more diffuse). The principal costs and gains of development resulting from town and country planning decisions, outside administrative costs, fall largely to the developer. In resource planning, the expensive costs of policy fall largely on the consumer and taxpayer, and whilst many of the gains might accrue initially to the farmer, they are to a large degree passed on to the agricultural support industries (Hill *et al*, 1988) and lost from the rural economy altogether. In the development of any new elements in planning for rural areas, the gainers and losers as a result of policy decisions must be overtly considered in policy objectives.

Finally, town and country planning has at its core, the *maintenance and improvement of the environment.* Certainly this, as this chapter has shown, is of increasing concern to resource planning, but still commands only a minority interest in the weight of policy mechanisms and resources within agriculture and forestry. Until such an objective becomes pervasive in both planning systems, the duality of planning for, and in, the countryside will never be more fully integrated.

Thus, in refashioning policies for the development and environmental quality of rural Britain there not only needs to be a concordance of rural *policies,* but a greater sympathy in policy *processes* between the two planning systems. It is hoped that the rural White Paper addresses innovations in policy *mechanisms* as a means of reducing the cleavage between resource planning and town and country planning in the countryside, as well as promoting more concordant policy objectives and intentions.

The Structure of the Book

The book is divided into three parts: planning issues in the countryside; the administration of rural affairs; and agriculture and the environment. In the first part of the book, concerned with planning issues, the chapter by *Paul Selman* notes some of the limitations of the traditional 'planning' conservation designations for conserving a broader rural ecology. Not least, these designations fail to tackle adequately ecological deterioration from agriculture and forestry. They also pay scant regard to the ecological value of the wider countryside and are protective rather than positive in approach. Ironically, a number of recent developments in rural policy may well act as a catalyst to the development of a more broadly based 'landscape ecological' approach to countryside conservation: declining agricultural fortunes provide an opportunity for a policy rethink about conservation of the wider countryside in terms of the 'rural estate', and informal conservation strategies provide a means of doing this.

In charting the roles that both natural and social scientists play in developing landscape ecological principles, Selman cautions against the over-dominance of natural science principles. Social science has a significant role to play through land use planning and, particularly, informal planning in asserting human values to countryside landscapes.

Gwyndaf Williams' chapter, in examining new housing development in South Lakeland, pinpoints some of the strengths and weaknesses of the town and country planning system in meeting local, rural development needs. To begin with, the 'no development ethic' has exacerbated housing problems in rural areas, particularly within traditional conservation designations. Restrictions in supply have forced up house prices beyond the reach of low income local people. Further, in the celebrated case of the Lake District in the 1980s government ruled that town and country planning was not empowered to deal with 'local needs' on the grounds that this planning system was essentially concerned with the *use* of land rather than the *user*.

Williams charts some of the initiatives that have taken place since the 1980s in South Lakeland to overcome some of the inherent impediments that town and country planning unwittingly places in the way of providing rural affordable housing. 'Exceptions' initiatives in planning policies have been successful in providing a limited number of homes for local people, but have done little to meet the needs of low income families. The chapter highlights the limitations of a planning system that, of itself, has no direct powers to bring land forward for development.

The social, economic and environmental impoverishment of villages as a result of the 'no development ethic' is a key theme of *Stephen Owen's* chapter. The failure of the planning system to ensure well-designed development has reinforced resistance to new buildings in the countryside. Experience over the past 50 years, where development has taken place, has shown poor design standards, often reflecting the transfer of inappropriate building forms from suburban settings .

New development in the countryside is essential for stimulating social and economic well-being, but many development plans, even at the district level, are not sufficiently fine-grained to accommodate the local distinctiveness of individual settlements. District-wide design guidance can encourage indifferent design in villages and, like restraint policies, can add to rural development problems rather than assist in resolving them. Town and country planning should be more interventionist in securing good quality design, for example, through Countryside Design Summaries and Village Design Statements, and should encourage local diversity at the smallest scale.

In the second part of the book, concerned with the administration of rural affairs, the chapter by *Alexander Mather* focuses on one characteristic of the development of two discrete planning systems for the countryside since the Second War. Not only were their remit and objectives different, but their organisational structures were at significant variance in a number of respects. Resource planning has been characterised by a number of independent sectoral agencies organised horizontally with little publicly available strategic planning, and certainly no mechanism for public participation. Town and country planning, on the other hand, has a more comprehensive framework, implemented through a vertical structure from government ministry through tiered local authorities to the parish.

Mather's paper provides a critical evaluation of the inherent limitations of the way in which aspects of resource planning have been organised and administered since World War II, and embraces recent organisational changes in both conservation and forestry. He covers issues of public accountability and sectoralism as well as the lack of sensitivity of monolithic national agencies to local geographical variation. The lack of sectoral integration in resource planning tends to lead to policy incompatibilities and does not effectively promote sustainability as a policy objective. Recent restructuring in the Forestry Commission and the creation of Scottish Natural Heritage have done little to ameliorate this situation.

The chapter by *Trevor Hart* provides an assessment of another layer of planning for rural areas that sits to a large degree outside either town and country planning or resource planning. Evaluation of the role of Training and Enterprise Councils (TECs) in training and employment creation in rural areas demonstrates a number of limitations in both planning sectors. The 'urban' ethos of TECs, and their requirement to follow nationally laid down objectives (particularly in relation to various performance indicators), makes them insensitive to the rural context in many instances. Even where specific initiatives are introduced for rural areas, they are often seen as little more than appeasement.

The impact of TECs on agriculture, an industry undergoing significant structural change and for which training and other forms of reskilling might be considered significant, appears to be slight. Clearly, their public profile in support of rural areas, at least relative to more traditional bodies such as ATB Landbase, needs to be improved. But also, part of the limitations of TECs' incursions into the countryside could well be attributed to the fragmented and underdeveloped economic base of rural areas.

The chapter by *Ian Hodge* evaluates conservation, amenity and recreation trusts. The evaluation shows that the way that they operate allows them to be identified as behaving more like private sector organisations in some instances, or the public sector in others. At times they can exhibit characteristics and objectives that are not to be found in the mechanisms of either the public or private sectors and yet have considerable value. These include, for example, the ability to think and act very long term and to act as an intermediary between market operation and state intervention.

Such trusts also exemplify some of the characteristics of the growth in 'informal' planning. Their objectives, ultimately, may be self serving rather than serving wider notions of the public interest. They also may be inefficient in duplicating roles and even in being in competition with each other. They run the risk of being essentially unaccountable, certainly to the wider public, where a small caucus of active members often can pursue their own interests in the context of a passive wider membership. Above all, in direct parallel with the growth in informal planning, there is no broad co-ordination or orchestration of these bodies, and their sum may remain less than the number of their individual parts.

The chapter by *Mike Kelly* and *Andrew Gilg*, focuses on one of those areas where the conventional remit of town and country planning in the countryside has been relinquished, to a large degree, in favour of a greater degree of agricultural autonomy. In the construction of agricultural workers' dwellings in rural areas most of the controls that would normally have to be met in a planning application for a new dwelling in the countryside do not have to apply. Despite this, such dwellings require approval by the appropriate planning committee, being subject to the condition of agricultural occupancy.

Their chapter provides an account of how applications for agricultural dwellings are considered by planning officers and committees and shows, through a case study in Devon, how decisions are not made along party political lines, but rather, how councillors with farming backgrounds exert undue influence on the decision-making process. The political influence of the farming community in rural development decisions, in this case study at least, still far exceeds their representation in the population, even the rural population, as a whole.

In the first chapter in the third section of the book, *Clive Potter* traces the evolution of environmental policy responses in agriculture from the mid-1980s. Although there were pressures for environmental incorporation in agricultural policy from this time, they only really gained institutional acceptance at the European level with the McSharry reforms of 1992. Potter attributes their adoption not only to the growing acceptance of an environmentally damaging agriculture but of a resource planning sector failing to meet its objectives. This was due, essentially, to the use of the wrong policy processes and instruments in seeking to achieve these objectives.

A commitment to the environment by the farming lobby is seen as a way of redirecting farm support away from compensation payments (paying farmers just because they are farmers) which are considered politically less defensible in the longer term. At least in the short term, agri-environment measures have become part of the policy framework for institutional resource planning. In the medium term, cross-compliance will have an important role to play in getting farmers used to being paid as environmental custodians, but in the longer term, the only satisfactory solution to securing environmental quality in the countryside is to decouple environmental payments from food production support altogether and make them part of a European *rural* policy framework rather than just an agricultural one.

Bill Slee's chapter explores a number of relationships between farm diversification and the environment. He notes that many authors, and particularly amenity societies, view both on- and off-farm diversification with suspicion in terms of its environmental impact, yet provides a number of examples where diversification can have positive environmental impacts. Such impacts are due not only to the diversification activities themselves (for example the agri-environmental schemes that are widely considered in this volume) but also due to farmers' attitudes. In questioning earlier research that posits that farmers invariably seek to diversify as a means of maintaining or enhancing income or capital value, he notes an increasing tendency for farms to be considered consumption units where their environmental and leisure values are of prime concern. In this context, the environment is commonly an objective of diversification.

Slee's chapter reinforces a theme developed earlier in this chapter. Much farm diversification still takes place outside full town and country planning controls. Indeed, as Slee himself notes, the principal initial spur to diversification in Britain, the ALURE package of 1986, actually slackened a number of procedures relating to development control on farmland. If diversification is to be compatible with environmental objectives, there is a strong case for them to be more fully embraced within the town and country planning system.

The chapter by *Martin Battershill* and *Andrew Gilg* explores the attitudes and motivations of farmers who actively participate in agri-environment schemes. In surveying farmers in these schemes in Devon, Cornwall and West Somerset, they explore the relative influences of geographical, attitudinal, socio-economic and farm system factors on the nature of their farming activity, and compare the findings with a fairly substantial literature on farm decision-making in relation to the environment. Whilst concluding that traditional farming methods are most likely to sustain conservation and environmental values, they note that most farmers' participation in schemes is not because of their inherent conservation aspirations *per se*, but rather, because of the funding that is offered to otherwise economically marginal farming practices.

This provides some indicators for the development of rural policy. Firstly, it would appear that imposing regulatory measures rather than incentives in pursuit of environmental objectives in marginal areas may well render a number of currently economically marginal farmers unviable. It also suggests, as the authors propose, that there is a need to reskill farmers in the importance of conservation and environmental objectives to promote their adoption in whole farm planning.

Helen McHenry's chapter, which explores farmers' perceptions of agricultural policy changes in the southern Scottish uplands, illustrates a number of important issues in rural land use change. Intervention by the State, in the shape of new rural policy measures, will always be tempered by those with the land holding interest. This interest in turn will be influenced by the culture and attitudes of, in this case, farmers and such a culture, to a large degree, will determine the success of policy. Farmers will seek to negotiate their position in relation to these policy measures, tending naturally towards a position that requires minimum change. Policies are likely to be most successful where they are perceived by farmers to require them to do more or less the same things, but in slightly different ways.

The chapter also illustrates two significant obstacles to the implementation of rural policy. The first is that farmers' perceptions of 'conservation' are likely to be very different from those of conservationists. Leaving the responsibility for the implementation of conservation or environmental polices to farmers may lead therefore to significantly different outcomes than were originally intended by policy makers. Secondly, the importance of the voluntary nature of policies is well illustrated. As long as there is no compulsion to join schemes such as ESAs, their uptake will always remain patchy and their overall intended effect less than complete

The chapter by *Charles Watkins, David Williams and Tim Lloyd,* provides a review and evaluation of another strand of policy that potentially impacts upon the environmental effects of agricultural practice, farm woodland and forestry planting. They review recent policy developments in this area, as part of the accompanying measures in the McSharry reforms, and summarise the current grant aid available to farmers under a number of different schemes. They then report on a survey in Nottinghamshire of farmers' uptake of, and attitudes towards, a variety of these schemes. In line with other researchers, they are able to report a generally negative attitude on the part of farmers to woodland planting, in part because of the long time horizon for woodland investment and the likely change to agricultural policy during such a period.

Significantly, too, farmers feel that the grant aid available for woodland planting is not sufficient to enter into schemes because of the relative return on other agricultural products brought about by market management and inflated prices. This again provides a good example of the lack of orchestration of different types of planning for the countryside: inflated agricultural prices inhibit environmental objectives (such as amenity tree planting) by rendering them less financially attractive than they would have been in a free market for food products. Both agricultural production and tree planting, because they are planned or directed by economic incentives, will be relatively successful by virtue of the relative levels of support offered to them. The success of either will be the result of a bidding process for public support in which the most lucrative is adopted by farmers, rather than as the result of integrated polices where multiple policy objectives might allow a balance to be achieved between these two competing land uses.

The final chapter by *Peter Gaskell* and *Mike Tanner* explores the most long-standing of the recent resource planning agri-environment measures, Environmentally Sensitive Areas (ESAs). They examine an issue that is clearly at the interface between resource planning and town and country planning: the conservation of the rural built environment. Whilst ESA policy has clear objectives for the protection of buildings in the conserved countryside, Gaskell and Tanner contend that the resource planning sector, with no tradition for buildings conservation, is particularly weak at fulfilling this part of its environmental objectives.

Difficulties in defining types of buildings and their condition have inhibited this conservation process, but difficulties also arise because many buildings are not actually owned by farmers in ESAs and, enduringly, these ESA schemes are voluntary. Farmers may simply choose not to embrace traditional farm buildings within such schemes. Revision, monitoring and a relaunch of ESAs in 1993 has led to some slight improvements in the conservation of the built environment, particularly with the introduction of conservation plans, but these cover only certain types of building and are not even compulsory for farmers who have opted to join ESA schemes. Ultimately, conclude Gaskell and Tanner, ESAs are still preoccupied with components of the landscape and these are principally elements of the natural rather than the built environment.

References

CAP Review Group (1995) *European Agriculture, the Case for Radical Reform*, Ministry of Agriculture, Fisheries and Food, London.

Copus A K and Thompson K (1993) The Budgetary Effects of the CAP reforms in the UK, in *Progress in Rural Policy and Planning*, Gilg A, Dilley R S, Furusseth O, Lowe P, McDonald G and Murdoch J, (Eds), Volume 3, Wiley International, Chichester.

Council for the Protection of Rural England (1995) *Taking Stock: Why Planning is Good for the Countryside*, CPRE, London, June.

Country Landowners' Association (1994) *Focus on the CAP*, a CLA discussion paper, the Association, London, September.

Countryside Commission (1993) *Design in the Countryside*, Technical Report 418, Countryside Commission, Cheltenham.

Countryside Commission (1994) *Design in the Countryside Experiments*, Countryside Commission, Cheltenham.

Countryside Commission, English Nature and the Rural Development Commission (1992), *Advice on Rural Strategies*, available from all three organisations.

Countryside Policy Review Panel (1987) *New Opportunities for the Countryside*, CCP 244, Cheltenham, the Countryside Commission.

Curry N R (1992) Nature Conservation, Countryside Strategies and Strategic Planning, *Journal of Environmental Planning and Management*, 35, 79-91.

Curry N R (1994) *Environmental Skills in Agriculture*, Final Research Report to ATB Landbase, ATB Landbase, Kenilworth, Warwickshire, September.

Curry N R (1995) *The Environmental Content of Landbased Skills Acquisition: A Response to Industry Needs?* Final Research Report to ATB Landbase, ATB Landbase, Kenilworth, Warwickshire.

Dalton G (1993) *CAP Reform: Its Impact on Scottish Farming*, Discussion Document, Scottish Agricultural College, Edinburgh, March.

Department of the Environment (1980) *Development Control - Policy and Practice*, Circular 22/80, London, HMSO.

Department of the Environment (1989) *The Future of Development Plans* Cmnd 569, London, HMSO.

Department of the Environment (1990a) Planning Policy Guidance Note 15 *Regional Policy Guidance, Structure Plans and the Content of Development Plans*, London, HMSO.

Department of the Environment (1990b) *This Common Inheritance*, White Paper, Cmnd 1200, London, HMSO.

Department of the Environment (1992) Planning Policy Guidance Note 7, *The Countryside and the Rural Economy*, London, HMSO.

English Nature (1991) *Rural Strategies*, internal memorandum, January, Peterborough, EN.

Harvey D (1994) *GATT, the CAP Reforms and the Future of British Agriculture*, University of Newcastle Upon Tyne, the Agricultural Society.

Hazel V and Savage R (1990) A Rural Development Strategy for Hampshire, *Journal of the Royal Agricultural Society for England*, 151, 66-77.

Hill B, Yung N and Brookes G (1989) *Alternative Support Systems for Rural Areas*, Wye College, University of London, Ashford, Kent.

Lowe P and Murdoch J (1994) *Introduction to Section III: Europe*, in Progress in Rural Policy and Planning, Gilg A, Dilley R S, Furusseth O, Lowe P, McDonald G and Murdoch J (Eds) Volume 4, Wiley International, Chichester.

Marshall B J and Miller F A (Eds) (1995), *Priorities for a New Century - Agriculture, Food and Rural Policies in the European Union*, Centre for Agricultural Strategy, University of Reading, CAS paper 31.

Ministry of Agriculture, Fisheries and Food and the Welsh Office Agriculture Department (1991) *Code of Good Agricultural Practice for the Protection of Water*, MAFF, London.

Ministry of Agriculture, Fisheries and Food and the Welsh Office Agriculture Department (1992) *Code of Good Agricultural Practice for the Protection of Air*, MAFF, London.

Ministry of Agriculture, Fisheries and Food and the Welsh Office Agriculture Department (1993) *Code of Good Agricultural Practice for the Protection of Soil*, MAFF, London.

Owen, S (1994) Fresh perspectives for village planning, *Town and Country Planning*, 63, 132-133.

Parsisson D, Hanley N and Spash C L (1994) *Cross Compliance of Agricultural and Environmental Policies*, Discussion Paper in Ecological Economics, Nitrate Pollution due to Agriculture, Project Report Number 2, Environmental Economics Research Group, Department of Economics, University of Stirling

Rural Development Commission (1991) *Rural Development Strategies*, internal memorandum, London, RDC.

Rural Development Commission (1993a) *Rural Development and Statutory Planning*, RDC Research Report number 15, Rural Development Commission, London

Rural Development Commission (1993b) *the Economy of Rural England*, RDC Strategy Review, Topic Paper number 4, Rural Development Commission, London.

Saunders C (1994) *Agricultural Policy: an Update*, Centre for Rural Economy, Department of Agricultural Economics and Food Marketing, University of Newcastle Upon Tyne, Working Paper 6.

Stansfield K (1990) Going for Green, *Public Service and Local Government*, 20, No 3, 32.

West Sussex County Council (1991) *A Nature Conservation Strategy for West Sussex*, County Planning Department.

Winter M, Gaskell P, Orme E and Short C (1995) *the Effects of the CAP reform on the British Countryside*, desk study number 1, the CAP and the Countryside Research Project, Countryside and Community Research Unit, Cheltenham.

CHAPTER 2

The Potential for Landscape Ecological Planning in Britain
Paul Selman

Britain has a long and, in many respects, exemplary track record in nature conservation. Despite the well-known limitations of statutory protection of critical countryside, there have been signal achievements in respect of science, site management and species recovery. Some of the conventional wisdom regarding species and site safeguard is, however, coming under challenge. First, international pressures (e.g. the European 'Habitats Directive') have forced a re-examination of the role of domestic sites in terms of their place within a wider geographical network, raising issues of their completeness, management and security of protection. Second, the continued loss of semi-natural habitat in undesignated areas has left some fragments of critical countryside dangerously isolated, turning attention to the importance of the 'wider countryside'. Third, agricultural surpluses have forced the consideration of alternative uses, or altered intensities of use, of large areas of land, thereby creating opportunities for re-shaping landscapes. Fourth, whereas landscape tastes tend to be conservative, and in particular have shown excessive deference to the 'Georgian' countryside, there is now a growing propensity to think in terms of landscape 'potential' rather than solely the inherited types of land cover. Fifth, there has been a recent rapprochement of nature and landscape conservation agencies, which had been divided (since the 1949 National Parks and Access to the Countryside Act) by an increasingly artificial and irrelevant boundary. The creation of Scottish Natural Heritage and the Countryside Council for Wales was echoed in late 1994 by a policy commitment to closer working arrangements between the Countryside Commission and English Nature.

These changes signal not so much a revolution in rural land use policy and planning as a context in which to give greater emphasis to the wider countryside, and to create conscious visions about landscapes of the future. Substantial change of this nature needs to be underpinned by reliable theory and implemented through a workable planning method, in contrast to the opportunistic and episodic approaches which have underpinned many, very worthy, localised countryside management schemes. The author has advocated landscape ecology as an appropriate theoretical basis; this may be defined as:

"the study of the spatial relationships and functional interactions between the component patches of an extensive and heterogeneous land area, and how these bring about changes of structure and function in the ecological mosaic over time".

(Selman, 1993; citing Forman and Godron, 1986 and Naveh and Lieberman, 1984).

The significance of the terms used in this definition will soon become apparent, but it is important to note the centrality of the notion of *scale* to landscape ecology, both temporal and spatial. The emphasis on diverse and extensive tracts of land, and the ways they change over time, should be a diagnostic hallmark of landscape ecological studies. Equally, landscape ecology explicitly recognises human intervention, including land use planning, treating it as a driving variable rather than an inconvenient complication. It is encouraging to note some initiatives in British land use planning which implicitly or explicitly draw on landscape ecological principles.

The Problem

The issues of habitat loss and fragmentation in countries with advanced agricultural economies have been extensively described. A key feature is the reduction in the extent of critical semi-natural vegetation, and the consequently smaller sized and more isolated remnant patches. This diminishes their viability as areas in which ecosystem processes (of birth, death, immigration and emigration) can be sustained:

"Human activity is not only reducing the size and number of remaining natural areas but also causing habitat fragmentation, which results in configurations, or arrangements, of these areas that are poorly suited to maintaining ecological function" (Smith, 1993).

The major causes of this attrition have been identified as agricultural intensification, afforestation, road building and urban development.

The consequences of rapid and broadly unsympathetic change in the wider countryside are serious for conservation strategies which rely predominantly on site specific approaches. In the British context:

"Since 1949, the main thrust of policies and programmes has been to protect an adequate amount of good quality habitat to ensure core areas for the survival of healthy populations of the native plants and animals....The view was that if the habitat was protected the species would look after themselves. In recent years it has been recognised that additional measures are required to ensure that as wide a range of species as possible survive throughout their natural range. In this connection the fragmentation and subsequent gradual reduction in size of certain habitats...is a major concern" (HMG, 1994, p64).

This response at the national level has been stimulated by statements arising from the Rio Conference on Environment and Development (UNCED, 1992), at which it was agreed that *in situ* conservation would partly rely on our ability to:

- regulate or manage biological resources important for the conservation of biological diversity whether within or outside protected areas, with a view to ensuring their conservation and sustainable use;

- promote environmentally sound and sustainable developm in areas adjacent to protected areas with a view to furthering protection of theseareas;

- rehabilitate and restore degraded ecosystems...through the development and implementation of plans or other management strategies;

- preserve and maintain knowledge, innovations and practices of indigenous and local communities enabling traditional lifestyles relevant for the conservation and sustainable use of biological diversity.

(extracts from sections a, e, f and j of Article 8 of the Biodiversity Convention; see Grubb *et al*, 1993).

There appears to be a high level of consensus that a sizeable part of the problem confronting conservation strategies is the absence of effective countryside protection measures in the wider countryside. Going beyond this, it may be conjectured that, in addition to wider safeguards, it is also essential to have a vision of the ways in which critical countryside might strategically be consolidated and reinforced.

The Opportunity

A hallmark of landscape ecology, then, is its concern to address issues of scale in the wider countryside. Scale is important in a *temporal* sense for, in the words of an American landscape ecologist:

"...recognition of the inherent tendency for change in nature transforms the perception of the landscape as a static pastoral entity into a more accurate recognition of the landscape's constant dynamism. The elements of a landscape are constantly cycling between immaturity and maturity because of natural and human disturbance as well as accumulated...stress" (Thorne, 1993).

By contrast, countryside management projects have too frequently treated sites on a one-off basis, lacking time-depth. Equally, *spatial* scale is important, as we need to understand the influence of landscape structure on populations and communities of species, and on the fluxes of nutrients and pollutants within the wider environment. Landscape ecology enables us to do this, as its scale of resolution is always at least "several kilometres wide" (Noss, 1983; Forman and Godron, 1986).

Large-scale thinking about purposive landscape change has rarely been possible in Britain, especially under conditions of prosperity and commercial investment in the basic rural enterprises of agriculture and forestry. However, the changing economic fortunes and policies of farming and forestry, especially in the context of GATT and CAP reform, have created conditions in which visions about landscape futures are both possible and necessary. Changes in the intensity or purpose of land management will inevitably lead to changes in land cover, and in some instances these may, fortuitously, have positive consequences. However, they may also lead to degraded and nondescript landscapes with little environmental or community benefit. Conservation policies thus need to include elements which are ambitious in terms of their spatial and temporal scales, and which couple practical conservation tasks with visions about the appearance and functions of the future countryside. Combined with this are wider environmental perturbations, such as climatic changes, whether natural or induced, and possible sea level rises: biotic movements likely to follow on from these will be severely hampered in areas where habitat is highly fragmented.

The possibilities of planning within these more strategic temporal and spatial scales are already starting to emerge. First, new policies, underpinned by public financial support, have been introduced. These include environmental conservation on farms, in respect of habitat features, nitrates and former set-aside land, and new multi-purpose forests (the 'National' Forest and community forests and woodlands). These are spatially extensive, if perhaps less impressive in terms of their impact on agricultural over-production: for instance, Environmentally Sensitive Areas (ESAs) covered, in 1993, 831,000ha in England (with a further 318, 000ha planned), 359,000ha in Wales, 1.4m ha in Scotland, and 131,000ha in Northern Ireland (with 117,000ha planned). Second, new planning mechanisms are being developed which enable the broader scale to be considered, and these are outlined later. Their problems of implementation, and over-reliance on voluntary participation, are well-known, but this should not deny their measurable achievements in practice. Comparable environmental projects have succeeded in other parts of the world - greenways in the USA (Little, 1990) or the 'green heart' system of the Dutch Randstadt (Harms and Opdam, 1990) for instance.

Indeed, it could be argued that approaches to landscape ecological design in the wider countryside are comparable to the designs of the great estates of the past couple of hundred years. The country estate had a landscape *gestalt*, in which the unifying visual and ecological features were greater than the sum total of the tenanted parts. The increase in owner occupation of farm units has unwittingly led to the unifying matrix of this countryside being fragmented: however socially desirable the dissolution of landed estates may be, some consequences are undesirable ecologically and aesthetically. The opportunity may now exist to re-capture a new 'rural estate', albeit one which is founded on more ethically acceptable and publicly accountable principles. The features of the 'traditional' estate and modern, 'landscape ecological' estate have some remarkable resonances, and are summarised in figure 2.1

Figure 2.1 Elements of the 'traditional' and 'landscape ecological' estate

'traditional' estate	'landscape ecological' estate
agricultural improvement	sustainable agriculture
visual satisfaction	regional 'imaging' of landscape
game cover	biodiversity
drainage/ willow planting	surface/groundwater hydrology
timber production	farm/community woodlands

The Science

The science underlying landscape ecology has been summarised by various authors, and this is not the place to rehearse the technical arguments (see, for instance, Selman, 1993; Thorne, 1993; Haines-Young *et al*, 1994a). Suffice to say that it is both controversial - in terms of its limited empirical base and validity as a coherent sub-discipline - and yet increasingly accepted, especially in Europe, as a conceptual and practical planning framework. In order to explore its applicability in the British countryside, it is useful to review some of the main avenues of scientific enquiry.

One key aspect of landscape ecology is its concern for the degree to which landscape elements are effectively connected or, conversely, isolated (Spellerberg and Gaywood, 1993). Thus, the overall structure of a landscape may vary in terms of its connectedness (physical completeness of linear features, such as hedgerows, and the number of ways in which they join habitat remnants) and connectivity (functional usage of connecting corridors, or even of apparently unconnected landscapes, by mobile species). Whilst many studies have produced alternative measures to reflect these properties, based on topological analysis, only a few have demonstrated convincingly that species actually use corridors for essential life-cycle functions. Some of these functions are negative, for example where corridors become death traps (the case of the northern spotted owl, Noss, 1993). As yet, no general rules exist for predicting the effects of changes in physical connectedness on the survival strategies of animal or plant communities. Nevertheless, many assumptions are made about the importance of linear features in landscapes, especially where critical semi-natural habitats have become geographically isolated - assumptions which are treated by some as a precautionary fail-safe principle, and by others as mythology.

Another key area of research has been that of the behaviour of populations of particular species in the wider landscape. Whereas population ecology has tended to focus on local communities, landscape ecology has focused on the 'metapopulation', that is, the cluster of sub-populations inhabiting geographically distinct patches, but which interact via processes of birth, immigration, death and emigration (BIDE). Given the complexity of studying metapopulation dynamics in the field, most studies have considered single species, and are thus of limited predictive use because they ignore the potential effects of competition with other species. In the future, therefore, multi-species approaches will be required. Similarly, many, especially American, studies are moving away from strategies designed to cater for named species (e.g. Ahern, 1991), towards those which consider 'guilds' of different species occupying similar niches and which have overlapping or complementary survival interests (e.g. Verner, 1984; Hellmund, 1993). Population studies must consider not only numbers, but also genetic variability, as species may otherwise lose the ability to evolve and adapt to changing ambient conditions.

Further research attention has focused on the characteristics and dynamics of habitat patches. These may vary in respect of size (larger is better?), shape (rounder is better, with elongated habitats being vulnerable to the external influences of a 'peninsula effect'?), and internal structure (complexity and multiple vertical layers are better?). Although a near-circular patch shape is often deemed desirable, crenulations around the perimeter will tend to favour 'ecotone' species, and several studies have considered the fractal dimension of landscape components, inasmuch as this approximates to a particular organism's perception of the risks and opportunities associated with a habitat boundary. Patches are defined by their demarcation within a matrix of more or less hostile 'managed' landscape; however, species will, to varying extents, be able to negotiate the spaces in between their favoured habitat patches, even in, or perhaps regardless of, the absence of connecting corridors. This will depend on the porosity - presence of 'stepping stone' patches - or permeability - moderate conduciveness, even though unable to sustain all life-cycle functions - of the matrix. Various studies also have attempted to quantify these properties. Thus, whilst traditional ecological research has tended to focus on process, there is a growing recognition of the need for a more pattern-based approach, given the importance of spatial and temporal patterns in influencing the distribution and behaviour of organisms.

Movement across the matrix or along corridors requires further research, but clearly the landscape pattern will influence spatial processes in a complex manner. Spellerberg and Gaywood (1993) note that critical influences on dispersal include the proximity of the colonisation source, presence of suitable niches for colonisation, and continuity of habitat. Some evidence exists for the diffusion of species along canals, roads and railways.

A further environmental topic which has interested landscape ecologists is that of hydrology, especially the ways in which watercourses and aquifers form both a natural organising principle for the subdivision of physical environments, and contribute to the spatial flux of energy and nutrients. Rivers have sometimes been chosen as the principal feature of greenway systems, partly taking advantage of the relative freedom from development pressures in corridors subject to risk of flooding. Binford and Buchenau (1993) note that the ecological benefits of riparian communities include their moist and fertile soils, well-developed and complex vegetation structure, and inherent dynamism. They consider that particular attention should be paid to chemical status, energy, temperature, and the capacity of riparian systems to stabilise and buffer fluxes in energy and nutrients. Overall, landscape ecological plans should have regard to:

- groundwater flow systems;
- parts of a groundwater flow system on either side of the groundwater catchment boundary;
- infiltration and related exfiltration zones;
- surface water catchment areas of different orders;
- parts of the surface water catchments of either side of a stream;
- upstream and downstream areas in surface water catchments (van Buuren, 1991).

A final main area of scientific enquiry has been that of informatics. In particular, the data capturing and processing powers of remote sensing and geographic information systems have enabled us to perceive large-scale landscape pattern and change in hitherto unimagined ways (Haines-Young et al, 1994b). The methods of land classification and land cover analysis which have emerged from the Institute of Terrestrial Ecology have also facilitated the more rapid and objective sampling and analysis of land use changes. The Countryside Information System, deriving from these advances, now assists in making targeted enquiries about environmental patterns and processes. These all contribute to the possibility of a landscape ecological perception of the countryside, and furnish wider frameworks within which more locally specific planning strategies can take place.

The Social Science

Whilst the substance and practical value of landscape ecology remains controversial with many scientists, it is nevertheless evident that the relevant scientific literature is burgeoning. By contrast, the contribution of social scientists is very limited. This is serious, as people inhabit, enjoy and manage landscapes, and any conservation strategy which ignores the human component is fundamentally flawed. In site-based ecological management, reserves could be controlled and managed directly by trained conservationists. In area-wide strategies, the responsibility must pass to lay custodians, and conservation actions must be compatible with the wider purposes of a landscape's 'insider' and 'outsider' communities. There are several contributions which social scientists should begin to make to landscape ecological planning.

First, they are in an excellent position to contribute to our understanding of cultural landscapes. Landscape ecology is especially relevant where environments are mosaic and heterogeneous; this chiefly arises where they have been altered by long periods of farm and woodland husbandry. The varied appearances of long-settled countries are produced by a blend of both natural and human ecology, and their retention requires the maintenance of an intricate balance of distinctive local conditions. It is abundantly clear that landscapes which have survived intact for centuries are now in imminent danger of disintegration, and with them the rich biodiversity brought about by low-intensity cultural management. There is an urgent need to record, understand and, in certain cases, protect or re-create cultural landscapes.

A second key area entails assisting policy-makers to target expenditure and action on the most worthwhile sites. Countryside policy has moved sharply away from a 'grapeshot' approach, to one of selectivity based on measurable indicators. Even agricultural expenditure, which has traditionally been based largely on equal access to all farmers, now recognises the need to target some expenditure on sensitive or vulnerable parts of the countryside. Targeting may take place on the basis of farms, farmers or land, and its effectiveness depends on a correct identification of the conservation resource and area boundaries (Potter et al, 1993). Social scientists still need to provide back-up for policy-makers and planners in matching types of intervention to landscape ecological zones.

A third focus of enquiry is that of the behavioural processes which underlie land managers' actions within cultural landscapes. Potter (1994) has identified the need to go beyond describing adjustment patterns which may only hold true for limited periods, to analysing longer-term trajectories and the more enduring properties which influence how farmers in different 'structural situations' may behave and react to future policy changes. Thus, he is focusing on the ways in which observed land use and landscape changes are linked to actual farming and socio-economic profiles. It is most improbable that landscape ecological plans will be implemented on a compulsory basis and, consequently, they will be highly dependent on a well-informed appreciation of the more subtle triggers to sympathetic land management.

Fourthly, the author has experienced in practice the problems of devising landscape ecological solutions in isolation from other planning considerations. Unless constrained in some way, new additions of patches and corridors to a fragmented landscape become arbitrary, and solutions are indeterminate. Successful planning will require clearly articulated objectives, which are agreed between multiple users of a particular zone of countryside. Here, social scientists have much to offer in terms of consensus-building and policy evaluation. Consider, for instance, a quote from Noss (1993):

"...the goal of a landscape strategy should not be to consider dispersal of all species. Indeed there are a number of species...whose dispersal must be actively thwarted to maintain native species composition in any given region. Whereas habitat modification by humans has imposed new barriers and has restricted movement of many species, it has facilitated movement of other species far beyond their native ranges...(creating) threats to biotic integrity, both within nature reserves and across the landscape as a whole". (he also cites Mooney and Drake, 1986 and Usher, 1988 writing on this theme).

This view is salutary as, in the absence of contrary objectives, many proposals would simply include measures designed to reduce fragmentation and increase connectedness. Solutions clearly need to be constrained by explicit aims. The kinds of objectives which are now being set by English Nature in their Natural Areas, and by the Countryside Commission in their Landscape Character Zones potentially form an effective basis for focused landscape ecological strategies.

Fifth, social science must provide the policy, planning and implementation methods by which landscape ecological solutions can be delivered. This implies both a set of well tested and researched policy instruments, and a planning method capable of integrating survey and analysis in the pursuit of land use designs. The amount of evidence on the workability of different approaches is variable. Numerous agricultural measures are now available which encourage the creation or retention of habitats or the reduction of agrochemicals, run-off and leachates. To these must be added management agreements for wildlife on farms which, in recent years, have become more positive and creative in nature. Several parallel measures exist for forestry. Quite a considerable amount of critical evidence is now available on their uptake and effectiveness. However, they have yet to be shaped into a genuinely integrated framework for managing extensive and contiguous areas over the long-term. Within the statutory planning framework, the increased recognition and formalisation of the role of planning obligations have clarified the scope for the creation of new landscape as a positive consequence of well-conceived development. This, too, needs a strategic vision, as well as its site-specific dimension. Some of the more recent work on countryside strategies (e.g. Curry, 1992), including the NRA's catchment plans, and zonal plans for community forests, appears promising. There is, though, a dearth of critical literature on the ability of these land use plans or, more accurately, supplementary planning guidance, to integrate with each other and attain a satisfactory level of implementation.

Sixth, landscape ecology has been characterised by its confused and ambiguous terminology; when the American jargon and Eurospeak have been stripped away, it is not always clear what its advocates mean or believe. The same phenomena have sometimes been labelled with different and opaque terms. A common terminology is necessary, and social scientists can assist, not only by clarifying the discourse, but also harmonising it with the well-established terms of urban and landscape design. This would probably also assist a convergence between the interests of science and aesthetics. Terms such as patch, corridor, matrix, permeability, variety, legibility, robustness and richness immediately spring to mind as potential keywords in a common vocabulary.

Finally, and perhaps most importantly, social scientists can ensure that the human viewpoint is fully represented in, and perhaps helps to mould, scientifically-inspired designs. Some intriguing developments have already been pioneered. The work of O'Riordan *et al* (1993) in the Yorkshire Dales showed that it is possible to engage active participation in landscape visions, and that future preferences need not simply be synonymous with sentimentality for the familiar. The use of group psychotherapeutic methods in the Greenwich Open Space study both demonstrated how public perceptions of landscape can help inform planners, and warned of the dangers of creating 'instant' patches of countryside divorced from their human associations (Burgess *et al*, 1988). More recent work by the Countryside Commission has entailed incorporating the findings of focus groups into their landscape character zones ('New Map'), and involved local people in 'planning for real' exercises in the Thames corridor. Public viewpoints, as with land use management, should be seen as positive formative forces rather than irksome complications, and a landscape ecological framework should be capable of accommodating them.

The Next Steps

Although landscape ecology remains controversial, it now has enough momentum, within a European context, to emerge as a guiding framework for the wider countryside. A substantial body of scientific evidence is now available, even if it does need buttressing in relation to the actual usage of alternative landscape patterns by specific groups of species. Thus, whilst our understanding of landscape ecological principles is still fairly crude, it is at least sufficiently robust to generate broad solutions within the blunt instruments of British countryside planning. Given the limitations of our influence over rural land use change, scientific theories can reasonably lack a certain degree of finesse, provided they yield general frameworks for reconstructing the ecological mosaic. It is very probable that these principles will become highly influential in determining policy objectives for 'natural areas' or 'landscape character zones'.

In this context, there is a danger that the scientific interest in landscape will dominate solutions, and that scientists' proposals may be poorly conceived because of poor definition of objectives or inadequate awareness of social factors. Social scientists need to respond to this challenge and, in particular, address the issues of:

- what we want;

- where we target, and

- how we do it.

Deciding *what we want* will require the attainment of a broad consensus for each area, reflecting the views of land managers, 'insider' residents and landscape professionals, balanced with current knowledge about fears, perceptions and usage of naturalistic landscapes. Fortunately, there is a growing literature on the methods of eliciting reactions to future environmental options, and of building these into design proposals. *Targeting* of policy measures is crucial to the attainment of landscape strategies, especially given that support to farmers and foresters in certain cases is increasingly selective. Social scientists have made a major contribution to the explanation of farmers' behaviour when running various enterprise combinations, on different sized farms, in contrasting parts of the countryside. Further application of this research will be critical in maximising landscape gains from limited financial inducements. *How we achieve* the implementation of landscape ecological plans will perhaps be the most difficult challenge. The lessons from community forests may not be wholly encouraging, but there is some basis for optimism in the evidence from countryside strategies generally. The most elegant scientific models of landscape optima will be irrelevant without a sound knowledge of the potential for integrated use of indicative planning, policy inducement and creative development control.

There is undeniably a strong interest in pursuing landscape ecological approaches to rural environmental strategies, and this is increasing under the influence of Europe. Whilst most of the attention to date has focused on scientific debates about the value of corridors or the spatial strategies adopted by different species, it is important that social scientists begin to contribute to the debate. Without their input, solutions may be impractical to implement, socially undesirable and unacceptable in policy terms. This would deny us the possibility of creating visionary, multi-purpose landscapes of the future.

References

Ahern, J (1991) Planning for an extensive open space system, *Landscape and Urban Planning*, 21, 131-146.

Binford, M and Buchenau, M (1993) Riparian greenways and water resources, in *Ecology of Greenways: design and function of linear conservation areas*, Smith, D and Hellmund, P (Eds.), University of Minnesota Press, Minnesota, 69-104.

Burgess, J, Limb, M and Harrison, C (1988) Exploring environmental values through the medium of small groups: 1, theory and practice, *Environment and Planning A*, 20, 309-326.

van Buuren, M (1991) A hydrological approach to landscape planning, *Landscape and Urban Planning*, 21, 91-107.

Curry, N (1992) Nature conservation, countryside strategies and strategic planning, *Journal of Environmental Planning and Management*, 35, 79-92.

Forman, R and Godron, M (1986) *Landscape Ecology*, Wiley, New York.

Grubb, M, Koch, M, Munson, A, Sullivan, F and Thomson, K (1993) *The Earth Summit Agreements: a guide and assessment*, Earthscan, London.

H M Government (1994) *Biodiversity: the UK Action Plan*, HMSO.

Haines-Young, R, Green, D and Cousins, S (1994a) Landscape ecology and spatial information systems, In *Landscape Ecology and GIS*, Haines-Young, R *et al* (Eds), Springer-Verlag, New York, 3-8.

Haines-Young, R, Green D and Cousins, S (Eds) (1994b) *Landscape Ecology and GIS*, Springer-Verlag, New York.

Harms, B and Opdam, P (1990) Woods as habitat patches for birds: applications in landscape planning in the Netherlands, in *Changing Landscapes: an ecological perspective*, 73-97, Zonneveld, I and Forman, R (Eds), Springer, New York.

Hellmund, P (1993) A method for ecological greenway design, in *Ecology of Greenways: design and function of linear conservation areas*, Smith, D and Hellmund, P (Eds), University of Minnesota Press, Minnesota, 123-160.

Little, C (1990) *Greenways for America*, Johns Hopkins University Press, Baltimore.

Mooney, H and Drake, J (Eds) (1986) *The Ecology of Biological Invasions of North America and Hawaii*, Springer-Verlag, New York.

Naveh, Z and Lieberman, A (1984) *Landscape Ecology: theory and applications*, Springer, New York.

Noss, R (1993) Wildlife corridors, in *Ecology of Greenways: design and function of linear conservation areas*, Smith, D and Hellmund, P (Eds), University of Minnesota Press, Minnesota, 43-68.

O'Riordan, T, Wood, C and Shadrake, A (1993) Landscapes for tomorrow, *Journal of Environmental Planning and Management*, 36, 123-148.

Potter, C, Cook, H and Norman, C (1993) The targeting of rural environmental policies, *Journal of Environmental Planning and Management*, 36, 199-216.

Potter, C (1994) Cultural landscapes in flux: an approach to understanding the processes of change, in *The Ecology and Management of Cultural Landscapes*, Selman, P (Ed), IALE-UK, 59-63.

Selman, P (1993) Landscape ecology and countryside planning: vision, theory and practice, *Journal of Rural Studies*, 9, 1-21.

Smith, D (1993) An overview of greenways, in *Ecology of Greenways: design and function of linear conservation areas*, Smith, D and Hellmund, P (Eds), University of Minnesota Press, Minnesota, 1-22.

Smith, D and Hellmund, P (Eds) (1993) *Ecology of Greenways: design and function of linear conservation areas*, University of Minnesota Press, Minnesota.

Spellerberg, I and Gaywood, M (1993) *Linear Features: linear habitats and wildlife corridors*, English Nature Research Report No. 60. Peterborough, English Nature.

Thorne, J (1993) Landscape ecology: a foundation for greenway design, in *Ecology of Greenways: design and function of linear conservation areas*, Smith, D and Hellmund, P (Eds.), University of Minnesota Press, Minnesota, 23-42.

UN Conference on Environment and Development (UNCED) (1992) *Agenda 21: Action Plan for the Next Century*, endorsed at the Earth Summit, Rio de Janeiro.

Usher, M (1988) Biological invasions of nature reserves, *Biological Conservation*, 44, 119-135.

Verner, J (1984) The guild concept applied to management of bird populations, *Environmental Management*, 8, 1-14.

CHAPTER 3

New Housing Development and Local Planning Policy in Pressurised Rural Areas: The Case of South Lakeland

Gwyndaf Williams

The role of new housing development in local housing markets has provided a focus for debate over the last two decades, dwelling in particular on the interface between the planning system and housing land release. Typically, housebuilders have criticised the planner's lack of appreciation of market requirements, and the planning system's inability to allocate sufficient land to meet residential demand. Local authorities, particularly in rural areas, are working to an agenda based on restraint, and aiming to meet local needs rather than accommodating additional growth. In the social housing sector, the demise of local authority housebuilding has led to a 'crisis of affordability', only partially compensated for by new housing association development, and the government's recent support for affordable housing provision through Planning Policy Guidance *Note 3 'Housing'* (DOE, 1992). Thus in both private and social housing spheres, the contribution of new housing development to meet the objectives of local housing strategies provides a particularly topical area for inquiry, particularly for rural areas.

The Study Framework.

Within this wider context an understanding of the relationship between planning policy, new housing development, and local housing markets would appear to be of both academic and professional interest, and this is the focus of this chapter. Relatively little empirical work has been undertaken in this field (Shucksmith, 1980; 1990; Williams, 1989; DOE, 1993; Barlow *et al*, 1994), belying the firm belief in the need for corporate approaches to local housing strategies which should meet both local housing needs and market demand (Audit Commission, 1992). Within the rural context, a main focus of recent work has been the Lake District (Shucksmith, 1980; 1990; Clark, 1982; Capstick, 1987; Lake District Special Planning Board, 1992), focusing in particular on the impact for local communities of market demand pressures, and the distributional consequences of strong planning restraint policies.

The focus of this chapter is the South Lakeland district of Cumbria, which provides an opportunity to evaluate the impact of new housing development both within and outside a national park setting. A principal aim of the research has been to monitor the effectiveness of local planning policy in relation to housing provision, and the contribution of such an approach to meeting the objectives of local housing strategies. This has involved a study of current statutory and informal policy documents, socio-economic information on housing and households, and a district wide survey of new housing development.

The survey included all new dwellings constructed within South Lakeland during the period 1986-91 on sites of over five units (excluding, due to survey constraints, information on smaller sites). The survey, carried out in association with the Cumbria Rural Housing Group, was conducted in the summer of 1993 by means of a postal questionnaire, with survey forms being delivered to 2255 dwellings on 120 sites, from which 1182 responses were received (274 being within the national park), a response rate of 52%.

The Planning and Housing Interface.

The Focus of National Housing and Planning Policy

The period since 1979 has been one of radical changes in terms both of housing policy and the development plan system. In terms of housing policy, the advocacy of market realities and the intention of reducing the scope of the public sector has resulted in the advancement of three main policy strands:

- promoting owner occupation as an ideological instrument, perceived to have a stabilising impact on society, and to result in more responsible citizenry. This has been facilitated through the continuation of mortgage tax relief to owners, and the promotion of the sale of council housing under the 'right to buy' legislation. Whilst undoubtedly successful (owner occupation increasing nationally from 57% to 67% in the 1980s; 1.5 million council houses sold 1980-94), the policy debate has begun to move on, with government acceptance that, although most people prefer to own, a substantial minority need or choose to rent;

- reducing and redistributing public spending on housing in line with 'what the country can afford', with capital spending on social housing being halved in the early 1980s. The Local Government and Housing Act (1989) introduced a new financial regime for local authority new housing provision with additional capital funding being increasingly channelled to housing associations. A by-product of such processes however, at least in terms of national expenditure, has been dramatically to increase the tax relief on mortgage interest repayments, and the payment of housing benefits through the social security system;

- changing the role of the local authority from being a housing provider to that of enabler, adopting a strategic approach to housing provision by other agencies (Audit Commission, 1992). Whilst it is anticipated that this role will involve close working relationships with other providers, commentators are not agreed whether this represents a 'disabling' of local authorities. It is quite clear however that the scale of enabling activity is increasing, but that this does not match the local authority's traditional role as provider, and that local authorities do not have the resources or freedom to act imaginatively at the local level.

In land use planning terms, whilst the 1980s were characterised by ministerial speeches expressing commitment to an effective planning system, a variety of reforms were introduced which were to result in the downgrading of development plans (seen as imposing costs on the economy and constraints on enterprise), and a simplification and speeding up of the development control process (Thornley 1991). However, the 1990s have seen an important shift in the government's approach, with the Planning and Compensation Act (1991) introducing a system of mandatory district wide plans, with up-to-date plans being perceived as providing the main component of the plan-led planning system and "an essential framework for development decisions"(S54A).

The Planning System and Rural Housing

Rural housing markets typically experience high levels of demand and a restricted supply, which has resulted in rising house prices and a wider crisis of affordability. Where rural population growth has occurred, it has generally resulted from net gains through in-migration rather than from natural increases, being both employment and lifestyle led: decentralisation of industry and commerce; commuter pressures; structural changes in the labour market (early retirement and self employment); leisure and second home demands; and retirement mobility. Local people are unable to compete within such a housing market due to low incomes, the level of external demand, and the shortage of housing supply both in tenure and type (Bishop and Hooper, 1991). Indeed, such competition has led to changes in the nature of rural communities, with much of the 'local/newcomer conflict' being based on social status (Cloke and Little, 1990), resulting in 'gentrification' and 'geriatrification'. This has consequences for the sustenance of local kinship networks, the loss of essential skills from the local labour market, and has repercussions for local service provision.

The planning system has operated a dual role in such a context, both acting to limit new development in the countryside, and attempting to facilitate the provision of housing to meet local needs. Restrictive planning policies (national parks, green belts) have ensured the implementation of tight controls on housebuilding outside the major settlements, and careful infilling controls within villages. Such policies have had profound economic and social consequences, effectively benefiting "the middle class, ex-urbanite country dwellers, and the owners of land designated for development, at the expense of the less affluent" (Shucksmith, 1990). However, early attempts by local authorities to introduce local needs policies in development plans (through occupancy restrictions) proved unacceptable to Government, on the ground that planning permission runs with the land rather than the occupier.

The introduction of the 'exceptions' initiative marks, however, a major change in government policy, with the acceptance that a community's need for affordable housing is a material planning consideration (DOE, 1989). This initiative aims to enable landowners to benefit the local community by releasing sites for affordable housing that would otherwise have no 'hope value' for development, with a policy on 'exceptional' planning permissions to be included in the framework of local development plans (Williams *et al*, 1991). Subsequent policy guidance (DOE, 1992) marks a further evolution of government policy by enabling local authorities to set overall targets for affordable housing provision, and to negotiate with developers for an element of affordable housing in private housing schemes (Barlow, 1993). The consequence of such policy developments is to give planners the potential for a more pro-active role in rural housing provision, even if they are still reliant on landowners and developers to put forward proposals, and housing associations to implement them.

The Role of New Housing

Since new housing provides no more than 1-2% of total housing stock every year, the nature of the local housing market is essentially determined by the existing range of second hand housing. However new housing, sold at an initial premium, is essential for ensuring the vitality of the local housing market, and for facilitating in-migration prior to subsequent readjustment within the local housing stock. Any study of the role of such new housing must focus on the structure and aspirations of households moving in, and the contribution that such housing plays in offering choice in the local housing market, and in the integration of local housing and labour markets. Previous work undertaken in the south of England (DOE, 1993) identified a dual circuit in the new housing market: those with relatively well paid, secure, professional employment with more than one household earner, who were typical occupants of new housing, and those with less secure, less well paid, lower status employment who were faced with intense competition to obtain housing within their reach, seeing lower market new estate-based housing developments as an initial stage in their housing careers.

Existing Research in Lakeland

The focus of previous research has been on the housing market within the
Lake District National Park, which is the planning authority for the area, but
covers substantial parts of the districts of Copeland, Allerdale, Eden, and
South Lakeland which are the housing authorities (see figure 3.1 below). In
the mid 1960s, the Special Planning Board, concerned at the continuing
decline in the area's population, agreed to a number of housing estate
developments within and around the larger settlements and a number of the
smaller settlements. Criticism grew over both design standards achieved in

Figure 3.1 - Local Administration in Cumbria

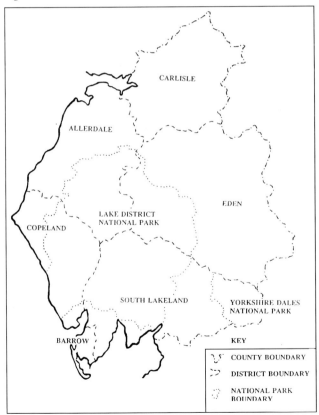

such developments, and the perception that the Board was neglecting the housing needs of locals. The Board argued that its powers under the Planning Acts could not in normal cases allow for a distinction to be drawn between the personal merits of one applicant and another, with the onus being placed on local housing authorities to accept responsibility for maintaining an adequate pool of housing available to let to local workers (LDSPB, 1992).

Realisation in the early 1970s of the impact of 'second homes' on local housing opportunities, led to the commissioning of a study on the use of the national park's housing stock (Bennett, 1976). Whilst the Board felt that its powers to acquire land for purposes other than access/recreation or conservation were sharply prescribed, it felt no similar inhibitions in its use of development control powers, and agreed to adopt a policy controlling occupancy of new dwellings through planning conditions. Whilst aware of likely criticisms on the legality of its control over house sales, it took the view that existing measures concerning the control over occupancy of agricultural and forestry workers dwellings could be used more widely to preserve the character of the area. It felt able to accommodate a policy which perceived the severe constraints on site approvals as providing an opportunity to target on meeting local housing needs.

This policy proved the most contentious section of the Cumbria and Lake District Joint Structure Plan (1980), with the Secretary of State overruling the Board on the legality of occupancy conditions on new housing (1983). He saw it as 'unreasonable' to deprive owners of their normal proprietary rights, and noted that the planning system was ultimately concerned with the physical use of land and not the status of land users. Other commentators have noted consequences for development land values of occupancy conditions, the inhibiting effects that this would have on both developers and building societies, and the distributive consequences of such an approach increasing pressures on existing housing stock (Shucksmith, 1980, Clark, 1982).

The Board looked again at demand and supply aspects within the park, noting the conflicting aims of physical conservation and restrictive development control policies, and its duty to safeguard the economic and social well being of local communities (Capstick, 1987). Finally, the Board initiated a further survey of the take-up of new housing developments, as part of the review process associated with the Cumbria and Lake District Joint Structure Plan (LDSPB, 1992). The main aim of the survey was to assess the extent to which different housing sectors had contributed to different housing market segments within the national park in the period 1975-1990. The study focused on open market housing, housing constrained by occupancy and other agreements, and housing association property. It then proceeded to examine the origin of both economically and retired households moving into new dwellings, and the relationship between residence and employment patterns. A secondary report looked in detail at the results from sites completed within the previous 5 years, attempting to illustrate market trends in recently completed developments.

Both reports confirmed the view that new open market housing is characterised by high levels of retirement and second home ownership (being over 70% in the latter report), involving considerable in-migration into the national park, and high levels of commuting for those economically employed. The picture was fundamentally different for housing with occupancy agreements (exhibiting a high proportion of starter homes) and housing association tenancies, both of which catered for a high proportion of local economically active households, with low levels of commuting.

Local Planning Policy and the Role of New Housing

Administrative and Policy Framework

Cumbria is predominantly rural, and includes the whole of the Lake District National Park and a small part of the Yorkshire Dales National Park within it. The Lake District Special Planning Board is an independent planning authority, and a structure plan authority in its own right. However, since 1980 the County Council and the Board have co-operated to produce a joint structure plan which provides the planning framework for the county. The first joint structure plan was originally submitted in 1980, and eventually approved with modifications in December 1983. Its housing strategy was primarily restrictive and policies were seen as 'holding policies' to limit growth especially in rural areas until detailed settlement strategies could be evolved. The plan proved highly controversial since it included a local needs housing policy for the national park, to be implemented by the use of occupancy agreements (policy 6.7). This was deleted by the Secretary of State, and the plan was subsequently reviewed, with the First Alteration being submitted in 1986 and coming into force in January 1988. This modified plan took forward and developed many of the policies in the original plan, in particular formulating a key settlement strategy. Subsequently, work commenced on the production of a new joint structure plan, the subject of an EIP in 1992, (with formal approval in late 1993), involving modification to the key settlement approach, and reinforcing its housing policies.

South Lakeland district council's area is complicated by the presence of parts of two national parks within its boundaries, with the national park authorities determining planning applications within their area and with the district council determining applications outside the parks, but being the housing authority for the whole of the district's area. During the study period the Board did not possess an approved district-wide local plan, but possessed two draft local plans - Cartmel and Furness Local Plan, South Westmorland Local Plan - covering the parts of its area outside the national park. In 1993, South Lakeland began the process of producing a district wide plan, with the initial consultation document expected by the end of 1994. The Board prepared a draft local plan for the national park area (1990), this being replaced by a series of interim policy statements (1991), which have in turn been superseded by a park-wide local plan, soon to be adopted.

Demographic and Socio-Economic Framework
South Lakeland is a predominantly rural district, dominated by the urban centres of Kendal, Grange over Sands, Ulverston, Windemere and Ambleside. It possesses a total population of 96,000, with a disproportionate number of residents over 45 years old (S. Lakeland 45%; Cumbria 41%;

national 37%), a consequent under representation of residents under 29 (S.
Lakeland 35%, Cumbria 38%; national 42%), and an average household size
of just under two (Cumbria 2.2).

Over the past decade, its overall population has increased by 3.1%
(Cumbria 0.4%), this being largely accounted for by significant in-migration
(+7.0%) in a situation of a negative natural increase (-3.8%). The strength of
the local economy, attractive environmental quality, and the ease of access to
the M6 for long distance commuting are undoubtedly contributory factors. In
terms of household structure, it is over-represented in relation to both
Cumbria and nationally in the extent of owner occupation, and under
represented in terms of local authority and housing association rental
properties, and has experienced a significant increase in owner occupation.

Between 1986-91 the housing market moved from a period of boom to
one of slump, but demand in South Lakeland was less affected than most of
the rest of Britain by the nature of external demand both for retirement and
for second homes. Prices stabilised over this period, but the existing high
values nevertheless deterred major elements of local housing demand, with
only a third of all Council Tax property valuations in South Lakeland being
under £52,000 and the advertised price of older two-bed terraced houses
being £50,000 in Kendal and £60,000 in Windermere (local press, April 1992 -
see figure 3.2).

Figure 3.2 House Price Bands in Cumbria (1992, numbers of houses)

Price (thousands)	Under £40	£40 - £52	£52 - £68	£68 - £88	£88 - £120	£120 - £160	Over £160
Allerdale	45	24	15	9	5	2	1
Barrow	61	22	12	4	*	*	*
Carlisle	34	26	19	11	6	2	1
Copeland	48	23	14	8	6	1	*
Eden	23	22	21	16	12	4	3
S Lakeland	14	19	22	18	15	6	6

The difficulties faced by local and first time buyers, usually on low wages, is well illustrated by South Lakeland District's current housing strategy (1994/95) which notes that only a tenth of the families on the council's waiting list have an annual household income in excess of £16,000, guaranteeing a mortgage for even the cheapest property. The authority has thus set a target of providing 140 new affordable homes annually for local people, targeted on rental housing. Arising from the recommendations of its specially convened 'Housing for Local People Working Party', the authority is committed to maximising the use of its own landholdings to provide affordable homes (sale of 11 sites 1991-93 for £95,000 to produce 170 new affordable homes), and concentrating its efforts on the provision of affordable homes through housing associations. Concern has been expressed, however, that even new rental schemes by associations are not meeting affordability criteria in relation to local low income employed households, with the example given of a recently completed scheme at Newbiggin, Kendal, which has two thirds of its 30 tenants on housing benefit.

Local Planning Policy for New Housing
During the 1980s, the strategic requirements identified in Cumbria for new housing appear to have changed, with sectoral deficiencies (family, elderly, single person, low income) becoming the main pre-occupation rather than overall shortages, and with the dilemma of balancing the need for new housing development against the responsibility of conserving the environment. The resultant strategy, particularly within the national park, is to restrict new development, and to favour the conservation of the environment over the promotion of development.

Within Cumbria's projection of the need for 23,000 dwellings between 1981-96, South Lakeland's provision was expected to be 4,600, of which 838 should be within the national park. In fact, South Lakeland's actual contribution was considerably greater than this (+50%), with its national park component being almost doubled. The role of new housing was seen as predominantly one of meeting local needs and demand (structure plan policy H9), particularly within the national park, where new development projections were based exclusively on changes to the indigenous population. Thus constrained, the district has had to concentrate the allocation of housing land in settlements outside the National Park, but adopting a more relaxed approach than that contained within the previous notion of key settlements, recognising that people may wish to have the opportunity to live in villages rather than the main towns (Cumbria County Council 1992, para 3.11). The National Park Local Plan (1994) stresses that its main objectives are to:

- ensure that the limited land available for residential development within the larger settlements and villages of the National Park is utilised to best advantage to strengthen rural communities by securing housing for local needs;

- provide a policy framework for development control decisions which will restrain further housing development unrelated to the identified needs of local people;

- assist and encourage all agencies to undertake housing schemes which will meet local needs for affordable housing and are undertaken in a manner which retains environmental qualities.

In terms of the two local plans outside the national park area (1981-96), the South Westmorland Local Plan envisaged a new housing requirement of 2,600, whilst the Cartmel and Furness Local Plan's requirements were 1,160 dwellings. The main feature of local plan housing strategies was to concentrate the majority of new housebuilding in and around Kendal, with a limited amount in Arnside, Kirkby Lonsdale, Milnthorpe, Ulverston and Grange over Sands. Significant housing development in the smaller settlements would be restrained. In both plans, specific policies were developed for small scale development in large settlements, new housing in villages, housing outside settlements suitable for growth, and conversion of redundant buildings.

New Housing Development.

Response to the postal survey was inevitably skewed in relation to the main urban areas within the district, due both to the focus of new housebuilding policies in recent years, and to the absence of sites of less than five dwellings from the survey. Thus, of the 1182 usable returns, 78% were from the district's main urban centres (Kendal 505, Ulverston 142, Grange over Sands 125, Windermere 120, Ambleside 70), 20% from the larger villages, and only 3% from the smaller villages and hamlets.

Consequently, the study is able to say little about the issues facing individual villages and hamlets, since the available data does not lend itself to such an analysis. An interesting facet of this study is that a quarter of all respondents (274) occupied dwellings within the national park area, and this will enable comparison to be made of any distinctive features of the housing market within and outside the park. Over two thirds of the respondents were first occupants, with the present dwelling constituting a 'main home' for 96% of respondents (91% in the case of national park respondents). It is quite typical for new residential developments to experience relatively rapid turnover at the initial stage, since new housing provides a useful 'stepping stone', particularly for incomers into an area. Such turnover is particularly well illustrated by respondents renting from housing associations (49%) and the private sector (32%), a minority of whom were first occupiers, significantly different from the 71% of respondents who were first occupiers in both owner occupied and local authority dwellings.

Not surprisingly, the private sector was the main contributor to new housebuilding, with 79% of all respondents being owner occupiers (10% local authority; 5% housing association; 3% private renting) this varying somewhat between respondents living within the national park (68%) and those residing outside (82%). Whilst this sector accounted for only three fifths of all new flats, it accounted for over 90% of all other dwelling types (87% of bungalows, 86% of terraced, 88% of semi detached and 98% of detached properties). Quite clearly therefore, the capacity of local interests to influence the form and function of new housing developments is limited by the strength of private market presence. Such provision is unlikely to meet the needs of the 1450 households on the local authority's waiting list (350 sheltered, 450 families, 650 single/childless couples), over 400 of which are currently sharing accommodation.

New Dwelling Characteristics

The most surprising feature is that over a third of all respondents lived in flats (see figure 3.3 below) attributable to the focus of recent social housing production (local authority and housing association), and to the dramatic expansion in the late 1980s of sheltered housing for sale. This is clearly a new facet of current rural and small town housing development strategies. Such a response may additionally be skewed by the fact that flat residents were predominantly retired (four fifths being occupied by respondents over 55), who may additionally have an increasing propensity to respond to such questionnaires. Indeed, 90% of all local authority respondents, and 70% of housing association replies were from occupiers of flats. The particular characteristics of the new housing market within the area is clearly evident from the fact that 63% of respondents to the study lived in dwellings of no more than 2 bedrooms.

Figure 3.3 Dwelling Types Within the Survey of Households

Type	Survey Response	National Park		Small Dwellings (1-2 bed).
		Within	Outside	
Detached	17.2	7.0	20.3	3.0
Semi-detached	14.6	10.6	15.9	41.9
Terraced	16.7	20.1	15.5	64.3
Bungalow	13.9	10.6	15.0	59.7
Flat	37.6	51.6	33.4	99.3

Moving on to consider the size of the property built, it is not surprising that almost all the one bed accommodation is in the form of flats, that over nine tenths of all bungalows, terraced and semi-detached housing have 2-3 bedrooms, and that two thirds of all detached housing have four bedrooms. It is clear that the new housebuilding market in such a pressurised rural area is not focused on the needs of first time buyers, since nine-tenths of respondent owners were already owner occupiers before moving. Indeed, on moving some former owners have entered local authority and housing association sheltered housing. In the case of former local authority tenants, 70% have moved within tenure, with only 18% becoming owner occupiers. New housing association tenants represented the widest diversity of previous tenures, and this reflects the variety of market sectors that such agencies attempt to cater for (see figure 3.4 below).

Figure 3.4. *Current and Previous Tenure*

Current Tenure	Previous Tenure				
	Owner	Council	Housing assoc.	Private renting	Tied/Other
Owner	89.7	1.9	0.3	5.6	2.5
Council	12.6	55.5	1.7	21.0	9.2
Housing Assoc.	25.4	15.3	15.3	28.8	15.3
Private renting	36.8	2.6	2.6	52.6	5.3
Tied/Other	40.0	5.7	-	31.4	22.9

Household profile

The household structure of respondents is not representative of those more widely in the district's housing stock (where 27% of residents are aged over 60) in that 45% are returned as retired households. The issue remains to be addressed, however, as to the extent to which this is a reflection of responses or the structure of provision of new dwellings. Thus it is not surprising that 37% of respondents were 1 person households (45% from respondents within the national park), resulting in an average household size amongst respondents of 2.1 (marginally larger than the district census figure of 1.97) and with only a quarter of all respondents living in households of three or more occupants (see figures 3.5 and 3.6 below).

The disproportionate significance of mature and elderly households in the survey response is clear from the analysis, being a major feature of all housing sectors except private renting. This population segment has provided the main focus for local authority housebuilding programmes over the past decade, and is one of two housing association target groups (the other being young families).

Such population profiles in new dwelling stock are reinforced by an analysis of the relationship between tenure and household size (see figure 3.7), where the owner occupied sector has significantly larger household size than other tenures, with the local authority sector catering almost wholly for the elderly in its new build programmes, resulting in the smallest household size.

Figure 3.5. House Type and Household Structure

Household type	Flat	Bungalow	Terrace	Semi	Detached
Under 35	22.0	4.8	33.2	32.0	8.0
35 - 54	10.1	9.5	21.7	19.3	39.4
55 - 64	32.8	23.7	12.2	11.5	19.8
Over 65	66.7	19.6	5.0	2.8	5.9
1 person	67.1	9.9	11.8	7.5	3.8
2 person	30.8	22.2	18.3	13.9	14.8
3/4 person	6.5	8.7	21.4	25.4	38.0
Over 4	-	6.1	15.2	27.3	51.5
Average household size	1.4	2.0	2.3	2.6	3.1
Pre-family	36.5	4.3	30.4	20.9	7.8
Young family	10.9	7.7	26.8	28.6	26.0
Mature family	14.1	15.7	20.4	15.2	34.6
Retired	63.4	19.7	5.4	4.0	7.5

Figure 3.6 Household Type

		Tenure					
	Survey response	National Park Within	Outside	Owner	Council	Housing assoc.	Private renting
Pre family	9.8	9.2	9.9	10.0	5.0	10.2	18.9
Young family	29.1	26.6	29.9	31.9	2.5	25.4	51.4
Mature Family	16.3	9.6	18.4	17.9	6.7	8.5	8.1
Retired	44.8	54.6	41.8	48.6	85.7	55.9	21.6

Figure 3.7. Tenure and Household Size

Tenure	Average household size	1 person	2 person	3-4 persons	larger
Owner	2.2	31.7	37.9	26.8	3.6
Council	1.4	66.1	31.4	2.5	-
Housing Assoc.	1.8	52.5	27.1	20.4	-
Private Renting	1.9	35.1	43.2	21.6	-
Tied/other	1.9	34.3	42.9	22.9	-

Further evidence of the differing contribution of the various providers of housing for meeting the district's housing objectives is unearthed by a breakdown of respondent age in relation to tenure (see figure 3.8 below). This clearly illustrates the focus of local authority provision for the elderly, housing association contributions to meeting the needs of young families and the elderly, and the private rented sector's role in relation to meeting the housing requirements of younger households.

Finally, in this section, it is appropriate to look briefly at the main reasons behind the move into new dwellings, as part of the initial evaluation of the role of new housebuilding in addressing both housing needs and market demands in such a diverse rural area (see figure 3.9 below). Whilst there are

Figure 3.8 Age Structure and Household Tenure

Tenure	Under 35	35-54	55-64	Over 65
Owner	21.4	32.9	11.1	34.6
Council	3.3	3.4	15.1	78.2
Housing assoc.	28.8	11.9	10.2	49.2
Private renting	59.4	18.9	-	21.6
Tied/other	34.3	20.0	14.3	28.6

clearly a multitude of reasons why people move, based on both voluntary and forced decisions, it is useful to put forward a tentative assessment of reasons given by respondents. The role of new housing in encouraging household formation is limited in this cultural setting, being given as a main reason for moving by only 11% of respondents, with new terraced property being the main outcome (46%). Much more significant were other stages in family life cycles, either in preparing for or in adjusting to retirement. For retirement related moves, the consequence was often a move into a flat (56%), the same being the output for households seeking a move to smaller dwellings (59%), or a wish to move nearer to the family (62%). For the relatively small proportion of respondents moving in order to gain a larger home, detached houses (51%) and semi detached properties (21%) were the main outcomes. For job related moves, the results were often the occupancy of detached (36%) or semi detached properties (22%), with the private rented sector being a particularly important sector for such moves (36%). Only a small minority gave the environmental qualities of the area as being the main reason in explaining their move. although this may have been significant in explaining retirement moves, particularly from outside Cumbria.

Figure 3.9 Main Reason for Moving

Reason	Survey response	National Park within	outside	Owner occupier	Private renting
Job related	17.4	5.9	20.9	19.1	35.1
Attractive area	7.3	7.8	7.1	8.7	2.7
Near family	9.2	12.6	8.1	9.5	8.1
Retire	21.7	28.5	19.5	19.9	16.2
First home	11.0	18.1	8.8	11.8	8.1
Smaller home	13.8	14.8	13.5	12.8	2.7
Larger home	10.6	3.0	12.8	12.9	2.7
Other	9.2	9.3	9.2	5.3	24.3

Housing History

In order to obtain a fuller appreciation of the contribution of new housing stock to local housing markets, it is important to make some comment on the housing history of respondents, paying particular regard to local and non-local mobility. In looking at the status of respondents, the vast majority of owner occupiers (83%) and council tenants (92%) were already household heads in their former accommodation, although 13% of current owners were formerly residing with parents. In the case of both housing association (28%), and privately renting households (32%), the role of shared accommodation, or living with parents, was however quite significant. Three quarters of the occupiers of new dwellings were formerly owner occupiers, with local authority (8%) and private renting (11%) being the only other significant tenures. Thus there is no evidence from this data that new housing in South Lakeland is meeting the needs of young and house-forming households, whether local or otherwise.

In terms of mobility patterns associated with occupying new housing, it is clear from the analysis that the vast majority of moves are from within Cumbria (63%), with the rest of North West England (14%) and South East England (7%) being other significant suppliers. Not unexpectedly, the vast majority of local authority (90%) and housing association (73%) respondents formerly lived locally (under 5 miles), whilst a significant proportion of owner occupiers (37%) were long distance movers (over 50 miles), with less than three fifths coming from within Cumbria. Long distance movers were more likely to move to detached properties and less likely to move to flats than local movers, and were thus likely to seek larger properties. By the same token, long distance movers were almost wholly owner occupiers with the local authority and housing associations being more significant in the case of local movers (figures 3.10 and 3.11). The three main reasons given for long distance moves were job related (35%), retirement (30%) and family (19%), whereas for local movers the search for a smaller home (21%), a larger home (20%) or a first home (18%) were the key ingredients in explaining the move.

New Housing and Employment Opportunities
Whilst job related moves accounted for less than a fifth of the main reason for moving, it is central to consider the employment status of new occupants, in order to evaluate the contribution of this segment of the housing market to wider socio-economic performance (see figure 3.12). It is clear from the

analysis that the sample of respondents has a disproportionate element of households who are not economically active, this being at its highest within the national park.

Figure 3.10. Location of Previous Home

Location	Survey response	National Park within	outside	Owner occupiers	Private renting
Under 5 miles	49.1	49.0	49.2	42.4	48.6
5 - 20 miles	13.8	13.4	13.9	14.6	16.2
20 - 50 miles	5.1	4.6	5.3	5.6	5.4
Over 50 miles	31.9	33.0	31.6	37.3	29.7

Figure 3.11. Local Movers Compared to Long Distance Movers

Dwelling type	Flat	Bungalow	Terrace	Semi	Detached
Short distance	42.2	13.4	15.5	14.5	14.3
Long distance	31.0	15.8	15.2	12.8	15.3
Bed number	1 bed	2 bed	3 bed	4 bed	-
Short distance	26.3	42.4	21.6	9.9	-
Long distance	14.4	37.8	29.1	18.8	-
Tenure	Owner	Council	Housing association	Private renting	Tied/other
Short distance	67.8	18.4	7.6	3.2	1.1
Long distance	91.8	1.4	1.1	3.0	2.7

Figure 3.12. Employment Status of Household Head

	Survey response	National Park within	outside	Owner occupier	Housing assoc.	Private renting
Employee	44.8	33.8	48.1	49.6	24.5	59.5
Self employed	6.2	6.7	6.0	7.2	3.5	5.4
Unemployed	1.8	2.2	1.7	1.1	7.0	2.7
Retired	45.6	55.4	42.6	41.1	57.9	21.6
Other	1.6	1.9	1.6	1.1	7.0	10.8

Respondents living in local authority property were most likely to be economically inactive (88%), whilst those in private rented property were likely to be most economically active. For those in employment, the socio-economic profile of respondents is clearly different from that seen for the district as a whole, with an over representation of managerial and professional employment amongst occupiers of new housing, and a much increased rate of retirement (see figure 3.13).

Thus new housing plays a limited role in meeting the needs of skilled non manual workers and manual workers, both groups being of central importance for the maintenance of healthy local communities in both rural and small town settings.

Of those in work, less than a tenth work from home, and thus for the majority significant work related journeys are necessary. However, nearly three quarters work within South Lakeland, with such journeys inevitably focused on the main towns

Figure 3.13. *Social Class and Job Status*

Social Class	District (Census)	Survey response	National Park Within	Outside	Owner occupiers
Managerial/professional	24.9	34.5	23.0	37.9	39.3
Skilled non manual	7.6	3.6	4.4	3.3	3.9
Skilled manual	16.5	9.2	9.3	9.1	9.8
Semi/unskilled	9.9	4.2	4.8	4.0	3.9
Retired	31.7	47.1	57.0	44.1	42.1
Other	9.4	1.5	1.5	1.5	-

within the area, with Kendal (45%), Barrow (10%), Ulverston (8%), Windermere (5%) being the main job related venues. In the case of owner occupied households, three quarters of those in employment work within a ten mile radius, but with a substantial 14% working more than 20 miles from home (figure 3.14). Clearly for almost all such travel, the economically active are almost entirely dependent on private transport in such an environment.

Figure 3.14 Job Location for Households Heads

Location	Survey response	National Park		Owner occupiers
		Within	Outside	
Same settlement	46.8	31.4	50.2	45.8
South Lakeland	28.3	41.9	25.3	28.0
Rest of Cumbria	13.2	8.6	14.2	14.1
Elsewhere	11.7	18.1	10.3	12.4

Evaluation and Conclusion

The research on which this paper is based has been primarily concerned with
the sphere of new housing development in a predominantly rural area which
is the focus of a multitude of pressures for land use and land allocation
changes (conservation/recreation/production), within the context of a
variety of development plan frameworks (structure plan, national park local
plan, district local plans). In such a context, the ability of local people to
compete in the housing market - particularly in the owner occupied sector -
has posed severe problems, due to the inability of the market to produce
affordable housing. This arises in a situation of sharp increases in land and
property prices, and a restrictive planning framework for development.

The role of the local authority has been predominantly restricted to
managing its own land resources to meet affordable housing objectives, and
to provide housing for local elderly households. Whilst housing associations
have also targeted this latter objective, they have also begun to introduce
development programmes focused on the needs of young families.
Emerging development policies by both the national park authority and the
district council have begun to reflect a new role for the planning system in
the provision of affordable housing, but this is unlikely to be of a sufficient
scale in such a restrictive overall environment.

The main objective of development strategy has been to focus housing
development pressures on the main towns and to a lesser extent on large
villages with services. This has been felt to best meet the needs of the local
workforce and prove less attractive to an immigrant purchaser (at least in
relation to new housing). Concentration on large sites in the main urban

areas has resulted in output of predominantly small units, with nearly two thirds of dwellings having 2 bedrooms or less, and with over a third being in the form of flats. The consequence of such output is that new housebuilding is not focused on the needs of first time buyers and young households, and social housing is targeted on the needs of the elderly. As a consequence, 45% of all responses were from retired households, and young working families were under-represented in the survey. Indeed, retiring, job related moves, and the need for housing to fit in with particular stages in the family life cycle were the main reasons given by respondents for their decision to move.

In terms of mobility patterns, it is clear that the new housing market has played a role in relation both to short distance mobility (half having moved under 5 miles) and to long distance migration (a third having moved over 50 miles). Short distance mobility was more likely to be associated with moves into smaller dwellings (and flats associated with the local authority, housing association, and private sheltered developers), whilst long distance migrants were almost all owner occupiers moving due for work, retirement, or family related reasons.

Occupation of new dwellings revealed an over representation of higher socio-economic groupings (as compared with the district average), and retired householders, and an under representation of local working families (either skilled or unskilled). In terms of employment opportunities, three quarters work within South Lakeland, concentrated largely on the district's main towns.

The overall conclusion is that whilst planning policy does appear to have been influential in controlling the location of new housing, and has significantly resulted in providing homes for local people, most of whom were already well established in the area, it has done little in terms of new housing provision to meet household formation needs, or the needs of ordinary working families. This must largely be met by the existing housing stock, itself under pressure due to its more dispersed nature from in-migrant households for retirement and second home purposes. Planning policy in the future will have to address such issues in a much more positive way, as a result of dramatic cultural changes currently taking place in rural areas.

The existing plan-led system, and the affordable housing provisions of Planning Policy Guidance *Note 3 'Housing'* (DOE, 1992) have failed to address the fundamental needs of existing local communities, whilst sustained market demand arising from continuing counter-urbanisation pressures are not easily accommodated within existing development control frameworks (RTPI, 1993). The widening social profile of rural communities, and the resultant problems of identity in an increasingly dual level social structure, will fundamentally challenge the balance of rural areas (Murdoch and Marsden, 1994; Marsden *et al*, 1993), and will be on the agenda of a variety of interests to be consulted on the forthcoming White Paper on the future of rural areas.

Notes

1. Households were classified as being 'pre-family' if they consisted of single or married couples without children (or with the household head under 35); 'young family' if the household had no children over 16 (or household head under 45); 'mature household' if one or more children were over 16, or whose children (if any) had left home; and 'retired household'.

References

Audit Commission (1992) *Developing Local Housing Strategies*, HMSO, London.

Barlow, J. *et al*. (1994) *Planning for Affordable Housing*, HMSO, London.

Capstick, M. (1987) *Housing Dilemmas in the Lake District,* Lancaster University.

Clark, G. (1982) *Housing and Planning in the Countryside*, Chichester Press, Chichester.

Cloke, P. and Little, J. (1990). *The Rural State? Limits to Planning in Rural Society*, Clarendon Press, Oxford.

Cumbria County Council (1992) *Cumbria and Lake District Joint Structure Plan (Deposit Draft)*, Cumbria County Council, Kendal.

DOE (1992) Planning Policy Guidance *Note 3 'Housing'*, HMSO, London.

DOE (1993) *New Homes for House Owners*, HMSO, London.

Lake District Special Planning Board (1992) *Housing Survey* 1991, LDSPB, Kendal.

Lake District Special Planning Board (1994) *Lake District Local Plan*, LDSPB, Kendal.

Marsden, T. *et al* (1993) *Constructing the Countryside*, UCL Press, London.

Murdoch, J. and Marsden, T. (1994) *Reconstructing Rurality*, UCL Press, London.

Royal Town Planning Institute (1993) *Rural Planning in the 1990s*, RTPI, London

Shucksmith, M (1980) *No Homes for Locals?* Gower, Aldershot.

Shucksmith, M (1990) *Housebuilding in Britain's Countryside*, Routledge, London.

Thornley, A. (1991) *Urban Planning under Thatcherism*, Routledge, London.

Williams, G. *et al* (1991) *Evaluating the Rural Low Cost Housing Initiative*, HMSO, London.

Williams, G. (1989) Monitoring Housing Market Demand in Local Plans, *The Planner*, 75, January, 11-13.

CHAPTER 4

Rethinking Village Planning and Design:
Articulating the Connections Between Social, Economic and Design Issues in Village Planning.

Stephen Owen

In preparing policies and plans for rural settlements it is important that planners recognise the connections between, on the one hand, the design of new development in villages and, on the other, the social and economic needs of village communities. A change of approach to village planning is needed that recognises and responds to these connections and is itself founded on an improved capacity to design rural settlements.

Three broad sets of objectives for village planning - environmental,[1] social and economic - command a significant degree of support amongst local communities, politicians, planners and commentators. In essence they are to secure:

- attractive settlements;
- a healthy local economy that offers opportunities for employment locally;
- access to affordable homes, facilities and services, and the maintenance of vital communities.

There are important connections between these sets of objectives that need to be explored and managed considerately through an integrated approach to village planning. Promoting good design in villages, as well as being an obviously desirable environmental objective in its own right, can also be a key factor in addressing social and economic objectives. Ironically, this is mainly because the design of so much development in villages permitted through the planning system in the past fifty years has been so inappropriate. The assumption that new development inevitably will be poorly designed has fuelled the widespread adoption of restraint policies in development plans for rural areas. By preventing all, or most, development throughout a policy area, restraint policies have inhibited the resolution of other important issues in village planning such as affordability of homes, employment opportunities and the protection of local services, many of which rely on new development taking place. In these circumstances it is arguable that planning policies themselves have intensified the problems experienced by village communities.

A false distinction has been created in planning between *development objectives* mainly intended to satisfy local needs and *conservation objectives* mainly intended to protect the physical characteristics of villages that are valued and considered worthy of protection. The planning policies of most local authorities covering rural areas respond to this false distinction by reinforcing conservation objectives at the expense of fulfilling development objectives (Punter, Carmona and Platts, 1994; Owen, 1995a).

Problems in Villages

The full range of environmental, social and economic problems facing rural communities has been articulated comprehensively elsewhere and is not repeated fully here. The following brief discussion is an outline of some of those problems, sufficient only to provide a context for subsequent discussion; it focuses particularly on unattractive development and the social and economic problems experienced by people on low incomes in rural areas.

Unattractive New Development

Unattractive new development has been recognised and recorded consistently as a problem in villages for the past fifty years (Council for the Protection of Rural England, 1995; Owen, 1995a). During this time the attractiveness, identity and local distinctiveness of many villages have been eroded, particularly during the building boom of the 1980s. Chiefly, this is a result of transplanting standardised and suburban building styles from urban to rural areas without responding to the character of villages generally or individual villages in particular. Private housing schemes in villages are often characterised by poor location, inappropriate scale in terms of their spatial extent relative to the grain of existing development, and standardised layout and design indistinguishable from that of housing schemes in the suburbs of most towns and cities. Typically, housing schemes are designed around specially constructed access roads that conform with local authority highway regulations, arranged in culs-de-sac of detached or semi detached houses, sometimes bungalows. Widespread reactions against the poor design quality, scale and pace of development derive at least in part from the growing strength of an articulate and influential 'environmental' lobby, mainly conservationist in character and middle income or above (Lowe and Murdoch, 1993). These reactions are symptomatic of an attitude that considers that any development will be prejudicial to village character - the so-called 'no development ethic'.

Adherents to the 'no development ethic' imply that *any* development in villages would be unattractive and should be resisted. This is clearly not the case; development is not intrinsically unattractive. Attractive villages that are the subject of conservation policies evolved through a process of development. The dynamic and, for many local residents, necessary process of physical change that responds to people's changing needs and requirements should not simply be arrested at one point in history. For a variety of reasons, however, and hopefully only temporarily, the ability to undertake good physical planning and design in the intimate context of the village has been lost.

Social and Economic Problems

A number of significant social and economic problems experienced by people living in villages have been identified and analysed over the past ten years. Work by McLaughlin for the Department of the Environment in 1985 was subsequently confirmed by a series of commissioned reports, most recently that of Cloke *et al* for the Rural Development Commission in 1994 (McLaughlin, 1985; Cloke, Milbourne and Thomas, 1994). These linked problems include:

- poverty;
- lack of employment opportunities, particularly for local people, and the predominance of low-paid work amongst the employed;
- lack of affordable homes for low income people and, increasingly, homelessness amongst young people;

- erosion of local facilities and services in villages, including shops, health care, child care and training, particularly for the young and elderly who become socially and physically isolated;
- poor accessibility to facilities and services elsewhere, particularly for women;
- less well-developed infrastructure in villages than in urban areas.

Of these problems, one of the most basic and crucial is poverty. Cloke *et al* (1994) confirm that the problems relating to poverty and deprivation identified ten years earlier by McLaughlin still exist in the same places and to the same degree. McLaughlin (1985) concluded, for instance, that 25% of rural households were living in, or on the margins of, poverty. The proportion of households identified by Cloke *et al* as living in poverty were generally of the same order in those areas covered by McLaughlin. Roberts (1994) argues that many local residents in villages, not just people living in poverty but also those living on low incomes, have experienced marginalisation or social exclusion in the face of the increasing domination by a very mobile and prosperous middle class whose lifestyle diminishes the viability of the rural services that form a lifeline for those on low incomes. The shortfall of affordable homes in rural areas in England between 1990 and 1995 was calculated as 80,000; completions during that period have not exceeded 3,000 per year (Clark, 1990). A survey by the Rural Development Commission in 1994 revealed the continuing erosion of rural services to the point at which 41% of parishes in England had no shop, 43% had no post office, 52% had no school, 29% had no village hall, and 71% had no daily bus service (Rural Development Commission, 1995).

Policy Responses in Development Plans

The failure to recognise the connections between sets of *problems* is replicated in a similar failure to recognise connections between *policies* in development plans. One of the effects of this second kind of failure is that planning policies themselves can create problems for people living in villages, or intensify problems that already exist. To demonstrate some of the problems caused by inadequately considered planning policies for rural settlements, two common types of planning policy are examined: *restraint policies* and *design policies*.

Restraint Policies

Resistance to physical change, based largely on an idyllic view of the countryside and its villages, has been a continuing feature of town and country planning since its inception, and also countryside policies more generally (Lowe, 1989; Curry, 1993). This resistance has intensified recently in response to increasing pressures for development in villages, mainly in the form of speculative housing within easy reach of existing towns and cities. Ironically, demand, like resistance, is stimulated by the same idyllic image of beauty and tranquillity that attracts people, particularly middle income or above, to the countryside. There are increasing pressures from commuters, from retired people moving from urban areas, and from people buying second homes or renting holiday cottages. Villages, particularly in lowland England, are under greater pressure for development than ever before (Countryside Commission, 1989).

Some development needs to take place in villages in order to provide affordable homes and local sources of employment for people on low incomes or unemployed. Local people who cannot afford to compete in the private housing market or travel long distances to urban areas for employment need access to employment and affordable housing locally. The difficulties they face are a consequence of a complex range of external factors including, specifically, government policies that prevent local authorities from building social housing for rent. These difficulties can be exacerbated by the widespread adoption of restraint policies that catch in their net affordable housing and local employment facilities as well as speculative housing development. In particular, restraint policies help to push up the price of houses well beyond the reach of most people on low incomes by restricting the supply of developable land against high levels of demand.

Restraint policies might be appropriate for some villages; more accurately, they might be appropriate for parts of some villages. They are certainly not appropriate as blanket policies for whole counties or whole districts. Settlement policies in both structure plans and district-wide local plans, should respond to the different needs and characters of individual villages. They should be more discriminating than the prophylactic policies that prevail at present. An examination by the author of structure plans and district-wide local plans for rural areas revealed that restraint policies continue to dominate both types of plan, usually in combination with key settlement policies and within a strongly conservationist policy framework (Owen, 1995a). Understandably, authority-wide approaches to both settlement policy and design policy predominate in most structure plans and many district-wide local plans, but little or no attention is paid to the place-specific needs or characters of individual villages either as an information source for authority-wide policies or as a basis for place-specific proposals.

One type of policy that addresses the housing needs of people on low incomes in rural areas is the 'exceptions' policy. Widely adopted in recent structure plans and district-wide local plans, exceptions policies are intended to respond to local housing needs by permitting low cost housing on land that otherwise would not have secured planning permission and which does not, therefore, have residential land value. This land is often located beyond the existing bounds of the physical fabric of villages and, in some instances, can lead to the destruction of the integrity of village character. Although endorsed by government policy guidance, exceptions policies are regarded by many planners as contrary to the plan-led system and to the application of proper planning criteria (Department of the Environment, 1992a). Exceptions policies represent an attempt to resolve, through manipulation of the planning system, serious housing problems that can be addressed effectively only through a change in government housing policies. Just as restraint policies can be viewed in part as seeking to fulfil environmental objectives but having deleterious social and economic consequences, exceptions policies can be viewed in part as seeking to fulfil social objectives but having deleterious environmental consequences.

The welcome and timely emphasis on encouraging *sustainability* as a basic principle in preparing development plans unfortunately could further aggravate some of the social and economic problems experienced by people living in villages. Much of the current guidance on sustainability, for instance Planning Policy Guidance *Note 13 'Transport'* is singularly focused on the need to reduce the use of the private car (Department of the Environment, 1993; 1994a; 1994b). The note counsels local authorities to promote development in existing urban areas, strengthening local centres that offer a range of services and discouraging any significant incremental housing in villages and small towns. By intentionally concentrating future development in urban areas, this would reinforce the effects of restraint policies that can inhibit the fulfilment of the social and economic needs of village communities. A more inclusive, and potentially more effective, view of what constitutes sustainable development would encourage rather than prevent development in some villages.

Design Policies

During the past ten years or so significant advances have been made in the development of *urban* design theory and practice. Urban design concepts and techniques, and their physical manifestations in the built environment, however, have been confined, as their title suggests, mainly to urban and metropolitan areas. There has been little parallel development of approaches to design in rural areas, particularly in villages. There is little evidence of either a contemporary culture of village design that pays simultaneous attention to continuity of tradition and response to current needs, or the confidence in design that would come from such a culture. Perhaps the most telling evidence for this lack of confidence is displayed in the common practice of banishing new housing, where it is permitted, to the least attractive villages, thereby revealing the depressing contemporary assumption that people's homes are likely to be poorly designed and should be located in unattractive surroundings. The confidence of planners in addressing matters of design was seriously undermined by government policy articulated in Circular 22/80 and subsequently in Planning Policy Guidance *Note 1 'General Policies and Principles'* which ruled that, in the main, design was the prerogative of developers rather than planners (Department of the Environment, 1980; 1988).

The examination of development plans by the author, referred to above, revealed a consistent approach to the treatment of design issues across a range of district-wide local plans for rural areas.

- Local plans contain few policies and little advice or even comment on the appearance of new development in villages.[2]
- Village envelopes predominate as the chief means of designating where development will and will not be permitted in villages.
- Negative rather than positive phraseology, specifying what will not be permitted, dominates most design policies.
- Whilst design policies frequently pay lip service to the need for good design, they rarely promote it effectively; expressions like, *"in all cases, development should not have an adverse impact upon the environment and should be sympathetic with the form and character of the settlement"* are all too common without further elaboration or positive guidance.
- More recent local plans are beginning to make reference to encouraging employment and responding to local needs for low cost housing, but without any clear means of achieving these objectives except, in the case of low cost housing, through occasional references to 'exceptions' policies (Owen, 1995a).

These findings are similar to those of Punter *et al* (1994), reporting on research commissioned by the Department of the Environment on good practice for design policies in development plans. This research concludes broadly that the coverage given to design issues varies greatly between district-wide local plans, with most plans avoiding either detailed coverage or prescription, and failing to relate design policy to context. More specifically, the key findings *inter alia* of the research are that district-wide local plans for both rural and urban areas generally:

- have a very low emphasis on design;
- are not good at expressing general design strategy;

- are poor at expressing analytical appraisal and the consultative bases of policies;
- fail to relate policies to a variety of local contexts;
- tend to resort to bland phrases advocating contextual design rather than clear statements of design expectations. The authors refer to 'motherhood' policies - simply seeking good quality design without specifying what good design might be;
- rarely support innovation or contemporary design quality.

The authors emphasise in particular the dearth of appraisal to underpin or inform design policies. Many so-called appraisals in individual villages are really surveys and remain descriptive, with no policy prescription or clear design principles likely to emerge from them.

Bishop (1994a) identifies the lack of any coherent strategic link between design and other aspects of environmental quality on the one hand, and between design and land use allocation and infrastructure on the other. Similarly, in its recent publication *Design in the Countryside*, the Countryside Commission (1993) claims that authority-wide policies in development plans have been unable to address the individual characters of different villages and the design of individual buildings. The Commission refers to a 'design gap'.

Some of the worst aspects of design in villages, particularly the standardisation and suburbanisation of housing development across both urban and rural areas, are consequences of economies of scale in the building industry, but some responsibility also lies with design policies. District-wide design policies for housing, in the form of design guides, often assume that suburban housing layouts and buildings styles will be adopted throughout the district, irrespective of the location of development and, implicitly, they encourage this practice. Bishop (1994a) concludes that most design guides have a narrow focus, fail to pay attention to buildings in context or to settlement patterns, and provide no framework by which practice could develop over time. There are no apparent links between local plan formulation and development control practice, and nothing that pays attention to local distinctiveness. In this sense it is possible to claim that ill-considered design policies, like restraint policies, can add to, rather than resolve, problems experienced in rural areas. Whilst strongly supporting the use of prescriptive design guidance, particularly in the form of supplementary planning guidance, the Council for the Protection of Rural England (1995) argues that guidance should be strictly relevant to individual localities and, preferably site specific.

Design ability generally remains inadequate amongst planners, not necessarily the ability creatively to design buildings and spaces, but an ability to evaluate design, to discriminate between good and bad design, and to coax good design from developers. Specifically, design skills that respond to the particular needs of rural settlements are almost entirely undeveloped. Whilst during the 1980s government policies discouraged local authorities from intervening in too much detail in the development process, particularly with regard to the form, appearance and detailed design of development, this should not disguise the fact that, had they been free to intervene to a greater extent, planners generally lacked the appropriate design skills to encourage high quality design in villages.

A Change of Approach to Village Planning and Design

The debate stimulated by the publication of the White Paper on the future of rural areas during 1995 represents an opportunity to re-appraise approaches to village planning and design. As a contribution to that re-appraisal, two aspects of a fresh approach are examined here: *rural settlement policies* and *rural settlement design*.

Rural Settlement Policies

The Rural Development Commission (1993) is at the forefront of a move towards a more positive approach to development in the countryside, an approach shared by a range of other influential bodies and individuals, including central government, albeit with different emphases and different degrees of commitment. Views seem to cohere around the following imperatives for rural settlement policies:

- the need for positive and strong land use policies, including land use allocations for specific land uses;
- the need to revive rural industries, particularly manufacturing and services, based partly on improved technologies and communications;
- the need to encourage the provision of affordable housing.

From 1990 onwards Government policy, promulgated through the White Paper *This Common Inheritance* and a series of Planning Policy Guidance Notes, has consistently pressed for a positive approach to development in rural areas (Department of the Environment, 1990). Research conducted by the Rural Development Commission (1993), however, suggests that planning authorities in rural areas apply over-restrictive and over-elaborate policies, thereby negating the positive approach to rural development advocated by government. In particular, the research suggests that planning authorities do not fully observe the advice of Planning Policy Guidance *Note 7 'The Countryside and the Rural Economy'* that a balance should be struck in development plans and development control decisions between development and conservation (Department of the Environment, 1992b).

In order to break into the process by which restraint policies can impede the fulfilment of social and economic needs, a change of approach to rural settlement policy formulation should integrate and reconcile environmental, social and economic objectives, acknowledging that their relative importance will be differently weighted in different villages. At the heart of policy making for villages there is a lack of disciplined thinking, a confusion of ends and means that results in the means to achieve some narrowly defined objectives impeding the achievement of other, broader, objectives. Specifically, restraint policies, the means to achieve particular objectives concerning the appearance of some aspects of the built environment, are impeding the achievement of broader social and economic objectives. Restraint itself, however, should not be regarded as an objective of village planning; it is one means of protecting certain valued aspects of the life and character of individual villages. Although robust policies are necessary to resist pressures for inappropriate and inadequately designed private housing in some areas, restraint justified by the need to protect attractive physical character is best exercised with greater discrimination than at present. In some villages, or parts of villages, where there is particularly high and consistent quality, and where the unity of the existing physical character can only be safeguarded by protection, restraint will remain the most appropriate planning response. But even here restraint should act as a policy framework rather than as an absolute constraint on development.

Rural Settlement Design

As a condition of introducing a more positive approach to the formulation of rural settlement policies it is essential to improve the quality of village design. This would enable changes to the physical fabric of villages to be planned to meet people's social and economic needs without detriment to village character. Indeed, an aim of village planning should be to *enhance* village character through the design of development.

A substantial initiative to improve the quality of design in villages is needed that extends the existing urban and metropolitan focus of urban design towards the particular design imperatives facing rural settlements.[3] Rural settlement design should have the vibrancy and confidence of established urban design practice, but fashioned specifically for the needs of villages (Owen, 1995b). Such an initiative should increase the capacity of planners and designers, in consultation with local people, to understand, analyse and cultivate the distinctive character of villages. Intimations in the discussion paper *Quality in Town and Country*, and elsewhere, of a reversal of the central government policies that, for the past 15 years, have discouraged local planning authorities from intervening in design decisions present an opportunity for such an initiative to be taken (Department of the Environment, 1994c).

Rural settlement design should be a positive antidote to the prevalent negative protectionism that is casting a dead hand over many villages and the lives of their less well-off inhabitants. It should deal with sets of relationships in which understanding and responding to context and pattern play a role at least as important as creating groups of buildings and enclosed spaces in the tradition of urban design; a process of adjustment to context through extended periods of time rather than architecture writ large and suddenly realised. Specifically, planning practice should be infused with greater design literacy based on understanding the natural and built character of villages and fostering confidence in design that comes from witnessing, and engaging in, good practice.

There is a case for some optimism. The need for better design in the countryside is being registered clearly at the national level through government publications and through influential commentary. Some of the most persuasive design advice in the countryside in recent years has come from government bodies, the Countryside Commission and the Scottish Office. In a series of publications, these two bodies have established the grounds for debate about design in the countryside, they have charted a direction for further action and they have offered practical advice (Countryside Commission, 1989; 1993; 1994; Scottish Office Environment Department, 1991; 1994) The Countryside Commission appointed BDOR Ltd to undertake an action research project with selected local authorities, other consultant designers and, most importantly, local communities, the first phase of which culminated in the publication of *Design in the Countryside* (Countryside Commission, 1993). Retrospectively, this report might be seen as a watershed in the evolution of a more positive and considered approach to rural settlement design. The Commission proposes a number of principles, criteria and practices to achieve high quality design and suggests, albeit tentatively, two new mechanisms for rural design, Countryside Design Summaries and Village Design Statements, both of which provide frameworks for design that allow untrained people as well as planners and other design professionals to contribute to improving the quality of design in villages.

Countryside Design Summaries, produced by local authorities, are appraisals of landscape, settlements and buildings covering sub-areas of a district. They offer broad guidance on the features of the area to which the design of development should respond, and they can be incorporated into district-wide local plans. Village Design Statements are appraisals of the character of individual villages produced mainly by local communities together with planning authorities. They offer explicit guidance about the setting to which any new development should respond in order to add to the character of the village.

The second phase of the research developed and tested Countryside Design Summaries and Village Design Statements through seven projects in different parts of rural England (Countryside Commission, 1994). One of the many conclusions derived from the evaluation of the projects was that these two new mechanisms would have maximum effect if they had status as supplementary planning guidance so that they were more fully integrated into the statutory planning system. A further conclusion was that they are flexible enough to respond to local circumstances, indeed, the outputs of the various projects were seen to be as diverse as the range of local characters. The report includes a series of recommendations including the preparation of a 'Workbook' for Countryside Design Summaries and guidance material on the production of Village Design Summaries. It is intended that this detailed advisory material will be produced in a further phase of the research.

Some local planning authorities are beginning to adopt the sorts of practices that recognise and respond to the individual character of villages in a positive manner. Shrewsbury and Atcham District Council (1992) and Cotswold District Council (1992), for instance, have supplemented district-wide plans with individual plans for most villages, including precise land allocations for development. In the latter case the plans are accompanied by an insightful design code that covers such matters as a sense of rhythm in street scenes and the significance of ancient plot boundaries. West Dorset District Council prepares a 'footprint' or master plan for sites in villages which developers must observe. On the 'footprint' the planning authority plots the proposed relationships between buildings and open spaces and includes an aerial perspective showing suggested design details (CPRE, 1995).

As well as intimations of a changing attitude amongst opinion-formers and policy makers, there is sporadic evidence in different parts of the country of good design being implemented. Increasingly there are examples of well designed, attractive housing that fits its village setting and, crucially, can be afforded by local people. A report on rural housing needs by Rural Voice (1994) presents four brief case studies of housing schemes intended to meet local housing needs. The case studies include an analysis of costs, processes of implementation and the involvement of the local community in decision taking. Although, from the illustrations provided in the report, the schemes appear to vary in design quality, one scheme in Abbotsbury, Dorset is a particularly good example of how high quality design can be achieved at low cost in an attractive and, therefore, challenging village setting. In its booklet *Local Attraction* the Council for the Protection of Rural England illustrates attractive and distinctive new housing in South Creake in Norfolk, Broad Chalk in Wiltshire, Calver in Derbyshire and Luccombe in Somerset There are also thoughtfully designed factories and workshops such as the David Mellor Factory in Matlock, Derbyshire that express their own clear sense of identity and function yet manage to be integrated harmoniously into their built and natural surroundings.

Conclusions

From the foregoing discussion of rural settlement policies and rural settlement design, a number of points have emerged that, in outline, provide the basis for a change of approach to village planning and design.

- There should be an integrated approach to identifying and responding to social, economic and design problems with an explicit recognition of the connections that need to be explored between the policy responses to these connected problems.

- The 'no development ethic' in the countryside should be eschewed as a blanket perspective in authority-wide rural settlement policies. Policies should respond to the social and economic needs of village communities and the physical character of villages through a positive yet discriminating approach to development. Restraint should be applied over whole areas only as a policy framework and should be applied to specific localities only where there is consistently high quality in the existing built environment.

- There should be a shift of emphasis from authority-wide policies towards place-specific proposals for individual villages and individual sites.

- Authority-wide policies will continue to be needed but they should be based on appraisals of the different capacities of individual villages to benefit from, and to absorb, development. Whilst they might incorporate design policies, care should be taken to ensure that, unlike some design guides, they do not themselves encourage blandness and standardisation.

- Where resources allow, separate plans for individual villages should be prepared as insets to district-wide local plans, including precise land allocations for development. Land use allocations should be accompanied by carefully considered criteria for the location, layout and form of development. Where appropriate, design briefs should be prepared to form a link between the overall policy guidance contained in district-wide local plans and analyses of the character of individual sites.

- At the scale of the individual village, proposals should be founded on a thorough understanding of, and response to, the distinctive character of individual villages, their natural features and built character. There is a need to cultivate amongst planners a better design appreciation at the scale of villages and small towns, and a fuller appreciation of the culture, problems and aspirations of local village communities.

- Where appropriate, planning instruments dealing with design in villages should be accorded the status of supplementary planning guidance so that they can link more effectively with the preparation and implementation of statutory local plans and more strongly influence the outcomes of planning applications and appeal decisions.

The framing of policies and proposals for village planning and design should be informed by a recognition and understanding of the connections between environmental, social and economic issues. Within this connected rural settlement policy framework, and contributing to it in an attempt to bridge the gap between policy and design, it is crucial to develop an enhanced capability in rural settlement design that is responsive to the needs of local people and the character of individual villages.

Notes

1. The term 'environmental' encompasses a wide range of factors, including many aspects of the natural environment. The main intention here is to concentrate on the design of the physical fabric of villages.

2. This confirms research undertaken by BDOR Ltd (1992) of a much larger sample of 35 local plans for rural areas.

3. Bishop (1994b) argues the need to move beyond the narrow construct of the urban designer to consider the applicability of principles and methods of urban design to the shaping and management of rural areas.

References

BDOR Ltd (1992) *Design of Buildings and Settlements in the Countryside*, unpublished report to the Countryside Commission.

Bishop, J (1994a) Planning for Better Rural Design, *Planning Practice and Research*, 9, 259-270.

Bishop, J (1994b) Rural Design and Urban Design: The Missing Link? *Urban Design*, 52, 5-7.

Clark, D (1990) *Affordable Rural Housing: A National Survey of Need and Supply*, Rural Development Commission/Action with Communities in Rural England, London.

Cloke, P, Milbourne, P and Thomas, C (1994) *Lifestyles in Rural England*, Rural Development Commission, Salisbury.

Cotswold District Council (1992) *Cotswold District Local Plan: Draft for Consultation*, Cotswold District Council, Cirencester.

Council for the Protection of Rural England (1995) *Local Attraction*, CPRE, London,

Countryside Commission (1989) *Planning for a Greener Countryside*, Countryside Commission, Cheltenham.

Countryside Commission (1993) *Design in the Countryside*, Technical Report 418, Countryside Commission, Cheltenham.

Countryside Commission (1994) *Design in the Countryside Experiments*, Countryside Commission, Cheltenham.

Curry, N (1993) Rural Development in the 1990s - Does Prospect lie in Retrospect? in Murray, M and Greer, J (Eds), *Rural Development in Ireland*, Avebury, Aldershot.

Department of the Environment (1988) Planning Policy Guidance *Note 1'General Policies and Principles'*, HMSO, London.

Department of the Environment (1990) *This Common Inheritance: Britain's Environmental Strategy*, Cmnd 1200, HMSO, London.

Department of the Environment (1992a) Planning Policy Guidance *Note 3 'Housing'*, HMSO, London.

Department of the Environment (1992b) Planning Policy Guidance *Note 7 'The Countryside and the Rural Economy*, HMSO, London.

Department of the Environment (1993) *Environmental Appraisal of Development Plans*, HMSO, London.

Department of the Environment (1994a) Planning Policy Guidance *Note 13 'Transport'*. HMSO, London.

Department of the Environment (1994b) *Sustainable Development: the UK Strategy*, HMSO, London.

Department of the Environment (1994c) *Quality in Town and Country*, HMSO, London.

Lowe, P (1989) The rural idyll defended: from preservation to conservation, in Mingay, G (Ed) *The Rural Idyll,*, Routledge, London.

Lowe, P and Murdoch, J (1993) *Rural Sustainable Development. Strategic Review* Topic Paper 1, Rural Development Commission, Salisbury.

McLaughlin,B (1985) *Deprivation in Rural Areas*, unpublished report to the Department of the Environment.

Owen, S (1995a) Local distinctiveness in villages, *Town Planning Review*, 66, 143-161.

Owen, S (1995b) Rural Settlement Design, *Urban Design*, 54, 9-11.

Punter, J, Carmona, M and Platts, A (1994) The Design Content of Development Plans, *Planning Practice and Research*, 9, 199-220.

Roberts, L (1994) Director's Note, *Rural Viewpoint*, Autumn, 2.

Rural Development Commission (1993) *Rural Development and Statutory Planning*, Research Report 15, Rural Development Commission, Salisbury.

Rural Development Commission (1995) *1994 Survey of Rural Services*, Rural Development Commission, Salisbury.

Rural Voice (1994) *Meeting Rural Housing Needs*, Rural Voice, Cirencester.

Scottish Office Environment Department (1991) *Planning Advice Note 36, Siting and Design of New Housing in the Countryside*, Scottish Office, Edinburgh.

Scottish Office Environment Department (1994) *Planning Advice Note 44, Fitting New Housing Development into the Countryside*, Scottish Office, Edinburgh.

Shrewsbury and Atcham Borough Council (1992) *Shrewsbury and Atcham Rural Area Local Plan Written Statement*, Shrewsbury and Atcham Borough Council, Shrewsbury.

CHAPTER 5

Rural Land Use in Britain: Agency Re-Structuring and Policy Adaptation*

Alexander S Mather

The last few years have witnessed the most radical changes in land use policies in Britain since the 1940s. World War II and the ensuing years gave rise to policies that prevailed with only minor adaptation until the second half of the 1980s and the structure of the government agencies responsible for administering rural land use remained essentially unchanged. By the late 1980s and early 1990s, however, some policies had been turned on their heads and extensive re-organisation of the agency structure was underway. Paradoxically, the agency structure in the sector in which policy changes have been most radical, agriculture, has undergone less change than that in the forestry and conservation sectors. This re-structuring is not yet complete, but it has progressed sufficiently far to give rise to questions of both cause and consequence: why has it happened, and what is its significance? More generally, what is the relationship between agency structure and policy adaptation and integration, and what has been the significance of agency structure for rural land use in Britain?

Policy Background

The objectives of the dominant land use policies in post-war Britain were to increase the production of food and wood, and hence to increase the level of national self-sufficiency in these products. In the food sector, the policies, in relation to these objectives, were highly successful, with the degree of self-sufficiency having more than doubled by the mid-1980s. Price support for farm products and grant aid for agricultural improvements such as drainage, combined with a vigorous government-financed programme of research and development, succeeded in encouraging a dramatic increase in levels of production. Afforestation both by the state and by the private sector with state aid transformed many upland parts of the country, with little detriment

---

* This paper was written before the author's appointment to a Regional Board of Scottish Natural Heritage and does not necessarily reflect the views and opinions of that organisation.

to the level of food production. By the mid-1980s, however, strong reaction was setting in to the production-dominated policies in both sectors. This reaction stemmed from different reasons. In agriculture, the source was the surpluses of food then being produced within the European Community, the costs associated with these surpluses, and the environmental impacts of intensive agriculture. In forestry, there was no question of surpluses in either Britain or the other member states (the former producing little more than 10 per cent of its wood requirements), but strong objections were levelled both at the environmental impacts of afforestation geared to wood production as its primary concern, and at the acceptability of subsidies being paid to rich individuals to establish forests. In both sectors, there was by the end of the 1980s talk of a 'post-productivism' era - the term not implying that production was no longer sought but indicating that it was no longer the sole or even primary concern.

Some policy reversals were dramatic. For example, grant-aid that previously had been available for removing field boundaries was now available for restoring them. Afforestation, which had previously been relegated to the poorest hill land, was now encouraged on arable land by the payment of a 'better land' supplement on planting grants. In short, policies in agriculture and forestry suffered their greatest upheavals for several decades. The changes, however, stemmed primarily from external pressures and perceptions, rather than from the agencies responsible for administering rural land use. The agencies, in general, tended to react to rather than initiate change.

Agency Structure in Post War Britain

During the 20th century, the usual pattern in Britain has been to establish new agencies in response to new issues and new pressures, rather than to add to the functions of existing bodies. There are cogent arguments in favour of this approach: if new functions are added to existing agencies, there is a risk that they are subordinated to the previously existing functions and that their effective discharge is therefore compromised. On the other hand, a separate-agency structure carries the risk of sectoral conflict and lack of policy integration.

While the agency structure has been simple in terms of land use sectors, it has been complex in terms of geographical pattern. Agriculture and forestry each had its sectoral administration. In forestry the structure was unitary throughout Great Britain, with the state forestry service, the Forestry Commission, being responsible both for state forests and for administration of private forestry. In agriculture, however, there was administrative, but not political, devolution, with different bodies in England, Wales and Scotland (MAFF, WOAD and DAFS/SOAFD[1]). The geographical pattern was further confused by the fact that the body responsible for wildlife conservation (NC/NCC[2]), had a Britain-wide remit, whilst those with responsibilities for landscape conservation and aspects of countryside recreation were the Countryside Commission (England and Wales) and the Countryside Commission for Scotland. A further complication was the political status of the agencies. The agricultural bodies were firmly within the realm of central government, having the status of government departments. The Forestry Commission was a government department but had a chairperson and board of commissioners. The conservation agencies were 'quangos', with chairs and commissioners, and operated under the aegis of sponsor departments, the Department of the Environment in England and the Scottish Development Department[3].

This agency structure has evolved incrementally, and is both complex and confusing. Two main features characterise its pattern. One is the geographical tension inherent in the contrasting pattern of Great British and national[4] responsibilities, and in the degree of centralisation. The other is the sectoral basis of organisation. By the late 1980s, both these features were being widely recognised as problematic. By the early 1990s, sectoral and geographical re-organisation was either underway (in the case of conservation), or was being advocated (in the case of forestry).

The Sectoral Approach

The sectoral approach is explicable in terms of the history of the emergence of each rural sector as a major issues. The urgency of the problems of timber supply during World War I, for example, led to the creation of the Forestry Commission as a separate entity, rather than as a sub-department of agriculture. After World War II, the pattern was continued with the creation of the Nature Conservancy and the National Parks Commission (later the Countryside Commission) rather than a single conservation body. Perhaps in an age of expansion, not just of food and wood production but also of numbers of nature reserves and national parks, a sectoral approach helped to serve a promotional purpose. Perhaps it was vindicated in terms of criteria such as increases in production and of forest areas. Its limitations and weaknesses were soon recognised, however, and by the early 1970s its shortcomings were being openly acknowledged. In 1972, the Select Committee on Scottish Affairs published a long and detailed report on 'Land resource use' in Scotland. The Committee referred to the four "heavyweight" agencies with land use responsibilities, and to its hope that a system of "constructive tension" would exist between them (Select Committee, 1972). The government, in its responses to the report, agreed that there was a need for closer liaison between the agencies, but the Select Committee's proposal that an integrative Land Use Council be established was rejected (SDD, 1973). Attempts were made to establish inter-departmental committees to promote liaison and integration in both Scotland and England, but the problems of the essentially single-issue approach adopted by the "heavyweights" became increasingly apparent down through the 1970s and 1980s.

Whilst expansion remained as the main characteristic of the agriculture and forestry sectors, the conservation agencies (and NCC in particular) were forced into an increasingly defensive role in attempting to safeguard protected areas such as Sites of Special Scientific Interest (SSSIs). Afforestation and land improvement for agriculture were increasingly impacting on valuable habitat and prime landscape. Major conflicts developed between nature conservation and agriculture or afforestation in various parts of Britain, including the Somerset Levels and the Berwyn Mountains (Lowe *et al*, 1986). In parts of northern Scotland, where very extensive SSSIs were being notified, the conflict between afforestation and nature conservation on the so-called Flow Country reached an impasse which could not be resolved within the existing sectoral agency structure.

Eventually, the local authority in the shape of Highland Regional Council was able to bring the opposing sides together and to secure a measure of agreement in the form of what amounted to an indicative strategy based on zones in which there would be presumptions for and against afforestation. The episode not only clearly illustrated the limitations of the sectoral approach, but also proved to be the trigger that led to the geographical and sectoral restructuring of the conservation agency. A single-sector British body, the Nature Conservancy Council, was replaced by a dual-sector Scottish body, Scottish Natural Heritage.

Agency Re-Structuring: Conservation

Government conservation agencies in Britain date from the 1940s. The legislative foundation was laid in the form of the National Parks and Access to the Countryside Act of 1949, which made provision for national nature reserves and other types of wildlife conservation areas throughout Britain, and for national parks and England and Wales. Different agencies, however, were established for nature conservation and for national parks. For the former, the Nature Conservancy was established by Royal Charter in 1949. For the latter, the National Parks Commission was set up, becoming the Countryside Commission in 1968 when additional responsibilities were allocated to it with the passing of the Countryside Act that year. A Countryside (Scotland) Act was passed in 1967, leading to the setting up of the Countryside Commission for Scotland (CCS). During the 1960s, the expectation of rapid and major increases in demand for, and participation in, outdoor recreation had led to a recognition of a need both for new types of countryside recreational areas outside the national parks, and for an enhanced framework for the administration of countryside recreation and conservation.

The shape and direction of nature conservation derived their initial character from wildlife conservation committees which in turn stemmed from the war-time debate about national parks (Sheail, 1976). Despite their origin, the wildlife committees' conclusions pointed to a separate state biological service, distinct from a national-parks agency. Although nature and landscape conservation had previously been considered together (for example by the Addison Committee of 1929-1931), at this critical juncture a structural distinction was established between the two, and was to survive for more than 40 years. Such a distinction is paralleled in few, if any, other countries.

Separate wildlife committees dealt with England and Wales on the one hand (the Huxley Committee), and Scotland on the other (the Ritchie Committee). While the Ritchie Committee supported the notion of a single biological service for Great Britain, it made it clear that the Scottish division should be devolved and separately financed, in recognition of the different conditions prevailing in Scotland. The Committee members were "convinced that wildlife conservation in Scotland can be fully effective only if it has the backing and whole-hearted support of the Scottish people generally" (Cmnd 7235, Part II). If this were to be achieved, a Scottish Division based in Edinburgh and working closely with other government departments in Scotland was essential. Ritchie was at pains to emphasise the practical benefits that could arise from wildlife conservation: wildlife assets, including in particular game, wildfowl and freshwater fisheries were already of rich economic value but could be improved and extended. Agriculture and forestry could benefit from research carried out on nature reserves. For example, reference was made to one prospective reserve in Sutherland which "could be the meeting ground of agricultural and ecological research, as far as moorland grazings are concerned" (Scottish Record Office AD 6/9/3/FC 9/3). In the Huxley Committee's report, on the other hand, the flavour is one of 'purer' nature conservation, with less reference to practical benefits.

Neither the geographical structure of the Biological Service nor the pragmatic and practical flavour of conservation which characterise the Ritchie recommendations was to survive. When the Nature Conservancy was established, a Scottish Committee was appointed, but the recommendation that the Scottish Division be run almost independently was, for practical purposes, ignored. Over the next three decades, both the name and the administrative/political status of the Nature Conservancy was to change. Its centralised character was, however, maintained intact. A narrow sectoral focus on nature conservation was accompanied by a wide geographical coverage. If anything, the focus narrowed further during the 1980s, when much of the NCC's energy was devoted to notifying and re-notifying Sites of Special Scientific Interest (SSSI) following the Wildlife and Countryside Act of 1981.

By the end of the 1980s, the stresses and strains arising from this narrow focus and high degree of centralisation were such that the structure could no longer hold. These pressures became especially severe in some peripheral parts of Britain, in which numbers and extents of SSSIs were large and where there were some local perceptions of the imposition of constraints on land management and development. Amongst the areas in which conflict emerged were the island of Islay, off the west coast of Scotland, and the northern part of Scotland, including Caithness and Sutherland as well as Orkney and Shetland. The controversy in northern Scotland in particular was a significant factor in the eventual re-structuring of the nature conservation agency.

Conservation conflicts in northern Scotland

In northern Scotland, the second half of the 1980s witnessed bitter conflicts between nature conservation on the one hand and agriculture and forestry on the other. The Nature Conservancy Council sought to protect the wildlife interest by opposing afforestation of peatlands and the conversion of moorland to improved pasture (Mather, 1993). The former issue became very heated in Caithness and Sutherland, and the latter in Orkney. In the conflicts, the NCC and FC were strongly supported and encouraged by their respective client groups, including notably the Royal Society for the Protection of Birds and the private forestry company, Fountain Forestry. To this extent the conflict was a national one, fought out locally in a northern battleground. Local land occupiers became increasingly disaffected as a result of the perceived constraints imposed on their freedom of action by the notification of Sites of Special Scientific Interest. Strongly negative sentiments were expressed about the imposition of SSSIs, and perceptions of the NCC as a distant body based in Peterborough did not help. In the northern Scottish controversies, there is little doubt that the role of the NCC was handicapped by both its sectoral and geographical characteristics. The former ensured that its stance was defensive and apparently inimical to local developmental interests, whilst the latter, despite the best efforts of its local staff, made it seem remote if not alien.

Political expediency may have facilitated the ensuing restructuring. Where afforestation or land improvement on SSSIs was opposed by NCC, compensation became payable in the form of management agreements. The expected costs arising from management agreements in Scotland appear to have disquieted Nicholas Ridley, then Secretary of State for the Environment. He is reported to have suggested that NCC operations be hived off in Scotland and that the Scottish Office - instead of the Department of the Environment - be responsible for its costs (Mackay, 1994). This move was made in autumn 1987, and was followed by Scottish Office consideration of merging the Scottish part of NCC with CCS. In 1989 a formal statement was made to Parliament: the government had decided that the NCC would be split into separate agencies for England, Wales and Scotland, and in the case of the latter two countries combined with the countryside agencies (Hansard (House of Commons) 11.7.89, Written Answers 484-85). Reference was made to the different circumstances and needs of conservation in the three countries, and to the allegedly inefficient and insensitive organisational arrangements that currently existed. By implication, the highly centralised and sectoral approach of NCC was now to give way to the more devolved and broadly based activities of Scottish Natural Heritage.

Scottish Natural Heritage

After a transitional year during which the functions of the former Nature Conservancy Council were taken over by a separate Nature Conservancy Council for Scotland, Scottish Natural Heritage was inaugurated in 1992. Legislative provision was made for it in the Natural Heritage (Scotland) Act of 1991: its aims were "to secure the conservation and enhancement of, and to foster understanding and facilitate the enjoyment of, the natural heritage of Scotland; and SNH shall have regard to the desirability of securing that anything done, whether by SNH or any other person, in relation to the natural heritage of Scotland is undertaken in a manner which is sustainable". In addition, SNH was required to balance the needs of agriculture, forestry and fisheries; the needs of social and economic development; and the interests of local communities and of owners and occupiers of land. In its first annual report, SNH referred to the closing of the gap between nature and landscape conservation "which many of us had long felt was unreal, and unrealistic" (SNH, 1993). The echoes of the recent conflicts resounded in the statements that the "natural heritage is not limited to particular sites or special areas" and that "our overall mission . .[is] . . to work *with* the people of Scotland" (SNH, 1993, italics added). Two characteristics that SNH has been keen to highlight are those of partnership (working with other bodies) and delegation of decision-making to regional and local levels.

Time will tell how successfully these approaches will translate into action, but from the outset there has been a clear desire to negate some of the criticisms heaped on its predecessor, the NCC. For example a Peatland Management Scheme was introduced in the Flow Country, whereby payments are offered to encourage traditional and extensive forms of management on SSSIs. Under the previous regime, a frequent criticism was that payments were made only where there was a threat of habitat damage (for example by afforestation). More broadly, the issue of soil conservation is being addressed. Under the previous regime this issue attracted little attention, perhaps falling between the ambits of DAFS and NCC. While, following on the Wildlife and Countryside Act 1981 and other legislation,

SNH inherited from NCC responsibilities for SSSIs and site protection in general, it has also attempted to project an image of wider concern for the natural heritage in general.

The setting up of SNH and the nature of its early performance clearly hark back to the opinions of the Ritchie Committee of the 1940s in terms of their general character if not of their precise detail. It is difficult to avoid the conclusion that the highly centralised but narrowly focused character of the NC/NCC had given rise to an unsustainable form of conservation.

Agency Re-Sructuring : Forestry

Symptoms of stresses and strains have also been apparent in the forestry sector. During the 1980s, serious questioning was addressed at the type, location and purposes of forests being created in Britain, but the ensuing policy adaptations were piecemeal and incremental rather than radical and comprehensive. The main trends can be summed up as a 'greening' of forestry policy, and a weakening of the primacy of wood production as a policy objective. Most of the policy modifications stemmed from external influences, rather than being initiated within the Forestry Commission itself. The role of the FC underwent significant change. Throughout most of its existence, it had been directly responsible for most of the afforestation effort in Britain. While it also undertook the administration of planting grants for the private sector, it was heavily involved in acquiring, planting and managing forest land. With the advent of the Thatcher government, it was made clear that most afforestation would now be carried out by the private sector rather than directly by the Forestry Commission itself. Furthermore, a programme of partial privatisation of FC land was begun. The relative roles of the Commission therefore changed, with that of forest ownership and production weakening and that of administration and regulation strengthening. The distinction between the Forest Enterprise and Forestry Authority functions thus became clearer, and this distinction did not always fit comfortably within the structure of the organisation.

The decade had opened with a call for a policy review (House of Lords,

1980) and, indeed, with a plea that the "objectives of British forestry policy should not be confined exclusively to the production of timber". It ended with a similar call, by the House of Commons Agriculture Committee in 1990. Eventually, in 1991, there was some response from government, in the form of a new policy statement. In this statement, the two main policy aims were stated to be the sustainable management of existing woods and forests, and a steady expansion of tree cover.

The 1991 statement failed to satisfy the critics of forestry policy. In 1993, for example, the House of Commons Environment Committee concluded that existing policy had failed to set adequate priorities for achieving multiple benefits in different forests and in different situations. It also considered that clarification in relation to EC policies was necessary, and that spatially-disaggregated policies were required, so that the different situations pertaining in the various parts of Britain could be more clearly reflected and accommodated. Fuller co-ordination of forestry with other rural policies was also urged.

Perhaps the most damning conclusion of the Environment Committee was contained in the apparently innocuous statement that "the change in emphasis, away from forests created purely for wood production, together with changing public aspirations for forestry, have developed at a faster rate than the institutional and administrative structures responsible for forest policies and practices" (House of Commons Environment Committee 1993). The sting in this statement is heightened by the fact that a restructuring of the Forestry Commission had occurred less than a year before the Committee's report was issued. That restructuring, partial though it may have been, was itself carried out in response to criticism of the functioning of the Commission, and in particular of its combined responsibility for functions of enterprise, promotion and regulation (House of Commons Agriculture Committee, 1990).

Forestry Commission

The thrust of the Environment Committee's conclusion is that the Forestry Commission's structure has failed to adapt to the changes in public aspirations and stated policies that have occurred over the years. These changes are extensive: some involve completely new functions and responsibilities, whilst others reflect changes in emphases. While secondary objectives of providing rural employment and insuring against a world-wide shortage of timber were identified from the earliest days of the Forestry Commission, recreational and environmental objectives were not formally added until 1960s and 1970s. Under the Countryside (Scotland) Act of 1967 and the Countryside Act of 1968, the Forestry Commission was given a general responsibility to "have regard to the desirability of conserving the natural beauty and amenity of the countryside". More recently, the Wildlife and Countryside (Amendment) Act of 1985 gave the Commission a more particular duty of attempting to achieve a "reasonable balance" between afforestation, forest management and timber production on the one hand, and conservation of landscape and wildlife on the other. The practical significance of such responsibilities and duties is debatable, but it is clear that critics of the Forestry Commission have not been satisfied that their formal expression in statute has been translated into practice. Nor, on the evidence of the House of Commons Environment Committee's report, have they been satisfied by the limited restructuring of the Commission that took place in 1992.

From 1 April 1992, the Forestry Commission was reorganised to make a clearer distinction between its two main roles. Its regulatory and promotional (including grant-aiding) function is carried out by the new Forestry Authority, which together with a Policy and Resources Group makes up the Department of Forestry. Forest Enterprise has responsibility for managing the Forestry Commission's remaining forests. These components of the Forestry Commission continue to be overseen and directed by its Board of Commissioners and Director-General. Unusually for a government department, which is its formal status, the Forestry Commission has a chairman and commissioners, the performance of the Board being "subject to ministerial direction" (Forestry Commission, 1992). The nature of the Forestry Commission is further complicated by the fact that as a government department, it "reports collectively and individually to the

Secretary of State for Scotland, the Minister of Agriculture, Fisheries and Food, and the Secretary of State for Wales" (Forestry Commission, 1992).

This institutional structure has not easily accommodated, or responded to, the changing demands and concerns about afforestation and forest management in Britain in recent years. The Forestry Commission has generally been reactive rather than proactive in relation to environmental issues in particular. For example, it was pressure from the, then, Nature Conservancy Council and voluntary environmental groups that helped to get the broadleaves issue on the policy agenda. Rightly or wrongly, the Commission has been perceived as being dominated by wood-production interests. The fact that commissioners are nominated from within the Commission (House of Commons Environment Committee, 1993) may have helped to perpetuate that domination. And although the activities of the Commission have been repeatedly scrutinised both formally by House of Commons committees and informally by a variety of bodies, the mechanisms of its accountability remain obscure in the eyes of many critics.

A further problem has been geographical structure. From the outset, the Forestry Commission has had responsibility for Great Britain as a whole, but not for Northern Ireland. For a time, separate committees dealt with Scotland, England and Wales, but when the Commission headquarters were relocated from London to Edinburgh in the 1970s even that acknowledgement of distinctive concerns in the different parts of Britain disappeared. It is perhaps ironic that the concerns about forestry and afforestation in the different parts of Britain have become even more distinctive since then. For example the broadleaves issue emerged in lowland England, while afforestation in upland Scotland gave rise to controversial issues of environmental impact and planning.

In short, the Forestry Commission has been perceived by many as a monolithic body which has been slow to respond to national and regional concerns and to concerns about objectives other than wood production. That this perception has endured despite recent changes in structure and policy is clearly reflected in the recent report of the House of Commons Environment Committee (1993). It recommended that:

"major changes be made in order that forestry in England[5] is sufficiently diverse, flexible and abundant to meet today's needs without compromising those of future generations. We believe that reforms are necessary at the highest level, by developing a forest strategy for the United Kingdom as a whole and within it separate policies for England, Wales, Scotland and Northern Ireland, as well as at regional level by developing indicative strategies for planning and managing new and existing forests. More particularly, there needs to be a clearer statement explaining the importance of trees for this country and their purpose: at present there is no formal process or framework for setting national priorities and objectives".

The chairman of the House of Commons Environment Committee has recently expressed disappointment at the government's response (UK Government, 1993) to the Committee's recommendations (Jones, 1994). In essence, the government accepted some of the detailed points but rejected the major proposals for separate national strategies for the constituent countries of the UK. The government has, however, subsequently produced 'Sustainable forestry: the UK programme' (UK Government, 1994). Following the UNCED Conference in 1992, the UK Prime Minister had made a commitment to produce a national plan to show how the government intended to implement the Forest Principles agreed at Rio. The sustainable forestry programme purports to "pull together the various strands of the Government's forestry policy and programmes into a coherent whole, taking into account the international principles and guidelines to which we are committed". Perhaps not surprisingly in such a document, little is said either about administrative structures or about internal variations within the UK.

Several features characterise the forestry policy climate in Britain during the 1980s. In addition to the overall 'greening' tendency, there has been a trend toward a proliferation of policy elements. The agricultural departments have introduced farm woodland schemes, whilst the Countryside Commission has promoted community forests and the concept of a National Forest. In effect these agencies were formulating their own forestry policies alongside that of the Forestry Commission. Another feature was the emergence of spatial or geographical issues in stronger forms than had previously been apparent. These issues had various dimensions.

At the regional level, indicative forestry strategies were introduced and incorporated into the planning system in Scotland at the end of the 1980s. At a different level, new attention was focused on urban fringes as locations where afforestation could usefully be undertaken. The Countryside Commission made much of the running on this issue. At a different level again, the Secretary of State for the Environment announced in 1988, in response to environmental interests, that there would now be a presumption against commercial coniferous afforestation in the English uplands. Such issues were probably influential in leading to the Environment Committee's call for spatial disaggregation of forestry policies, perceiving the structure of the Forestry Commission and of existing policies as too monolithic.

Like the Nature Conservancy, the Forestry Commission had been set up as a British body with assurances that intra-British distinctiveness would be recognised by separate divisions. Like the Nature Conservancy and its successor agencies, the Forestry Commission in practice became increasingly centralised, albeit eventually with a British headquarters in Edinburgh. Like the conservation agency, the Forestry Commission was characterised by a narrow focus (afforestation geared to wood production) and a wide geographical coverage. Like its conservation counterpart, it appears to have been insufficiently flexible and insufficiently sensitive to geographical variations to adapt successfully to the changing circumstances of recent years. While the degree of restructuring may as yet be less than in the case of the Nature Conservancy Council, the trend is clearly in the same direction.

Agency Structure and Sustainability.

The basic structures of land-use administration in Britain date from an earlier age with circumstances and concerns quite different from those of the late 20th century. Today, a central concern is that of sustainable development, and not least of sustainable use of environmental resources. David Pearce contends that two of the main obstacles to sustainability in the UK are institutional structure and failure to integrate and co-ordinate policies (Pearce, 1993). The sectoral structure of land use administration, with built-in tensions (whether 'constructive' or not) would seem to exemplify his contention, and the lack of policy co-ordination is all too apparent. For many years the basic policies operated by the main agencies were in clear conflict, with one agency offering incentives for, for example, the drainage of wetlands whilst another sought their protection. At the same time, there were clear gaps in the sense of important environmental issues falling between the remits of sectoral agencies, with the result that they were largely ignored. One obvious example of this general point is that of soil conservation.

A sectoral agency structure has impeded but not prevented the adaptation of land use policies and their co-ordination and integration. Over the last few years there have, however, been signs of partial convergence of policies, in spite of the sectoral nature of agency structure. Previous reference has been made to the objectives of Scottish Natural Heritage and to the 1968 and 1985 additions to forestry policy. In 1986, a new Agriculture Act placed a duty on the agricultural departments to strike a balance between:

- the promotion and maintenance of a stable and efficient agricultural industry;
- the economic and social interests or rural areas;
- the conservation and enhancement of the natural beauty of the countryside;
- the promotion of the enjoyment of the countryside by the public.

The primacy of food production within agriculture has weakened, just as has that of wood production within forestry. With this broadening of concerns, the appropriateness of the essentially single-sector agency structure fades. Whilst some convergence of policy objectives has occurred within the existing agency structure, the stresses that have occurred in the conservation and forestry sectors in particular have been very apparent. It is arguable that a different agency structure might have accommodated policy co-ordination more readily. The emergence of SNH from NCC and CCS is perhaps only the first chapter of a continuing saga of restructuring. Perhaps here there is an exemplification of the notion that experiments are first tried in the peripheries of states, and then transferred to the core (Flowerdew, 1982): the consideration given in 1994 to the possible merging of English Nature and the Countryside Commission would seem to be in line with this view[6]. The House of Commons Environment Committee, however, advocated a much more sweeping reform, with the setting up of a combined ministry of environment, agriculture and rural affairs. However logical this might be, it is probably unlikely to happen in the foreseeable future, but a significant step towards it would be the establishment of a single agency for agriculture, forestry and conservation. It remains to be seen whether the recent manifestations of restructuring will ultimately lead to this state of affairs[7].

The agency structure that has been in place during much of the second half of the 1900s has certainly not facilitated policy co-ordination and integration. Nor has it facilitated the introduction of policies conducive to sustainability. The "constructive tension" which for several decades existed between the sectoral agencies tended to give rise to a defensive stance on the part of the conservation agency, rather than to the incorporation of conservation attitudes in the mainstream policies of the agricultural and forestry agencies. Perhaps that tension, and the underlying agency structure which it reflected, was more suited to objectives of protection or preservation than of sustainability. It is true, of course, that a lack of integration of agricultural and environmental policies is not a feature peculiar to Britain. It has also occurred in some other countries and at supra-national levels, notably in the European Community. Indeed, OECD has concluded that "it is clear that administrative arrangements exert considerable influence and, in many countries, are impeding the development of integrated policies" (OECD, 1989). There are signs, however, that shifts are underway (OECD, 1993), for example with the introduction of 'agri-environmental measures' in the CAP reforms.

The narrow focus of the single sector agencies has not been the only point of criticism. Sensitivity to geographical variations has been another major concern, not just in relation to conservation in northern Scotland, but more generally in forestry matters, as the recommendations of the Environment Committee suggest. It is also noticeable that member states of the EU were invited to devise national, regional or zonal programmes under the 'agri-environmental' measures. In other words, scales at levels below that of the state have been attracting increased attention. Along with the general trend towards the broadening of policies beyond single-sector foci, there has been one of increasingly recognising regional variations within Britain.

This combination of widening sectoral concern but narrowing geographical focus would seem to call into question the long-term prospects for the survival of the type of single sector GB agencies that have dominated rural land use policy for close on half a century. Supra-national (EU) influences are growing, not only through the Common Agricultural Policy but also by means of the Habitats Directive and the possible evolution of common forestry policy. At the same time, awareness of intra-British variations has strengthened. Perhaps the intermediate, i.e. British, scale is doomed to become less decisive. Whether further restructuring will occur, and whether it will foster policy integration and the drive for sustainability, remains to be seen. The expectation, however, is that the answer to these questions will be positive.

Notes

1. MAFF Ministry of Agriculture and Fisheries; WOAD Welsh Office Agriculture Department; DAFS Department of Agriculture and Fisheries for Scotland (now SOAFD - Scottish Office Agriculture and Fisheries Department).

2. The Nature Conservancy Council replaced the Nature Conservancy in 1965.

3. Now the Scottish Office Environment Department.

4. 'National' here refers to England, Scotland and Wales separately.

5. The Committee's remit extended only to England, although many of its general observations applied also to other parts of the UK.

6. The Secretary of State for the Environment announced in October 1994 that it had been decided not to proceed with a merger of the Countryside Commission and English Nature. Instead "a programme of closer working is to be developed" (Hansard, House of Commons, Written Answers, 17 October 1994).

7. Following a structural review, a proposal was announced in May 1995 for a regrouping of responsibilities within The Scottish Office which would bring together agricultural and environmental affairs. At the time of writing, a final decision had not been made.

References

Flowerdew, R (ed.) (1982) *Institutions and Geographical Patterns*, Croom Helm, London.

Forestry Commission (1992) *The Forestry Commission of Great Britain*, FC, Edinburgh.

House of Commons Agriculture Committee (1990) *Land use and Forestry* HC16, HMSO, London.

House of Commons Environment Committee (1993) *Forestry and the Environment,* HC 257 1992-93, HMSO, London.

House of Lords Select Committee (1980) *The Scientific Aspects of Forestry*, HL 381, HMSO, London.

Jones, R (1994) National Forestry Strategy Required, *Land Use Policy* 11: 124-127.

Lowe, P, Cox, G, MacEwen M, O'Riordan T and Winter, M (1986*) Countryside Conflicts: the Politics of Farming, Forestry and Conservation*, Gower/Temple Smith, Aldershot.

Mackay, D G (1994) *Rural Land Use Agencies in Scotland*, Unpublished PhD thesis, University of Aberdeen.

Mather, A S (1993) Protected Areas in the Periphery: Conservation and Controversy in Northern Scotland, *Journal of Rural Studies,* 9: 371-84.

Organisation for European Co-operation and Development (1989) *Agricultural and Environmental Policies: Opportunities for Integration*, OECD, Paris.

Organisation for European Cooperation and Development (1993) *Agricultural and Environmental Policy Integration: Recent Progress and New Directions.* OECD, Paris.

Pearce, D (1993) *Blueprint 3 - Measuring Sustainable Development.* Earthscan, London.

Scottish Development Department (1973) *Land Resource Use in Scotland; the Government's Observations on the Report of the Select Committee on Scottish Affairs*, Cmnd 5428, HMSO, Edinburgh.

Scottish Natural Heritage (1993*) Annual Report 1992-93*, SNH, Edinburgh.

Scottish National Parks Committee and the Scottish Wildlife Conservation Committee (1947) *National Parks and the Conservation of Nature in Scotland*, Cmnd 7235, (Ramsay/Ritchie Committees), HMSO, Edinburgh.

Select Committee on Scottish Affairs (1972) *Land Resource Use in Scotland*, HC Paper 51, 1971-72, HMSO, London.

Sheail, J (1976) *Nature in Trust: the History of Nature Conservation in Britain*, Blackie, Edinburgh.

UK Government (1993) *The Government's Response to the First Report from the House of Commons Select Committee on the Environment*, Cmnd 2259, HMSO, London.

UK Government (1994) *Sustainable Forestry: the UK programme*, Cmnd 2429, HMSO, London.

Wildlife Conservation Special Committee (England and Wales) (1947*) Conservation of Nature in England and Wales* (Huxley Committee), Cmnd 7122, HMSO, London.

CHAPTER 6

Rural Training & Enterprise Councils -
Local People Influencing Local Decisions?

Trevor Hart

Employment in rural Britain has been undergoing some fundamental changes. While employment in agriculture has continued its long decline, recent years have seen new patterns of economic activity emerge. Rural areas have seen growth in manufacturing employment and the emergence of new forms of employment in the service sector (Fothergill and Gudgin, 1982; Cloke *et al*, 1994). However, this positive picture of the rural economy is balanced in a number of studies which place stress on the problems faced by businesses and workers in rural areas (see, for example, Errington *et al*, 1989; Cloke *et al*, 1994; ACORA, 1990). In summary, these are seen as including: a persistent problem of a lack of jobs and a lack of choice of jobs; problems associated with the availability of personal services, particularly transport and childcare; the urban location of most business services, particularly training; the small size of many rural businesses and the high proportion of self-employed; and the geographical dispersion of businesses and residents. Allied to this, rural areas have experienced many of the recessionary pressures affecting the rest of the country, giving rise to increasing levels of unemployment and underemployment. There have also been doubts expressed about the quality of many of the new jobs which have been created, with a significant proportion of low paid, insecure, seasonal or part-time work associated with some of the growing sectors. Clearly, there are significant variations between rural areas: indeed, Errington *et al* (1989) usefully point out that, in employment terms, there is no such thing as a "typical rural area".

Most of the research on which these pictures of Britain's rural economy are based dates from 1990 or earlier. The 1980s had seen the development of a number of policy responses to economic change, some of which - notably Rural Development Programmes - had a specific focus on rural areas, while others were nation-wide in their application. It is the view of Cloke *et al* (1994) that the "problems of rural employment have not yet been solved by rural development policy responses in England". More recently, there have been a number of changes in economic development policy, with a reformulation of local authorities' powers and a restructuring of central government spending and agencies. A major change to emerge, following the White Paper *Employment for the 1990s*, has been the establishment of Training and Enterprise Councils (TECs). In the last four years, a network of TECs has been established across England and Wales. Launched with a clear remit to change Britain's much-criticised training culture, they have increasingly taken on a broader role in economic development.

The aim of this chapter is to explore how these bodies relate to the individuals and organisations that make up the communities that they serve, and in particular to consider how they are responding to the distinct problems faced in promoting the economic development of rural areas. It touches on two long-standing issues associated with government funded programmes focused on rural areas. First, does the level of funding available to TECs allow them to address adequately the problems associated with meeting the needs of dispersed rural communities? Second, are these local communities able to exercise any effective influence over the nature of the programmes managed and delivered by TECs, to ensure that they meet the needs of the locality? The latter point is perhaps particularly important, given the absence of a "typical rural area" to act as a model for action.

In seeking to address these questions, this chapter draws on material gathered for a study commissioned by the Employment Department (Haughton *et al*, 1995a) into the relationship between TECs and their 'non-employer stakeholders'. This term encompasses a wide and varied range of organisations, including local authorities, trades unions, representative bodies for local communities and business, voluntary organisations, and training and education providers. The study was carried out in early 1994 and consisted of three inter-related pieces of research: a postal questionnaire survey of the Chief Executives of the (then) 75 TECs in England; a series of interviews with a number of national representative bodies and a review of analytical and advisory material that they have produced; and five case studies of individual TECs, to examine the evolution and practice of working relationships in greater depth.

The chapter first gives some essential background for the subject, and then gives a summary of the results of the research at the national level. These national results are important as they provide a picture of the constraints and pressures shaping the national framework within which rural TECs have to operate. The final section then attempts to draw out particular issues affecting the relationships of TECs with rural communities.

Background

The concept of TECs was announced in the White Paper *Employment for the 1990s*, published in 1988. Their task was summarised as being (p40):

"to contract with Government to plan and deliver training and to promote and support the development of small business and self-employment in their area."

Initially, TECs were essentially an institutional development (Bennett, 1993), rather than being concerned with radically reshaping established programmes concerned with training and enterprise. They have been established as companies limited by guarantee, with a board of up to fifteen people. At least two thirds of the board members must be "employers at top management level drawn from the private sector." (Employment Department 1988, p41). These board members are chosen not as representatives of their organisations, but as individuals with particular skills and knowledge valuable in guiding the operation of the TEC, particularly at the strategic level. TECs do not run training programmes themselves, but sub-contract these activities to local providers in much the same way as the area offices of the Training Agency before them. However, the White Paper noted that, in future, contracts would be performance-related and linked to the achievement of specified targets.

Perhaps the two key features of this institutional development are the stress placed on decision making at the local level, and the leadership role assigned to the private sector. The localist perspective is strongly emphasised in the White Paper (p39), while the involvement of employers is intended both to emphasise the importance of training to employers as a whole, and to ensure that the range of training services provided by the TECs is more relevant to the needs of employers.

By late 1991, the complete network of TECs was in place. Their size varies considerably, with some having small populations and workforces, like the Isle of Wight and St Helens, while others, such as Devon and Cornwall and Manchester, are of a considerable size. While these variations can be said to reflect the diversity of their local areas (Employment Department, 1994b), differences in size are reflected in budgets and staffing, and thus, to some extent, in capability.

The major part of TECs' budgets continues to be devoted to youth (YT) and adult (ET/AT/TFW) training, with these two elements accounting for 71% of TEC expenditure in 1993 (Employment Department, 1994a). A significant development in this area since TECs were launched has been the increasing importance of a TEC's performance in influencing its level of funding. In particular, a growing amount of funding - between 25 and 40% in 1993/94 - is closely related to the immediate results of TEC activity (output related funding - ORF), and in particular the success of the TECs' mainstream training programmes. As well as successful employment placements on completion of training, considerable emphasis is placed on progress towards achieving the National Education and Training Targets (NETTS): so, for example, ORF would be related to a certain proportion of trainees achieving an NVQ at Level 2 on completion of their training.

Further emphasis on measuring TEC performance will come into play from 1995, when the first 'licensed' TECs will be operating under new contractual arrangements between TECs and Government. TECs awarded the three year licences will enjoy something akin to 'preferred supplier' status and consequently their annual contract negotiations with government should be shorter: they will also enjoy some other benefits, such as a greater freedom to spend their reserves. These new arrangements are "designed to support, ensure and to demonstrate continuous improvement in TECs' performance, value for money and accountability." (Employment Department, 1994c, p1). The criteria for awarding a TEC a licence are: the strength of its strategy as expressed in its corporate plan; its strategic impact, including progress towards education and training targets and the level of partnership the TEC has achieved with other key local agents; a number of outcome and cost indicators for the main training and enterprise activities; and an assessment of the TEC's 'capability' to meet local and national requirements throughout the three year period of the licence, taking in areas such as finance, competence of its staff, and its influence over its constituency.

At the same time as there has been ever closer monitoring of the TECs' performance, there has been an increase in their responsibilities, contributing to an increasing interest and involvement on the part of TECs in local economic development. This increasing involvement has meant an increase in the amount of partnership activity for the TECs, a feature further emphasised by the creation of Integrated Regional Offices for central government departments, and the launch of the Single Regeneration Budget.

Generally, the documents and developments reviewed above lack specific references to the particular issues facing the development of training and enterprise activity in rural areas - principally issues related to access to training and differences in employment structure. Clearly, however, working with rural communities may require distinctive approaches from TECs, and developments such as local government review - confined in England to the 'shire' areas - and the increasing importance given to output-related funding have the potential to generate serious impacts on the work of rural TECs. Such impacts may show themselves in contrasts between more urban and more rural TECs, or between the urban and rural parts of a TEC's area. They will also have an influence on the relationships between a TEC and its stakeholders.

TECs and non-employer stakeholders: the national context

The Employment Department's *Guide to Planning* (1989, p3) outlined the main rationales for TECs engaging with employer and non-employer stakeholders

"A TEC's primary customers are the businesses that operate in its area and local people. As a consequence, organisations which represent local people and businesses or their interests will be important stake-holders in the work of a TEC. Providers of vocational education, training and support for enterprise will also be significant stake-holders. Stake-holders will want to share and help shape a TEC's vision and will be vitally interested in playing their part to achieve this goal. Indeed the chances of a TEC realising its vision will be substantially reduced if these stake-holders are not actively consulted and involved."

It was the main objective of the research on which this chapter is based to assess the TECs' consultation and involvement with non-employer stakeholders.

Identifying non-employer stakeholders

As part of this research, TEC Chief Executives were asked to identify the key non-employer stakeholders in their areas, and the results are shown in figure 6.1. All saw local authorities as key stakeholders, but a significant number saw only a limited role for Industry Training Organisations, trade unions, community groups and the voluntary sector. Only four TECs saw the individual - the unemployed person, the trainee or others - as a stakeholder, with the implicit assumption being that the voluntary and community sector in particular would act as a link to individual views and interests.

Working relationships between TECs and local authorities were generally found to have been good, but there was also a certain amount of distrust and suspicion that emerged from the evidence. In part, this can be attributed to initial and recurring 'turf wars' between TECs and local authorities (Haughton *et al*, 1995b): there is also some evidence that these tensions were exacerbated by a lack of sensitivity on the part of TECs in their dealings with local government. More generally, however, a more positive approach to partnership working is emerging. This trend is no doubt partly attributable to lessons learned by TECs in their early years of operation, delivering mainstream programmes, but there is also an increasing requirement by government for partnership working in new initiatives, most recently in the development of proposals for 'Business Link', one-stop shops for business advice and support.

Figure 6. 1: Key non-employer stakeholders - TEC Chief Executives survey response

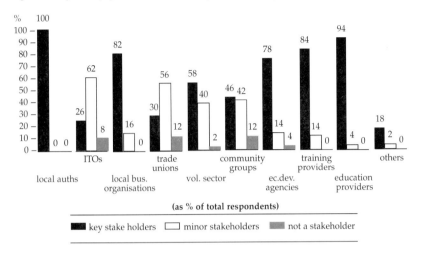

(as % of total respondents)

■ key stake holders ☐ minor stakeholders ▨ not a stakeholder

In the case of the voluntary sector, its fragmented nature often proved to be something of a problem for TECs: one TEC noted the problems inherent in dealing with over 2000 voluntary organisations in its area. Where local co-ordinating or umbrella bodies exist, their boundaries do not always coincide with those of the TEC, and such bodies do not always have the capacity to represent the diversity of the local voluntary sector in a coherent manner. Individual voluntary organisations often face an added difficulty in their relationships with the TEC, in that they can be contracted to the TEC as a training provider, as well as seeking to play a wider representative role. The study found the voluntary sector to be the source of some trenchant criticism of TECs, perhaps reflecting an underlying difference of philosophy: as one respondent put it:

"Community groups are uncomfortable working with the contract culture that the TEC is working with".

Such a judgement was sometimes reinforced by drawing an unfavourable comparison with the approach adopted by the TECs' predecessors, the area offices of the MSC, which were felt to be more 'community minded'.

The study found substantial evidence of TECs investing resources and staff time in ensuring that networks are strengthened with individual sectors of stakeholders. The case studies also revealed very high levels of consultation by TECs with the wide group of organisations encountered. However, this activity had not been able to dispel fully the feeling among many organisations that they came some way behind employers in importance and influence, in the eyes of the TECs.

Mechanisms and structures for communication and co-operation

TECs have a number of means of relating to their non-employer stakeholders. Board members have been assigned a role of forging links with the community, as well as with business; most TECs have developed a variety of sub-board structures to draw in the expertise of non-employer stakeholders; publicity and marketing also have a part to play in developing communication; in addition, more informal means can be used, relying on the interaction of TEC staff with outside individuals, organisations and networks. The case studies in particular revealed a rich variety of approaches, and a pattern of steadily increasing effort by TECs.

Board members are chosen for their individual expertise, and not as 'representatives' of specific groups of stakeholders. The research suggested that as far as the wider community is concerned, there is some doubt about the role of board members - in terms of their influence over the officers, who many see as effectively running the TEC; in terms of a lack of clarity about their remit; in terms of how they were selected; and a questioning of whether the voice of a non-employer board member carries the same weight as that of an employer member. While there was no evidence of employer and non-employer members consistently occupying different camps, there was evidence that each group felt that they brought different qualities to the board:

"they [private sector members] have highly developed business skills, poorly developed community skills. The TEC is the first time they find themselves in a broader stream: it's a salutary experience" (local authority TEC board member).

The research revealed a wide diversity of approaches to the development of sub-board structures. For example, a TEC in one area operated with only three sub-committees, while in another there were eighteen panels, most of which were based around industrial sectors. The most radical approach found was one involving the establishment of a TEC Council of 100 members, which is the ultimate 'ownership' body of the TEC and is responsible for selecting TEC board directors at an annual meeting. In the eyes of stakeholders such structures suffer from the same shortcomings as TEC boards, and particularly a lack of clarity about their level of influence and doubts about their accountability.

Although TECs devote considerable effort to publicity and consultation, this was not always seen to be productive. The glossy and sometime glamorous image that some TECs project may have been counter-productive in forming relations with some non-employer stakeholders, while several respondents felt that TECs too often elided consultation and public relations. The irritation that this can create was illustrated by a voluntary sector organisation in one of the case study areas:

"They are very into status and everything has to be big and glossy and grand ..... The annual event is the AGM, held in an expensive marquee with silk lining and chandeliers: It is like a royal wedding reception!"

All of the case study TECs put considerable effort into consultation, but this may have been undermined by a widespread doubt among non-employer stakeholders that their participation in such activity had any tangible impact on what the TEC decided to do. The findings of the Chief Executives survey indicated that most TECs could point to some circumstance in the past twelve months where non-employer stakeholders' views had influenced their plans or strategies: however, only two TECs were able to identify areas of their activity where non-employer stakeholders' views would be sought before a decision was taken.

Patterns, problems and possibilities

While the research suggested that TECs are gradually improving the quality of their working relationships with non-employer stakeholders, there is great variability between TECs as to how much they have achieved. Many bodies consulted in the research framed their comments on local TEC performance in the context of a lack of freedom of action that the TEC was felt to have, being constrained by a national procedural and financial framework:

"Influence on the TEC agenda is essentially top-down, because it is delivering a product on behalf of the Department [of Employment] that is already defined by the Department" (TEC officer).

Other barriers to effective contact revealed in the Chief Executives' survey were found in: the multiplicity of stakeholders that TECs had to deal with; time and resource constraints on TECs; political and territorial issues connected with the establishment and functions of TECs; some continuing mistrust and suspicion of TECs on the part of non-employer stakeholders; and sometimes a simple difficulty in understanding how to communicate with the TECs, given unfamiliarity with their mission and methods of working. Clearly, a solution to these problems requires an effort to be made by both TECs and stakeholders.

A country-wide perspective gained from the national surveys did not reveal any clear differences between more urban and more rural TECs on the basic questions, such as who they identified as being key non-employer stakeholders, methods of communication or barriers to effective contact. However, it did identify a number of TECs taking specific initiatives to try to relate more effectively to their rural context: these were echoed and amplified by the case studies.

TECs in the rural context

While the legislative framework for TECs, and the subsequent operational guidance, may have lacked any great rural dimension, the existence of specific rural issues affecting their working was recognised at an early stage by the TECs themselves. The main sign of this was the setting up, in September 1991, of the Consortium of Rural TECs. Twenty seven of the seventy four English TECs are members and, in the words of its mission statement, it "exists to help its members meet the training and enterprise needs of rural areas". It is principally financed by members' subscriptions, but with support from other interested organisations such as the Rural Development Commission. Among its objectives is that of "raising the significance of the rural dimension at national level, and within the work of member TECs". In furtherance of this objective the Consortium commissions research, participates in development projects and is developing a resource base for use by its members: part of this resource is to be found in the identification of the 'best practice' of its members.

There are some clear examples of rural TECs recognising the particular issues that they face:

"the rural communities, with their predominantly agricultural base, often restricted opportunities, transport facilities are poor, employment choices are limited and accessibility is a problem." (TEC Director, 1993)

The nature of the key issues in training and enterprise in rural areas has been established by a number of studies, some of which were noted in the introduction to this chapter. A key example is that undertaken in 1988 for the Rural Development Commission and published under the title *Employment and training in rural areas* (Errington *et al*, 1989). It summarised the position (p54) as:

"rural businesses, rural employers, rural employees and the rural workforce as a whole are at a significant disadvantage compared to their urban counterparts. This disadvantage stems largely from the small size of rural firms and their distance from existing training providers."

Small businesses are only one of the many groups of stakeholders with whom the TECs will need to work if they are to make an impact in rural areas. Many non-employer stakeholders are also small and will face similar handicaps to small firms - limited resources and limited capacity to engage with the TEC, in consultation or programme delivery. The success with which TECs deal with the particular problems of rural areas can powerfully influence the level of success that they achieve in forging relationships with stakeholders. The research identified a number of factors, related both to TECs' methods of working and to the framework within which they operate, which act to inhibit the full achievement of this success.

A question of style?

Partly because of the political rhetoric surrounding their launch and partly because of the very nature of the concept, tension between TECs and non-employer stakeholders was always a possibility. In the words of a voluntary organisation in one of the case study areas:

"The TEC has arrived on the scene and a lot of people say this is the cuckoo in the nest. ..... The most negative view of them is as an imposed body, and everyone has to move over to make room for them".

Given this context, TECs clearly needed to be careful over matters of style and of presentation: this was proved to be true in the case study rural areas.

In many rural areas, there is in all probability a certain amount of innate conservatism. This is perhaps typified by a quotation from a local business reproduced in a case study in TEC's *Economic and Labour Market Review*: "I am fairly conservative about the area. I don't want it to expand at any faster rate. We do need to grow .... (but) I don't want anything to change": such attitudes are not confined to the business community. The combination of this type of attitude with the remit that TECs were handed at their launch - to achieve some sort of cultural change with regard to training - indicates that rural TECs would have to have operated particularly carefully if no local sensibilities were to be disturbed.

There was also some evidence that TECs were insufficiently aware of the potential tension that exists between 'the city'/main town and the rest of a rural county, often corresponding with their area of operation. Rural TECs are typically based in the main urban centre, which is also home to a large proportion of the area's population, public administration and employers. As such, the urban influences that it represents can be seen by some to exercise a disproportionate influence over the TEC's policies and operations over the whole of its area. While this tended to be dismissed by TECs as parochialism, when allied to the 'glossy' approach that TECs are felt to use, it had a tendency to generate suspicion among some stakeholders. So, in one of the case study areas, there was some general unease among stakeholders at the approach of the "city-minded people" that the TEC was alleged to employ. This was felt to be a reflection of the all-out attempt to court the private sector - essential if the TEC was to achieve its mission of effecting a cultural change - but had the result of alienating many of its other stakeholders, by presenting the wrong image and speaking the wrong language:

"Part of the problem is that the TEC has been very image and marketing led, which people from the voluntary sector tend to be wary of" (local government officer).

While it may be difficult to support such assertions with hard evidence, these attitudes are not conducive to the development of effective working partnerships.

Getting to grips with rural issues

The research revealed a variety of initiatives being undertaken to address the rural dimension of individual TECs' work. There were a number of sectoral or area based initiatives focusing on specific rural matters, such as the impact of changes in the agricultural industry. In some cases, these initiatives were embedded in the formal sub-board structures of the TEC, through the establishment of separate panels with a specific responsibility for consulting on the issues locally and for monitoring the impacts of TEC activity. Examples were found of the appointment or identification of an officer with a remit to develop links with rural communities and to better inform the TEC about "rural needs and activities". There was also a variety of approaches to developing partnerships with rural agencies to address more effectively rural training and economic development needs: examples include Leicestershire TEC's Rural Issues Task Group and Lincolnshire TEC's Rural Action Team. Such initiatives were in addition to partnership building which has arisen through TECs' participation in Rural Development Programmes or in the course of involvement in putting forward bids to Rural Challenge.

Although many TECs can point to moves towards establishing a formal priority for rural issues, and to a number of initiatives such as those outlined above, this did not convince stakeholders that there was a real understanding of rural problems. In the research this was often articulated by stakeholders with the contention that TECs lacked a 'feel' for rural matters:

"[Initially they] parachuted in people with largely urban business backgrounds. Urban business in [TEC area] is important - they're the big players. But 40% of the county lives in parishes of under 3000 population: until you've seen and understood this network of villages it's hard to take on board the difficulties of delivering a service" (voluntary sector organisation).

This perception was often related to a perceived failure on the part of TECs to appreciate fully the problems of access and mobility. While TECs indicated an awareness of transport and access problems in rural communities and reflected this in policy statements in corporate plans, stakeholders sometimes doubted that the true costs to the TEC of following through with such policies were adequately accommodated in budgets.

This is not to say that TECs do not attempt to make special provision to meet the needs of rural stakeholders. In one case study area the TEC could point to having established 21 rural outreach centres: others have invested in various forms of mobile provision, and travel contingency budgets exist. However, the fact that in most rural TEC areas the majority of youth and adult trainees are from the main urban centres, taken together with the nature of the national funding regime within which the TECs have to operate, was seen by some to lead to lead to a lack of sensitivity to the practical problems that are faced by trainees in rural areas:

"It's very difficult to get them to appreciate the special nature of providing youth training in a rural area. They don't really appreciate the problem. They're city-minded people who think you can just hop on a bus." (training provider).

Needs and resources

The 'small firm problem' identified in *Employment and training in rural areas* is not confined to businesses alone, but affects many of a TEC's stakeholders, who are similarly short of resources and capability. For example, it extends to including the small size of many training providers. Although rural areas typically possess a number of large training organisations - colleges, ATB Landbase, for example - these are often based in the urban centres serving their rural hinterlands. In the rural areas away from these centres, training providers are likely to be small organisations. While this can offer advantages associated with small businesses generally, such as flexibility, new requirements for meeting quality assurance standards or providing the accredited standards of workplace support required by NVQs can often seem uneconomic or otherwise prove difficult for organisations with few staff. The problems posed for small suppliers of services to TECs by guidelines such as those encompassed by *TEC quality assurance: supplier management* (Employment Department, 1993) have been addressed by a recent study by REPLAN for the Consortium of Rural TECs (CORT, 1994a): it concluded that TECs would need to take account of the special problems of small organisations in meeting new standards, and "What is required is the recognition that small suppliers will require initial support to enable them to ensure and maintain compliance." (p6)

Whether TECs deliver such support depends both on their willingness to do so and on their ability to do so: the latter element is substantially influenced by the nature of the funding mechanism for TECs. While individual TEC budgets are determined by negotiation between the TEC and the Employment Department, this negotiation takes place within a framework determined by national guidelines. The base is provided by the national allocation of public spending to TEC functions, which is then distributed on a regional basis. Within the allocations to ED regional office areas, the level of funding for individual TECs is related to historical ED spending levels in that area and to the size of the TEC's various client groups. This method of allocation results in over half the membership of the Consortium of Rural TECs being placed in the bottom third of English TECs with regard to total budgets, standardised by the size of their working populations (Twomey *et al*, 1994). Their dissatisfaction with this outcome is clearly illustrated in the 1993-94 Annual Report of the Consortium which states that it "continues lobbying to highlight the unfair advantage that the Government gives to urban areas as compared to the high needs of rural areas" (CORT, 1994b).

While such allocations may reflect variations in need as related to levels of unemployment, they may also point to a limited capability to meet rural needs. The increased importance being given to output related funding (ORF) seems likely to do little to enhance the capability of rural TECs. It has always been difficult to deliver training and enterprise services in rural areas in both an effective and an economical way, for the reasons outlined in *Employment and training in rural areas*. The criteria used in determining ORF and the 'tariffs' included in the new contractual relationships being established between TECs and ED - looking at unit costs for delivering YT and TFW - will not favour rural TECs. Indeed, concern about the effect of ORF on their operations has led the Consortium of Rural TECs to commission a study into its impact, due to report in 1995.

In terms of relationships with stakeholders, any such limitations on resources will clearly do little to improve matters. The use of output related funding measures has particular implications for those training providers and organisations dealing with disadvantaged groups who are more difficult to place in work and take more time and money to achieve a given level of vocational attainment: these concerns were strongly voiced in our rural case study areas. More generally, the further limitations that were placed on the capability for local action by the tight specification and monitoring of TECs activities were shown to act to undermine good working relationships:

"They have limited scope to reflect the views of other local bodies and to reflect the peculiarities of [TEC area]" (local government officer).

The extent to which stakeholders' interests are reflected in a TEC's programmes and actions can also be influenced by the capability of stakeholders and their representatives to put their case and to influence the TEC. While, like most rural areas, the case study areas had a dense network of community organisations, they were in many instances highly fragmented, and representative and umbrella bodies, such as RCCs or CVSs, were often poorly resourced. Several noted the demands made by regular and effective engagement with TEC processes: these included the time needed to study and understand the volume of paper relating to programmes and policies, as well as the cost and difficulty of getting to meetings in the (often distant) 'city' base of the TEC. Although there was some recognition of these problems by the TECs - for example, by having 'outreach' area-based meetings and indenting on the contacts of rural board directors - there is perhaps a specifically rural barrier to effective consultation and accountability stemming from the problems faced by rural representative organisations.

This was also true of another important stakeholder - trade unions. In one case study area, a trade union board member had to resign when his union area of operations was effectively doubled, making it impossible to fulfil his responsibilities on the TEC board. In this case, the TEC concerned regarded trade unions as an important means of reaching a wider group of stakeholders, including the unemployed, but is conscious of the limited and declining capacity of trade unions to fulfil this role:

"outside the main urban areas there are fewer and fewer senior trade union people on the ground locally" (TEC officer).

However, even if these problems of resources and capability can be overcome, the question remains as to how far rural non-employer stakeholders are able to exercise any real influence over the policies and actions of their local TEC, given the limitations on local autonomy facing all TECs.

Conclusions

Although many TECs have devoted a significant amount of effort to developing their local working relationships, there are a number of issues which need attention if TECs and non-employer stakeholders - in urban or rural areas - are to achieve a productive partnership. Improved communication, transparency and clarity of purpose on the part of TECs are still important in many cases, if the necessary foundation of understanding is to be established among non-employer stakeholders. However, even if these local issues were addressed, there would remain to be addressed a number of issues related to the national model on which TECs operate. In particular, the contrast between the ever tightening control and monitoring of TEC spending and performance, and the image at launch of "local people influencing local decisions", is not at all helpful in establishing good working relationships between TECs and stakeholders. The move to 'licensed' status and the development of a national code of practice on accountability (by the TEC National Council) are just two of the current initiatives aimed at contributing to progress in tackling this problem. However, the code of practice will only emerge in draft form in early 1995, and a reading of the guidance on the new contractual framework for TECs (Employment Department, 1994b) does not suggest a dramatic increase in local autonomy will be available to the licensed TECs. In the words of one TEC chair:

"TEC licensing - I look on it as a Treasury means of controlling the TECs. Yet another layer of control - detailed control. Merely an additional control and we're over-controlled already".

Within this national context it seems that there are some issues which can have particular impacts on rural TECs. Although conclusive research evidence is not yet available, it appears likely that a move towards increasing the importance of output related funding and the approach on which it is based will not help rural TECs to deliver the required services to dispersed rural communities. It has long been a contention of agencies advocating the cause of rural areas that the additional costs of servicing the needs of these communities are rarely fully recognised by public sector funding regimes. The move towards increasing the importance of output related funding appears to repeat a familiar pattern and as such is unlikely to make working relationships between TECs and rural stakeholders any easier.

However, the research identified several rural TECs which are making substantial efforts to identify and include a rural dimension in their activities. Nonetheless, some of these efforts are open to the criticism that, by setting up specific channels to deal with rural matters or by isolating the rural themes in their activities, they are only succeeding in marginalising rural issues and rural stakeholders: this echoes a concern found among other 'special needs' groups covered by TECs.

Clearly the important question for many stakeholders is whether the existence of the various consultative mechanisms and partnership arrangements actually affect the nature of a TEC's work programme or influence its methods of working. Past experience with major central government initiatives for rural areas, such as Rural Development Programmes, suggests that it is difficult for local agencies to exercise much influence or leverage over the programmes of agencies whose priorities and agendas are set elsewhere. The close scrutiny and monitoring of TECs against nationally based targets and standards does not suggest that they will move away from this established pattern. This tends to add to the national perception of TECs as only nominally locally based institutions which are effectively controlled from the centre, lacking the capacity to enter into a true partnership. More recently, there has been a growing concern about the political accountability of local QUANGOs such as TECs, an issue touched on - but not yet addressed - by the Nolan Committee (Committee on Standards in Public Life, 1995).

Thus, having suffered handicaps at the outset in their dealings with non-employer stakeholders, stemming from the rhetoric surrounding their launch and an often overly aggressive style of operation - perhaps particularly inappropriate for many rural areas - TECs now face a further problem of a general perception of them as unaccountable bodies lacking in local autonomy: this problem can only be exacerbated by the rigidity of operation of the national funding model. Only time will tell if changes which are being made to their (contractual) relationship with central government will act to improve or impair this image in the eyes of the non-employer stakeholders who can play a large part in helping them achieve their original mission.

Notes

The research on which this work is based was funded by the Employment Department, and carried out with colleagues at CUDEM, Leeds Metropolitan University and at the School of Geography at Manchester University: however, the views expressed here are entirely the responsibility of the author.

References

ACORA (1990) *Faith in the countryside*, Churchman Publishing, Worthing.

Bennett R, Wicks P and McCoshan A (1993) *Local empowerment and business services: Britain's experiment with TECs*, UCL Press, London.

Cloke P, Milbourne P and Thomas C (1994) *Lifestyles in rural England* (RDC Research report No.18), Rural Development Commision, Salisbury.

Committee on Standards in Public Life (1995) *First report of the Committee on Standards in Public Life*, Cmmd 2850-1, HMSO, London.

CORT (1994a) *QA and the small rural supplier of services to TECs*, Consortium of Rural TECs, Leicester.

CORT (1994b) *Annual Report 1993-4*, Consortium of Rural TECs, Leicester.

Employment Department (1988) *Employment for the 1990s*, Cmnd 540, HMSO, London.

Employment Department (1989) *Guide to planning*, ED, Sheffield.

Employment Department (1993) *TEC quality assurance: supplier management*, ED, Sheffield.

Employment Department (1994a) *TECs - Action '93: progress through partnership*, ED, Sheffield.

Employment Department (1994b) *TECs: Towards 2000*, ED, Sheffield.

Employment Department (1994c) *TECs - The new contract framework: 3 year licences*, ED, Sheffield.

Errington A, Bennett R and Marshall B (1989) *Employment and training in rural areas* (RDC Research report No.3), Rural Development Commission, Salisbury.

Fothergill S and Gudgin G (1982) *Unequal growth: urban and regional employment change in the UK*, Heinemann, London.

Haughton G, Hart T, Strange I, Thomas K and Peck J (1995a) *TECs and their non-employer stakeholders* (Research series No.46), ED, Sheffield.

Haughton G, Peck JA and Strange I (1995b) *Turf wars: the battle for control over English local economic development*, mimeo.

TEC Director (1993) Lincolnshire TEC aids rural communities, *TEC Director* 16, 16-17.

Twomey J, Tomkins JM, and Topham N (1994) Allocation and need in the distribution of training budgets: the case of English Training and Enterprise Councils, *Regional Studies* 28, 495-510.

CHAPTER 7

Conservation Amenity and Recreation Trusts:
A Private - Public Continuum*

Ian Hodge

Conventional analysis in environmental economics concentrates on the application of regulations and incentive policies which can lead private decision-makers to incorporate environmental values into their decision making. Occasionally, although unfashionably, consideration may be given to the potential for public ownership and management. These approaches are based on an assumption of a world comprised of profit maximising firms, utility maximising households and government agencies. This analysis disregards an important and growing role payed in a variety of sectors of the economy by non-profit organisations.

The conventional distinction between the public and private sectors is breaking down. It has perhaps always been something of a convenience with many marginal cases, but recent years have seen a steady blurring of the division to the point where we must at least recognise a continuum rather than a dichotomy. The erosion of the distinction is a consequence of a recognition of the limits of government on the one hand and of the limits of the 'free' market on the other. It is a change taking place throughout the economy, in the UK and beyond. Private firms now contract to undertake tasks which have previously been regarded as the exclusive role of the public sector: managing prisons, collecting rubbish or cleaning hospitals. At the same time, private organisations act as agents for government policy, such as in the areas of social services and housing. The limits are no longer clear.

This chapter reviews the role of non-profit organisations in the ownership and long term management of land for the provision of countryside benefits; the wildlife conservation, landscape and recreation benefits which are enjoyed by the wider public. We term these organisations Conservation, Amenity and Recreation Trusts (CARTs). They are non-profit organisations which aim to generate conservation, amenity and recreation

* This paper derives from reserch undertaken on a grant from the Levehulme Trust and conducted with Janet Dwyer. We are grateful to the Trust for making the work possible but the author takes sole responsibility for the views expressed in this paper.

benefits for the public through the ownership and management of rural land. What sets CARTs apart from many other contemporary landowners is that income generation from land is secondary to their principal land management objectives.

After a very brief description of these organisations and their scale, we outline the range of forms taken between purely private and purely public organisations. We then consider whether the conventional models of private, market-oriented organisations and of public agencies can be applied to them. The evidence indicates that neither is directly applicable. CARTs have particular characteristics, both strengths and weaknesses, linked to their non-profit status. However, they adopt a variety of forms, representing a continuum between the private and public extremes so that there can be no simple, single model to which they may be expected to conform. This presents problems as to how we should evaluate CARTs as a method for generating countryside goods as against more usual approaches of incentives for private managers or of direct public ownership. The final section of the chapter indicates some of the difficulties involved in seeking an adequate indicator of CART performance and concludes that in practice there will be a variety of assessments, by members, donors and government agencies and departments, that engender the beginnings of a quasi-market test for the success of individual organisations.

CARTs and the Rural Environment

A variety of non-profit organisations are playing an active role in respect of the management of the rural environment. CARTs represent a significant and growing form of institutional land ownership and management in the British Isles, controlling just over 0.4 million hectares. Collectively, CARTs have a combined membership of some 3.1 million (though this double-counts individuals who are members of more than one trust), a staff of over 2,000, and a financial turnover approaching £110 million. They are discussed in much more detail in Dwyer and Hodge (1995).

Amongst these organisations, The National Trust is by far the largest, accounting for about half of the total turnover. Its properties cover over 230,000 hectares and it is one of the largest landowners in the country. It has a membership of 2.2 million. Since the 1930s, the Trust has followed a policy of acquiring large country houses and their estates and it has also played a key role in their preservation. It has also acquired important stretches of countryside and coastline. There is a separate National Trust for Scotland.

Also of significant size is the Royal Society for the Protection of Birds, owning about 73,000 hectares. Both of the National Trust and the Royal Society for the Protection of Birds were founded over 100 years ago. A third major element, operating at both national and county level, is the network of Wildlife Trusts affiliated to the Royal Society for Nature Conservation. Together these County Trusts own nearly 60,000 hectares. In addition to these large and well-established groups, there is a growing number of other local and national organisations that operate as independent CARTs. Some 122 such CARTs together own or have assumed long-term management responsibility for a further 50,000 hectares of open land in the British Isles. This has risen from about 20,000 hectares in 1978. The average age of these organisations is very low; the median is 9 years and the mode is 2.5.

The Non-Profit Continuum

CARTs take on a wide variety of organisational forms, ranging from those which are close to private organisations to those which are close to certain level of government, particularly local government or to particular government agencies.

The private end of the continuum

Some CARTs are close in form to wholly private organisations; there are two main types. A number of private estates have been converted to charitable trusts (Boddington, et al, 1989). In order to do this it is necessary to demonstrate that the property is managed with an accepted charitable objective for public benefit. Permanent preservation of lands and buildings of beauty or historic interest or conservation of the natural environment have been accepted as possible charitable objectives. The donor family may retain an interest in the property, members may act as trustees or as a tenant to the trust, although it is necessary to demonstrate that the family does not benefit financially from the value of the income of the trust.

Other CARTs more closely resemble private clubs to the extent that they are established and operated by a group of individuals with a common interest. This common interest is sometimes stimulated by a threat to the local environment or an opportunity for its improvement. There are many local amenity societies which are active in defending their local areas and a few of these own land. Other CARTs have been formed at the initiative of a very small number of individuals with drive to promote particular types of environmental improvement. Indeed, many of what are now large national trusts began in this way, including the National Trust which owes its formation one hundred years ago to the commitment of three or four individuals. By definition, of course, CARTs have the objective of acting for public benefit, but in these types of group the 'public' may be represented by a narrowly defined interest group with potential conflicts with a wider 'public' interest.

The public end of the continuum

At the other extreme in the public/private continuum are CARTs which operate closely to the public sector, often involved in activities which might otherwise have been undertaken within the public sector. A particular feature of the growth of independent CARTs in the last ten to fifteen years has been CART formation through public sector bodies - local government or quasi-government agency. The Groundwork initiative is an example of this kind of CART formation. Groundwork was originally set up through the initiative of the Countryside Commission to undertake projects for local environmental improvement, particularly in urban fringe areas. The Commission provided funding and a central support body for the establishment of local environmental improvement and amenity trusts around the country, developed in close financial partnership with Local Authorities. Currently, a central Groundwork Foundation acts as 'enabler' to bring local trusts into being, funding staff appointments and encouraging them to develop their operations in partnership with local government and local industry. It is intended that the local trusts gradually integrate sufficiently into local communities and local economies to become self-supporting within a few years. However, the initial underpinning by Countryside Commission and Local Authorities, and the continued support of Groundwork HQ by the Department of the Environment, have been crucial factors in the development of the Groundwork Trust network across England and Wales.

Another kind of public formation occurs when a public authority sets up a CART in order to manage land and other assets. Often public sector agencies and local governments have acquired land of conservation value in various ways, through planning gain arrangements or incidentally to other activities, which is then passed onto a CART for long term management. This has occurred with respect to new towns, such as Milton Keynes and Telford and with Welsh Water which established the Elan Trust. Often these trusts retain close links with local government and government agencies through the appointment of trustees from these bodies.

Given this diversity, it is perhaps surprising that alternative models of CART operations may be proposed. In terms of conventional analysis, these tend to be based on existing views of the private and public sectors.

Free Market Environmentalism?

One interpretation of the role of CARTs is that they represent a 'free market' phenomenon (Anderson and Leal, 1990). In order to fulfil a free market role they would act similarly to clubs, acquiring property rights on behalf of their members by means of member contributions and for the benefit of their members. Certain conditions would need to be met if such organisations can be expected to be effective in providing countryside benefits on a market basis. These would include a membership with a common interest towards which operations can be directed and excludability with respect to the benefits, i.e. that non-members can be excluded from participating in the benefits generated, so that the problem of free-riding could be minimised.

Thus we would observe these organisations taking actions:

- to meet the demands of their members and to exclude non-members from the benefits wherever possible,
- to raise a substantial proportion of their costs from the beneficiaries of their operations, particularly from members,
- to operate under similar trading conditions as other market organisations or at least as non-profit organisations and
- to be established by entrepreneurs in response to market-type opportunities.

Objectives of CARTs and interests of members

Some CARTs do not have a membership and so these must fail to meet the first condition. Those that do still, by definition, have objectives which provide public benefit. But this does not exclude the possibility that they may operate primarily to provide benefits for their own membership. In this case we may interpret such organisations as operating as private clubs whose activities generate external benefits of some sort, i.e. the public benefit may be incidental the pursuit of the interests of the membership. However, the evidence appears not to support this as a general interpretation.

One of the most obvious potential benefits which the County Trusts can offer to members is access to the Trust reserves. However, in practice this is not fully exploited. Half of all reserves are freely open to the public, while only 19 per cent are open only to members. The remainder are either open by prior arrangement or closed to all visitors. To some extent this reflects the practical difficulties of restricting access to members, many reserves have public rights of way across them and the fact that the costs of exclusion or of collecting admission charges are high relative to the likely income. But, more importantly, it also reflects a philosophy of these organisations that they are concerned to promote environmental values to a wider public and not just to serve their members. Publicity advertising for potential members tends to stress the opportunities for members to work for conservation and companionship above the any exclusive opportunities to enjoy access to nature reserves.

This is not to say that individual members do not take account of self interest in deciding whether to join an organisation. Bull (1990) has undertaken a survey of members of three County Wildlife Trusts and found evidence that trust members were motivated by personal self-interest. There was a preponderance of middle class and of newcomers to rural areas amongst the membership who may place a priority on the potential benefits from the trusts' activities of lobbying to protect the countryside. There was also evidence of members tending to live close to trust reserves, although there was no information as to whether these reserves were open to the general public. On the other hand, the most important reason given for joining the trust was to support the trust's aims, suggesting a desire to contribute to the provision of a public good.

The position of the National Trust is somewhat different. The 1907 National Trust Act explicitly states that the Trust shall promote 'permanent preservation for the benefit of the nation'. However, its properties attract significant numbers of visitors to sites, commonly country houses and their grounds, from which non-payers can be excluded and for which there are significant admission charges. Membership, which gives free access to properties, is therefore much more attractive. This suggests an explanation for the scale of membership. However, it also owns other property, open countryside and coastline from which it is much more difficult to exclude non-payers. In such areas, there are usually no charges for admission although there may be for car parking, often depending upon the honesty of visitors. The report on the Trust's constitution by Lord Oliver (National Trust, 1993) concludes that the Trust is not directly subject to the control of its members: they are not members of a club, but rather subscribers to a charitable work. The Trust is for the nation as a whole, including generations yet to come. Thus, similarly, the organisation is primarily committed to the national interest even though individually the members may be influenced by opportunities for personal benefits.

Sources of finance

A second characteristic of 'free-market' organisations is that they would be largely funded by the beneficiaries of their activities. This implies independence from government grants. Figure 7.1 shows the sources of operational income for some different organisations: independent CARTs, County Wildlife Trusts and the National Trust. These figures should be regarded as illustrative as the differences in accounting conventions make direct comparisons difficult. In particular, in the National Trust and County Wildlife Trusts accounts, appeals income and legacies are included separately. In 1990, for the National Trust, these comprised some £24m, equivalent to 30 per cent of operational income.

Figure 7.1: Percentage sources of operational income

	Independent CARTS+	County Wildlife Trusts*	National Trust#
Membership	8	22	37
Admissions	-	-	10
Donations	11	13	1
Government grants	27	31	10
Enterprises	26	25	8
Rents	17	-	14
Investments	8	9	20
Other	3	-	-

Notes: + 1989/90 accounts of 41 CARTs for which data available.
  * 1988/89 accounts for 47 Trusts
  # 1990 accounts

Incomes are drawn from a variety of sources and there is considerable variation between organisations, especially amongst the independent CARTs. The table does indicate the relative importance of membership and admissions charges to the National Trust in comparison the other organisations, particularly to the independent CARTs which derive little income from this source. Both the independent CARTs and the County Wildlife Trusts receive nearly one third of operational income from the state. The National Trust is able to achieve a greater proportion of its operational income from direct users of its properties, nearly half of its income derives from membership and admissions charges. It is less dependent upon grants from the state, although the accounts do not include any allowance for gains to the Trust from property accepted in lieu of capital taxes.

Special legal status

A third characteristic of free market organisations is that they should operate under similar trading conditions. Again this is not always the case in practice. While these organisations generally enjoy taxation benefits as charities, the National Trust and National Trust for Scotland hold particular powers which are not available to other private organisations in the UK.

First, the National Trust has the power to hold land inalienably. This means that, under the National Trust Act, 1907, property so declared may not be disposed of by the Trust and it may only be acquired compulsorily by the government by consent of parliament. It applies this power to that part of an estate which is both of the highest landscape or historic quality, and which is also essential to the preservation of the core of the property and its surroundings (National Trust, 1983 p48). This places the Trust in an advantageous position with respect to potential donors who will want to be reassured that property given will be preserved in perpetuity.

Second, the Trust has a statutory power to covenant land without the requirement that other private organisations have under English law of owning adjoining property. This is equivalent to the powers which organisations have in the USA to enter into conservation easements (Hodge, Dwyer and Castle, 1993). This means that the Trust can control land uses without full ownership. These powers give the Trusts a competitive advantage over other organisations with similar aims and, indeed, they have achieved a remarkably large proportion of the conservation market.

Establishment through the state

Finally, we may expect that CARTs would be established by entrepreneurs in response to an identified opportunity. We have already seen that while this is the case in respect of some organisations, it by no means always the case. Many CARTs have been established through the public sector essentially to undertake what have been conventionally regarded as public rather than private sector operations.

Collective action in the market

Voluntary organisations are making an increasing contribution to conservation initiatives in the countryside. But they are not doing so on a 'free-market' basis. While many organisations do show some characteristics of market organisations, few if any exhibit them all. Their development is substantially dependent upon the state in a variety of ways; in terms of funding, their institutional basis and their establishment.

CARTs as an Extension of Government

If CARTs are not a 'free market' phenomenon, can we therefore regard them as artificial extensions of government? There is little evidence to support this interpretation either. In fact, a number of CARTs formed through the public sector have had the specific aim of distancing CART operations from their parent organisation. There are a number of reasons for this.

Organisations within the public sector are often limited in the range of actions which are permitted or which would be acceptable to public sector organisations. One example is the East Cumbria Countryside Project (ECCP) which is involved with a variety of countryside improvement projects and operates as the local agent for the Woodland Trust, managing its woods, and for the Countryside Commission, as agent for the Pennine Way in the area. The ECCP arose initially from a rural economic development initiative and depends considerably on financial support from government agencies and from local government. Indeed, its staff are formally employed by Carlisle City Council. And yet its independent status offers a means of avoiding bureaucracy and it benefits from being perceived by the public as separate from the local authorities. It also has the flexibility to try out new ideas, such as arts events.

In the United States in particular (Endicott, 1993), private conservation organisations are typically seen as being able to act in support of government conservation objectives as opposed to the more general view in the UK that government agencies act in support of private organisations. Private, non-profit bodies can generally act more quickly than is possible in the public sector. While private organisations may be able to apply financial reserves almost immediately in response to an opportunity to purchase land, in the public sector it may be necessary to obtain political approval or even hold a referendum to determine whether funds can be used for this purpose.

There are also generally limits to the way in which deals may be arranged in the public sector which do not constrain private organisations. For instance, some public sector bodies are not able to bid at auction or to pay for land by instalments. Landowners and potential donors would also often rather deal with a private sector organisation. This means that a private organisation may be able to come to an agreement with a landowner to acquire a property in such a way as to maximise the tax advantage or to buy property under conditions which are acceptable to the owner, perhaps allowing him to remain in occupation of the property. As a result, it is quite common in the United States for private organisations to undertake land purchase and for them subsequently to resell property to government.

Private organisations may also be more successful in attracting donations from individual and corporate donors for land purchase and management. People wishing to ensure the long term conservation of their property are often willing to donate it to conservation organisations to this end. However, they may be reluctant to make donations to government bodies, especially local government, due to a fear that government objectives may be unduly influenced by short term political expediency.

Thus, while CARTs may be heavily dependent upon government in a variety of ways, they are also separate from it and this separation adds to the capacity of a public/private partnership to advance conservation interests.

Some Strengths of the Non-Profit Continuum

CARTs have important characteristics then which distance them from both the public and the market sectors. These attributes may give them particular value with respect to conservation objectives.

Acting for the long term

It is sometimes argued that government should intervene in the market in the interests of future generations. Pigou (1920) commented for instance that:

"It is the clear duty of government, which is the trustee for unborn generations as well as its present citizens, to watch over and, if need be, by legislative enactment, to defend, the exhaustible natural resources of the country from rash and reckless spoilation."

However, it is not at all clear that governments do in practice generally place greater weight on long term benefits and costs than is the case in the market sector. Perversely, one of the more recent arguments which has been used for seeking private finance for large infrastructure projects, which would historically have been funded through the public sector, has been that long term finance should be raised through private markets where investors are prepared to take a long term view. Electoral pressures encourage governments to weight benefits and costs according to the electoral cycle which means looking at a maximum of five years ahead. Of course, this is on the assumption that voters will respond to the benefits which are immediately available to them rather than to promises of benefits which will become available in the future. Thus the pressures on governments to take a short term view stem from the short term preferences of private individuals as voters, although it may be reinforced by a scepticism concerning the credibility of government promises in general.

We may then ask who does speak and act on behalf of future generations if neither the private nor the public sector? Clearly this is a role adopted by a variety of non-profit organisations and CARTs can implement this view in the management of their own land. In this context, the distinction between CARTs and clubs is an important one. CARTs do not simply aim to generate benefits for their own membership. They seek to provide public goods to a wider population and that population includes future generations. However, we should bear in mind the relatively limited influence that CARTs may have in total in promoting a long term view.

The place of entrepreneurship

The distance of CARTs from the public sector allows the flexibility for environmental entrepreneurship. It is particularly difficult for public policies to stimulate the creation of a mix of conservation goods. It is considerably easier for environmental policies either to prevent changes from taking place or else to stimulate land users to conform to a standard package of measures. However, variety is an important component of the conservation of the countryside, in distinct contrast with the uniformity which has been engendered by European agricultural support policies which have guaranteed prices for agricultural products.

The creation of variety depends upon some level of entrepreneurship, to bring resources, ideas and information together, to organize them and to take risks. In this context, the risk of undertaking unsuccessful projects may lead to a loss of membership and of public sector support, putting the future of the organisation at risk, rather than the conventional financial risks. CARTs offer a framework within which environmental entrepreneurs can seek out and experiment with new forms of conservation management and address new conservation demands. The inflexibility of the public sector and the public good nature of the outputs limit this type of operation within the public or market sectors.

Policy by intermediary

The successful provision of public benefits can often require detailed information commonly not available to individual landholders. For example the achievement of conservation goals depends on information both about the ecology of the habitat being managed and about the agricultural system which is operated within it. In some circumstances, guidelines for management can provide sufficient information for a farmer to achieve conservation goals without a detailed understanding of the ecosystem involved. However, in other circumstances, for instance where habitat is being re-created or where a rare habitat is being protected against external pressures, then a more proactive form of environmental management may be necessary. This would involve a more regular monitoring of the ecosystem and review of the appropriate management responses. Management of this sort requires a range of skills which are not always available to the particular farmers who happen to be owners of the relevant conservation sites and may be difficult to write into contractual agreements. Similarly, provision of appropriate public recreation facilities needs to recognise the wider patterns of land use and the demands within the local population.

While most policy mechanisms are directed towards existing owners, an alternative, and less direct form of mechanism is therefore for the state to promote the actions of organisations, in this context CARTs, which have objectives in common with those of the state. This may be done in terms of grants for the purchase of land, contributions towards labour costs and the tax relief generally available to non-profit organisations.

The non-profit organisation will still have an incentive to seek out least cost ways of generating and protecting the conservation and other values under its particular circumstances. It will be prepared to trade off costs against wider public gains. Therefore such organisations will seek out new methods of achieving their goals and will respond to changes in relative prices and technology. They often specialise in particular types of benefit, such as the protection of birds, or may focus their efforts within a particular area. In this way, although they may be relatively small organisations, they can build up a level of expertise within their own particular specialism. The position is likely to be different from that of a farmer who is persuaded to undertake a particular type of land management in response to the financial incentives offered to him through an environmental contract. The farmer will have an incentive to meet the terms of the contract at minimum cost and it will be necessary for a government agency to monitor such contracts in some detail. This suggests that the conservation organisation will require less detailed monitoring than a conventional farmer and that in the longer term it would be likely to develop more cost-effective methods of conservation management.

While not generally recognised as a coherent policy strategy, the state has played a key role in the development of CARTs and it seems inevitable that the scale of the movement would be considerably smaller in the absence of state support. In this sense the policy by intermediary approach is already adopted, but with little overriding strategy.

Some Limits of the Non-Profit Sector

There are of course limits to the potential of the non-profit sector. First, the objectives of CARTs may well not match those of the state precisely. They may respond first to the interests and priorities of their members or trustees rather than to priorities as perceived by government. The degree of matching between the objectives of the organisation and those of the government will vary considerably between different sorts of organisation and it will often be appropriate for government incentives to be directed towards those with the most similar aims and used to influence both the form and scale in which they operate. Thus, the trade-offs made may not reflect the relative priorities chosen politically and monitoring may be needed in the public interest.

Further, small organisations with a largely inactive membership or board of trustees may be susceptible to capture by a subset of the membership which seeks to modify the type of action being taken. Thus the actions taken may not in practice reflect the stated goals of the organisation. And even while the objectives pursued in practice may conform to those of the government, the organisations may simply be inefficient. Those people responsible for administration may be well informed about and committed to conservation, but less qualified for and less interested in financial management and administration. This may be a particular problem where there is a significant dependence on voluntary labour in running the organisation.

Finally, there is an element of competition between CARTs and there can be no guarantee that the more socially valuable types of organisation will be successful. While they make efforts to avoid direct competition in the sense of competing at auctions for land, there is inevitably some element of competition for public funds, for entry fees and for government grants.

The Evaluation of CARTs

As we have seen, CARTs represent an increasingly significant mechanism for the delivery of countryside goods. They receive substantial sums of public money, both through private donations and through government grants.

How then may these non-profit organisations be evaluated as mechanisms for promoting the enhancement of the rural environment, in contrast with incentives for conventional private landholders or direct public ownership? Not only do CARTs lie at different locations between the public and private sectors, they also take on a wide range of forms. Can they be guided towards preferred organisational forms?

Some CARTs are organised along democratic lines with decisions taken by a membership, others are governed by trustees appointed in various ways. In some, considerable decision-making powers are delegated to professional managers, in others control is retained by non-professional representatives and trustees. Some direct their operations towards the interests of a membership, others concentrate on meeting wider public goals. Given the range of objectives and activities, there can be no single ideal form. For some the advantage of economies of size is important, for others a small scale enables them to be responsive to local interests. There is likely to be strength in diversity. Some CARTs will grow and gain advantages from their scale. But there will always be a place for small local and experimental groups which respond to local concerns and which act as a testbed for new and alternative institutional arrangements, taking different locations on the public/private continuum. How then can we evaluate the operations of CARTs?

In the market sector, profit represents a reasonable indicator of performance, provided that government policy takes account of the major externalities. In the public sector, evaluation is more difficult. Despite the development of valuation techniques, valuation of benefits of public sector programmes remains limited. However, if it is assumed that the objectives of public programmes are set by the political process, then cost-effectiveness becomes an important criterion. However, it has been argued that one of the strengths of the non-profit sector is that organisations can set their own objectives and determine their own methods of meeting them. Thus an evaluation should take account of both what is achieved and the costs involved. Any formal analysis is further complicated by the emphasis of conservation for the very long term. Not only does this raise problems of choosing a discount rate, it also creates uncertainties as to what preferences and constraints will be relevant.

One possible indicator of performance might be the extent to which an organisation can attract financial support for its activities from the general public, either through membership fees or donations. And this will be important in determining the success of an organisation in terms of its growth and financial security. But it is a limited indicator of the social value of an organisation's activities. The different nature of the benefits offered to the public is a significant factor influencing their fund-raising potential and the attractiveness of different sorts of conservation does not necessarily reflect their social value. There are wide variations in the extent to which the benefits can be captured by donors and hence the incentive for free-riding. The amount of funds raised is in any case only a reflection of the capacity to control inputs rather than a reflection of the production of outputs.

The evaluation of CARTs is likely to remain qualitative. It should be possible to build up experience by examining the performance of organisations in similar circumstances through the use of performance indicators and measures of cost-effectiveness. It may be possible to make comparisons between achievements of different types of participant in schemes such as Environmentally Sensitive Areas or Countryside Stewardship. But the institutional differences will also make direct comparisons difficult.

In practice, the survival and success of individual organisations will depend upon their ability to convince potential donors, be they public or private, personal or corporate, that they can offer valuable outputs in a cost-effective way. Thus individual CARTs will be judged in a number of different fora against a variety of criteria. Organisations will develop links with particular sponsors, although there will be risks involved where they become excessively dependent upon too narrow a range of sources of support. Those that fail to do this will fail to survive. Where this happens, there should be some mechanism for insuring that a failure of an institutional form does not lead to a loss of conservation assets. In any case, the role of CARTs must be seen within a broader conservation movement that also includes important contributions from the private and public sectors.

References

Anderson, T L and Leal, D R (1991) *Free Market Evironmentalism,* Westview Press, Boulder.

Boddington, M A B, Miles, C W N and Surtees RNV (Eds.) (1989) *Charitable Land Trusts: Their History, Nature and Uses,* Land Trusts Association.

Bull, C J (1990) Popular Support for Nature Conservation: The Attitudes of County Conservation Trust Members, *Built Environment* 16 (3) 203-217.

Dwyer, J and Hodge, I (1995) *Countryside in Trust: Land management by conservation, amenity and recreation organisations,* John Wiley and Sons, London (forthcoming).

Endicott, E (1993) *Land Conservation through Public/Private Partnerships,* Island Press, Washington D.C.

Hodge, I D, Dwyer, J and Castle, R (1993) *Covenants as a Conservation Mechanism,* Monograph No. 26, Department of Land Economy, University of Cambridge.

National Trust (1983) *Arkell Report,* National Trust, London.

National Trust (1993) *Oliver Report,* National Trust, London.

Pigou, A C (1920) *The Economics of Welfare,* Macmillan, London.

CHAPTER 8

Farmers, Planners and Councillors:
An Insider's View of Their Interaction

Andrew W. Gilg and Mike Kelly

This chapter is based on all too rare collaboration between an academic and a practising planner and thus casts a pragmatic eye over some of the more structuralist interpretations of the planning process provided by academics observing the process from outside. It is based on research which examined the concession whereby agricultural workers' dwellings can be exempted from most of the strict controls on new houses in the countryside by so called 'agricultural occupancy condition' permissions being granted (Gilg and Kelly, forthcoming; Kelly and Gilg, forthcoming). The research collected data from seven sources but this chapter focuses on one of these - informal records of the decision making process gathered via a participant observation of the workings of the Planning Committee of North Devon District Council between October 1990 and January 1993. In general, the chapter concentrates on some of the practices adopted by those seeking planning permission via the preferential route offered by the 'agricultural occupancy condition' permission. In particular, it seeks to explain how an 'implementation gap' between policy and actual decision making evolves in the sometimes surreal world of the planning committee of local district councils in England.

Difficulty in putting policy into practice has been a long acknowledged fact in rural planning commentaries. For example, Blacksell and Gilg's (1981) study of development control in four different areas of Devon, and Cloke's (1987) collected series of essays revealed an implementation gap in various rural policy areas. Very few of these studies, however, have examined the agency by which the policy implementation gap occurs. In recent years attention has been focused on 'structural' factors, while before this, analysis centred on the numerical and spatial analysis of symptoms rather than causes.

In the 1990s though, attention has turned to a view of planning as a struggle between key actors following the pioneering work of Short *et al* (1986). This approach has since been developed by Murdoch and Marsden

(1994). Explicit in both these pieces of work is an assumption that the planning committee provides an arena for arbitrating between powerful interests. However, this arena is one in which certain groups are more powerful than others. The research reported in this chapter aims to test this assumption by examining the role played by rural councillors with an agricultural background, in achieving favourable outcomes for those planning applications that they deem to be in their specific area of interest.

This chapter thus aims to provide an example of just how powerful both local and human influences can be, and also how single issues such as agricultural dwellings can still cut across other structural divisions, for example, party political preferences. In this case farmers were seen, via a participant observation exercise, to unite around the single issue of 'looking after farming interests'. Other cases in recent years have highlighted various attempts to impose 'locals only' housing policies by a number of rural authorities. The present chapter is thus set within this wider debate concerning the degree of discretion local planners and councillors should be given in interpreting national planning legislation. In order to do this the chapter is structured as follows: methodology of the participant observation exercise; the political make up of North Devon District Council; the decisions taken; decision making strategies; the conflict between approved policy and exceptions granted; the case of applications recommended for approval; party politics; and conclusions. Three issues in particular are examined: first, the degree to which decision making has been, and continues to be, biased in favour the agricultural sector; second, the extent to which local human agency can subvert national policies; and third, the causal factors which may explain the implementation gap between policy and practice.

Methodology of the Participant Observation Exercise

An 'observer participation' exercise was undertaken by one of the authors which sought to examine decision making by elected representatives on applications for agricultural dwellings. Throughout the exercise the practitioner was in many ways in a unique position regularly to observe at first hand the decision making behaviour of key individuals at district council level. In his professional role as Area Planning Officer the practitioner regularly attended the three-weekly committee meetings of the Planning Committee at which the applications under study were considered. The officer was accordingly expected to appear at those meetings, his presence as a result gave no occasion for comment or question and neither councillors nor other officers were aware of the observer participation that was being carried out. Further, it would not be unexpected for notes to be taken of discussions carried out during the course of the committee meeting. As a necessary prelude to the exercise, the officer already had the benefit of a knowledge of the background of the councillors, the structure of the agenda and the procedures and working practice adopted by the committee (for example, Standing Orders relating to the 'moving' of applications from the non-contentious to the contentious parts of the agenda or referral to Full Council). All the relevant pre-committee and post-committee meetings at which any amendments and matters arising were discussed were also attended as a matter of routine practice.

The practitioner was also acquainted, or had ready access to, the appropriate national policy background summarised in figure 8.1, the development plan context outlined in figure 8.2, relevant legislation, case law, site histories, applications and appeal decision letters together with background papers not normally accessible to an outside researcher. The decisions on individual planning applications (policy outcomes) were, therefore, able to be assessed in the light of a detailed background knowledge.

The Political Make Up of North Devon District Council

According to the 1991 census, approximately 1300 primary sector workers are employed within the district, the overwhelming majority of those in agriculture. The number is declining but at a slower rate than the national average. Agriculture, however, remains the predominant land use and source of finance for land management in the district.

The political constitution of the Council may be said to reflect the rural character of North Devon District. Between May 1991 and May 1995 when the research was carried out, a Liberal Democrat majority of twenty six out of a total of forty four councillors made up the ruling group on the Council. Additionally, a significant element of longstanding Independent representation (sixteen seats) coloured the political profile of the district, particularly so for the rural wards. The balance of two remaining councillors represented the Conservative Party and formed a second party political group on the Council.

Two Liberal Democrat councillors were professional farmers whilst six of the sixteen Independent seats were retained by farmers or horticulturalists, a total of eight out of the Council's forty four councillors. Professional farmers accordingly made up over eighteen per cent of the District Council's elected representatives although less than two per cent of the district's populace were directly employed in agriculture. The same overall ratio was reflected in the composition of the Planning Committee where five of the twenty six members were professional farmers.

Following the May 1995 local government elections the Liberal Democrat majority increased to thirty seats with the balance being made up of thirteen Independents and a single Conservative councillor. Eight of the forty four members of Council again are directly employed in agriculture, three (Independents) having been returned unopposed, a further three having been re-elected to the same wards (two Independents and one Liberal Democrat), one having been re-elected but to an adjoining ward (as a Liberal Democrat successfully challenging one of the two post-1991 Conservative councillors) and one newly elected (Conservative) member replacing a deceased (Independent) councillor who was also from an agricultural background. The Conservative incomer, an established farmer with many years experience as Chairman at parish council level, takes his place on the newly formed District Council as an 'Individual' in that a sole party representative cannot formally constitute a political group. The number of councillors with an agricultural background sitting on the newly formed Planning Committee has increased to six members.

Figure 8.1 New Houses in the Country - Chronological Summary of Ministerial Policy Guidance

Date	Title	Content
1950	'Notes on the Siting of Houses in Country Districts'	Guidance confined to siting rather than the justification for new houses in countryside.
1960	Circular 22/60 'New Houses in the Country'	Superseded earlier advice and emphasised requirement for a 'special need to live on a farm'.
1969	Development Control Policy Note 4 Development in Rural Areas'	Agriculture identified as a 'vital national interest'. Reiterated the need for strict control over new houses and also the preservation of good quality agricultural land unless 'there is a special need in the particular case'. The protection of the countryside 'for its own sake' was not identified.
1973	Circular 24/73 Annex A 'Agricultural Dwellings'	Stressed the requirement of agricultural need for new farmhouses, advised on the assessment of such a need and the siting of dwellings. The use of occupancy conditions was identified as a 'safeguard against the misuse of planning permission'. Circular remained in force until publication of the revised PPG7 in 1992.
1976	Circular 75/76 'Development involving Agricultural Land'	Followed the White Paper 'Food from our own Resources' (Cmnd. 6020). Drew attention to the loss of productive agricultural land to development and need to protect land of 'higher agricultural quality'.
1980	Circular 22/80 'Development Control -	Replaced over sixty previous circulars. Reiterated objections to the extension of urban development into the countryside and advised on the desirability of policy and practice protecting agricultural land from development.
1984	Circular 15/84 'Land for Housing'	Advised on the allocation of an 'adequate and continuing supply of land for housing' while stressing a commitment to the conservation and improvement of the countryside.
1987	Circular 16/87 'Development Involving Agricultural Land'	Superseded circular 75/76 in light of changing conditions and agricultural surpluses. Emphasised the 'continuing need to protect the countryside for its own sake rather than primarily the productive capacity of the land'.
1988	PPG 7 'Rural Enterprise and Development'	Outlined the importance of a healthy rural economy and the desirability of encouraging enterprise while continuing to protect the countryside.
1991	Circular 7/91 'Low Cost Rural Housing'	Provided guidance on affordable rural housing schemes.
1992	PPG 7 (revised) 'The Countryside and the Rural Economy'	Cancelled circular 16/87. Reiterated a sound rural economy as the best protection for the countryside and the guiding principle that 'development should benefit the rural economy and maintain or enhance the environment'. Differentiated between agricultural land quality and the desirability of protecting the 'best and most versatile agricultural land' together with landscape diversity, wildlife habitats, historic features and non-renewable resources. Annex E set out the most detailed ministerial advice to date on the erection of agricultural dwellings.

It will be appreciated from the above scenario that councillors with a professional agricultural background are significantly over-represented on the Council. It may be conjectured at this stage that an applicant for planning permission for an agricultural dwelling is thus able to rely on disproportionate representation in the local decision making arena from

Figure 8.2 Agricultural Dwellings - Summary of Development Plan Guidance

Operative Date	Development Plan	Contents
1st. May 1981	Devon County Structure Plan	Guidance tightened pre-1974 criterion of 'agricultural need'. Submitted Policy 5P8 in 1979 Written Statement in cases of acknowledged proven need the construction of new houses in rural areas but the approved Policy SE8 referred only to 'an *acceptable* agricultural or horticultural need'. The submitted policy was however retained unchanged by the Secretary of State.
30th. July 1987	Devon County Structure Plan (First Alteration)	Also acknowledged that 'in cases of proven need, agricultural dwellings may be required outside settlements'. Written Statement substituted the criterion of '*proven* agricultural or horticultural need' in Policy SE8 in order to strengthen the policy in circumstances of 'continuing pressure for development in rural areas'.
31st. March 1994	Devon County Structure Plan (Third Alteration)	Secretary of State introduced a new Policy CDE1 in light of changes in national policy signalled by Circular 16/87 and the revised PPG7 issued after submission of the Alteration but retained test of a '*proven* agricultural, forestry or horticultural need'.
15th. September 1994	North Devon District Local Plan (Consultation Draft)	Consultation Draft refers to '*proven* agricultural or horticultural need' consistent with Policy CDE1 of the Third Alteration to the County Structure Plan. Further detailed criteria introduced - functional and financial tests relating to the viability and sustainability of enterprise; siting, design and access guidance.

their fellow professional councillors compared with his/her non-agricultural or 'urban' counterpart. Nonetheless, it would not be expected that five members could have any consistently effective influence on a Committee of twenty six members. However, the rest of this chapter shows that the minority wielded a wholly disproportionate influence when their own interests were involved.

The Decisions Taken

A total of sixty eight new applications for agricultural dwellings were recorded during the participation exercise. Out of that number no less than seventy per cent were placed on the 'contentious' part of the agenda (i.e. those applications formally presented for discussion) by reason of the officer recommendation conflicting either with the parish council recommendation or 'third party' (members of the public etc.) representations received.

The majority of the applications, sixty nine per cent, received parish council support in contrast to the thirty two per cent recommended for approval by the District Council's planning officers. The finding is highlighted by the thirteen per cent of applications recommended for refusal at parish council compared with the fifty seven per cent recommended for refusal by officers at district council level. In the latter respect it should be noted that in all cases where there was a difference of opinion between a parish council and the officer recommendation the application automatically became a 'contentious' item and was placed on the relevant part of the agenda as an application for determination by members rather than a delegated decision to officers.

An examination of the parish council decisions revealed three clear trends: first, parish councils tended to support applicants in their parishes for agricultural dwellings; second, this support was continued at the district council level by the district councillor who represented those wards; while third, in the absence of any effective third party objections to the proposal (specifically, in only 15 per cent of cases) the only dissenting voice to such proposals was the recommendation of the planning officer.

Out of the total of 68 applications observed, 39 applications were initially recommended for refusal, 22 applications were recommended for approval and seven applications were initially recommended for deferment. Five of the latter were subsequently recommended for refusal. However, notwithstanding the 44 applications recommended for refusal only 28 applications were finally refused whilst 37 were approved and three were withdrawn. The final results are summarised in figure 8.3.

Use of standard statistical tests (Chi-square) confirmed the departure of the observed frequencies (member decisions) from the expected values (officer recommendations). Specifically, the null hypothesis that there was no evidence of bias in member decision making was found to be invalid whereas the alternative hypothesis that a statistically significant degree of bias existed in the decision making process appeared to be validated.

Figure 8.3 Observer Participation Summary

Total new (Agenda parts A3 or A4) applications	68
Applications recommended for approval	24
Applications finally approved	37 (27 + 10)
Applications recommended for refusal	44 (39 + 5)
Applications finally refused	28 (19 + 9)
Applications finally withdrawn	3

The analysis accordingly confirmed the initial perception of the writers in highlighting what appears to be a marked weakness in the policy implementation process - policy as interpreted by planning officers is not being put into practice in a substantial number of cases notwithstanding the long established and seemingly unambiguous nature of the policy in question which at County level has been progressively strengthened since its inception in 1959.

It is now appropriate to examine just how a small group of councillors, five out of twenty six members, were so able to subvert the policy context, and to win over the remainder of the committee to their viewpoint.

Decision Making Strategies

The decision making behaviour of members highlighted a number of strategies for overturning a recommendation of refusal at officer level, and demonstrated how farmers often used arguments which, although plausible if taken at face value, often concealed a tactic designed to change the decision making agenda towards one more suited to the applicant's case. These strategies are considered below.

'The farmer knows best'

The first argument employed by members may be described as 'the farmer knows best'. The agricultural members of the Planning Committee assert their superior knowledge of farming in support of a particular application. Thus, for example, in the course of debate on one proposal for an agricultural dwelling an 'agricultural' councillor advised "those of us in farming know the inconvenience of farming from away ..." Further examples occurred during the discussion of a second application on which occasion another agricultural member asserted "I can understand the need to overwinter at ... with the differences in land".

On a further application the same councillor remarked "I suppose they (other members) know very little about farming. That's the problem ... an absolutely genuine and sincere applicant. I do beg of you to give this young man who lives in the parish your support". Other examples from agricultural councillors include the comments "it seems that some people who know nothing about farming now know a lot" , the passing remark that "common sense should prevail - it's an ideal place" over the siting of a livestock building and the demonstration of local knowledge when advising on one application " ... always used as a nursery unit for young farmers in the parish; rented land from the Clinton Estates pre-war for such a purpose. Clinton Estates sold land in late fifties or early sixties to pay off death duties and the present field was acquired by the applicant and used for stock rearing".

In a further case an agricultural councillor, a professional horticulturalist, supported an application for two dwellings on a horticultural holding. The councillor commented "listening to the debate I find it hard as horticulture is described as a background industry. Not so - a controlled environment with air, water, humidity etc. Been there a long time. 1992 approaching (a reference to the single European market?). What do we do? Put every impediment in the way with no distinction between agriculture and horticulture. Security also a need with chemicals etc ... when things go wrong I know what its like. Appraisal says a case for one at present then when finished for two". The councillor in question had recently been elected to the council as a Liberal Democrat and asserted his professional experience and expertise in support of the application for two dwellings on the holding. Of note, the two applicants attended the meeting and it is most probable that the councillor realised the applicants were present in the committee chamber. The application appeared late on the agenda and by that time the applicants were almost the only public remaining in the chamber. Furthermore, passing reference had been made to their presence during the course of the debate. Acknowledgement of the attendance of the applicants may perhaps also be inferred by the content of the debate on the application which conveys the impression of members sympathetic to the requirements of the applicants and a desire to help applicants who had previously been described by the same councillor as "honest and respected" local men.

Additionally, the agricultural appraisal (a technical submission accompanying the application which examines the functional and financial merits of the application) may be called into question or the appraisal quoted selectively. These criticisms were again levelled by the agricultural members of the committee with the exception of one application where the former chairman of the committee (from a rural ward) described the particular appraisal submitted in support of the application as "seven pages of drivel". The application was submitted by the county council which may or may not have been a relevant consideration, particularly in the lead up to local government reorganisation and possible unitary status for the authority! Alternatively, the officer's reading of the appraisal may be questioned, as in the case where one agricultural councillor pointedly commented "the officer cannot read ... didn't look at appraisal" before offering the further observation that "councillors ought to look for themselves rather than accept the recommendation of officers".

A recurrent theme arising from the debates over applications involves the issue of farm diversification. In one instance an agricultural councillor supported the application (for a dressage arena) and advised that the applicant had "diversified away from milk which failed. Conversion will tidy up site and provide employment". A second councillor commented that the authority "will get more applications like this in the future and should encourage it if employment will be created".

Similarly, the wider restructuring of agriculture may be identified as a cause for applications. Thus for example, a "a shift in farming policy" was specifically cited by an agricultural member as the reason for one application for an agricultural dwelling. A further application, recommended for refusal at officer level, attracted the comment from an agricultural member that "if stock on the holding there should be supervision. Have sympathy - unless land is occupied and used the countryside will degenerate - one can do everything in the countryside but farm".

The observer participation exercise also highlighted the problem of farm fragmentation and the splitting up of holdings, which may involve selling off the original farmhouse and farm buildings as separate parcels from the holding. Specifically, no less than nine of the sixty eight applications provided examples of the pressures for agricultural dwellings arising from the fragmentation of holdings.

Personal circumstances

The individual circumstances of applicants may also present a persuasive argument to other members for supporting an application. Thus, to one agricultural councillor, a particular application should have been approved as the applicant was "a retired farmer unable to continue farming due to poor health but wishes to remain on the holding and in the locality". Other examples include "giving the applicant the benefit of the doubt" or the comment from the local agricultural member that he was "more sympathetic towards the owner (the applicant) than officers in this case as he is trying to make a living". One professional farmer who moved approval of an application argued that it was "quite unusual for farmers' sons to want to go into farming - a rare example of going for a dwelling at farm who owns a piece of land in the village ... better than a bungalow half a mile up the road. Better on planning grounds".

The local applicant

The argument is strengthened if the applicant is local. Thus, four applications attracted support from members on the grounds that the applicant was from the local area. It will, however, be appreciated that in policy terms there should be no sound planning reason for differentiating between applicants on such a basis. In the latter respect the findings of the enquiry (Lees, 1993) into the planning system in North Cornwall serve as a recent reminder of the need to determine planning applications on sound planning grounds.

The 'local' argument highlights the influence of shared interests between applicants and councillors. The connection of applicants with the area and the wish to remain on the family holding accordingly present themselves as reason enough to justify consent for an additional agricultural dwelling on a particular holding. Thus, for example, one agricultural member outlined the applicant's personal circumstances and added "110 acres of original farm left in a will. A need to look after it - the right should be given to farm this land". To redress the picture is a quotation from an urban councillor relating to a proposed agricultural dwelling to the effect that "either you have a policy or you do not ... the personal side should not come into planning".

Delaying tactics

In the event that a move to approve a particular application may not succeed one option open to members is to move a deferment of the application. Reasons put forward may include the need for a further agricultural appraisal presumably this time supporting the application, the need to clarify the applicant's precise intentions, or the desirability of resolving secondary considerations such as siting, access or design. As an indication of the significance of such a strategy, out of the thirty nine applications originally recommended for refusal by officers, no less than thirteen were deferred by members, of which seven were deferred specifically for a Site Inspection.

Thus, for example, one farming member observed "officers fault that we are faced with this situation - invested heavily in the farm - not asking for approval but for a site inspection".

Concessions over secondary issues

A further strategy open to members seeking to support an application against a recommendation of refusal is to suggest conditions or amendments to the application to overcome the concern of officers. The stationing of a mobile home for a temporary period provides a common example. A second option put forward is that of the erection of agricultural building(s) prior to construction of a dwelling as a demonstration of the applicant's sound intentions and willingness to invest capital in the development of the farm holding.

The granting of temporary consent prior to the establishment of a viable holding has been highlighted by the Council for the Protection of Rural England (1990) as a particular cause for concern. A short term consent, albeit for a 'temporary' mobile home, nonetheless establishes the principle of agricultural accommodation on the particular site. That consent may be renewed, perhaps on several occasions, prior to the applicant seeking consent for a permanent dwelling on the site.

One example from within North Devon District highlights the difficulties over 'temporary' agricultural caravans. Consent for a mobile home was initially granted in 1981 against an officer recommendation of refusal; the consent was renewed in 1984 and again in 1986 before expiring in 1988. At the time the last renewal was determined the authority informally advised the applicant that no further renewal would be approved. Notwithstanding that advice, the mobile home remains on site at the time of writing (1995) and highlights the difficulties in enforcing temporary consents at the expiry of the time period.

A total of four examples were identified from the observer participation exercise. Thus, in the course of one debate a professional farmer specifically recommended that a mobile home be approved "until a dwelling is constructed".

Such a strategy effectively seeks to bypass the main policy objection concerning the principle of a dwelling on the site and diverts the debate to secondary considerations such as siting, design and access. In this way it may be argued that some concession to the officer's concerns has been made whilst securing the main requirement for the applicant, the principle of a dwelling on the site.

The Conflict Between Approved Policy and Exceptions Granted

The observer participation exercise also illustrated examples where applications were recommended for approval by officers but which otherwise would have been presented for refusal had it not been for the restraints imposed by policy. Thus, one case centred on the circumstance whereby the applicant had previously attempted to sell on the application site with the benefit of outline consent for a dwelling without any land. On renewal of the consent, supported by an up-to-date agricultural appraisal which again argued the need for a second dwelling to serve the holding, the site was again put back for sale on the open market. A second instance concerned an application for stock sheds which was recommended for approval but which attracted the comment from the local, non-agricultural, member that the application was a "a try on ... a prelude to a dwelling on the site". In response the officer was obliged to stress the need to consider each application 'on its own merits' rather than on the grounds of what might follow.

This of course highlights the constraints imposed on an authority's professional staff when they advise councillors on the adopted policies, and also accents differences in behaviour between officers and councillors. The issue is one worthy of further study but it is interesting to speculate about what degree of discretion is legitimate or desirable in the actions of either the officers or councillors of an elected authority. The working assumption made throughout this paper is that officers recommend in accordance with policy and that such advice has accordingly been offered in the wider 'public interest'. Considerations such as the personal circumstances of applicants highlighted in the preceding section may consequently not be viewed as 'material' within the meaning of the section 70 of the 1990 Town and Country Planning Act. Specifically, in order to be 'material' such considerations have to be relevant to the wider interests of the community as well as related to legitimate land use matters.

It will, however, be appreciated that an alternative argument could be put forward to the effect that irrespective of whether councillors determine applications consistent with officer recommendations or contrary to that advice, such decisions have nevertheless been made in the interests of the wider community by the elected representatives of that community.

The Case of Applications Recommended for Approval

Applications with a recommendation of approval by contrast are rarely challenged. This finding is of interest in two respects. First, the fact that such applications are not called for discussion, or transferred to the contentious part of the agenda for discussion, probably indicates tacit approval of the recommendation by councillors. Second, neither rural nor urban members of the Planning Committee transferred or called any application for an agricultural dwelling which had been recommended for approval. Thus, in contrast to their rural colleagues, those members from the urban authorities did not choose to exercise their right to challenge officer recommendations of approval.

However, once an application has been called and is the subject of debate a contrast in outlook between members is highlighted by the participation exercise. Thus, for example, one application attracted the comment from a Barnstaple councillor "I've yet to hear any members, particularly farmers, complain that planning permission should not have been given (for agricultural dwellings)". A second application moved for approval by an agricultural councillor elicited the remarks from the same urban councillor "I've heard the argument from farmers before" and "I don't believe that you give planning permission if you're local and you don't if you're not". Drawing on the same theme a rural but non-agricultural councillor commented "it would be different if it was a local farmer applying".

Party Politics

Throughout the observer participation exercise there was little evidence of party politics. Indeed, the only case where party concerns were evident centred on a non-agricultural dwelling in a rural parish represented by the leader of the ruling Liberal Democrat Group. The application was for a bungalow to house a local man and had become the centre of considerable discussion leading to a request from the ruling group that the authority draw up a specific policy to provide for such development. Even so the Chairman of the Planning Committee, although a member of the same group, requested that his vote be recorded against the proposal. In this instance the findings would appear to support those of Fleming and Short (1984) from their study of development control decisions in Bracknell District Council that 'party politicisation is rarely recognisable at the level of local government planning'.

It may also be noted that Group meetings were not as a matter of practice held prior to meetings of the Planning Committee. Thus, although the organisation of the District Council had altered following the May 1991 elections with the emergence of a ruling party, the 'politicisation' of the authority was not overtly translated into the planning arena. However, overall the authority did become politically structured with an organisational structure along party political lines reflected in the political control of the committees. The observer participation exercise does not, therefore, suggest that the decisions of the planning committee over agricultural dwellings reflect the political imperatives of the elected members and in particular of the ruling Liberal Democrat group.

This is not perhaps surprising in that applications for agricultural dwellings are not likely to raise or reflect on wider party political issues. What, however, did occur following the May 1991 elections was the displacement of councillors by Liberal Democrats, a quantitative trend reflected in the national arena by the replacement of the local Conservative Member of Parliament by a Liberal Democrat the following April and reinforced at the local level in the subsequent May 1995 local government elections.

The politicisation of local government since local government re-organisation in 1974 has been documented (for example, Young and Davies, 1990). The more 'rural' authorities have been characterised in the past as the subject of non-party control. However, insofar as applications for agricultural dwellings are concerned, whilst the leading group made up the majority representation on the Planning Committee (with committee places allocated on a proportional basis) holding the Chairmanship and Vice-Chairmanship, the impact of any political control on decision making appears to have been muted. The reality is well illustrated by the observer participation survey. The latter confirmed the high proportion of such applications successfully challenged by councillors at meetings of the Planning Committee. Every agricultural application that was called for discussion was called by a member with an agricultural interest. Those councillors comprised six Independent councillors and only two Liberal Democrat councillors.

Furthermore, the observed behaviour of councillors at meetings of the Planning Committee would appear to belie any notion that the decisions have already been decided prior to the meeting itself, whether at a meeting of the party group or on a more informal basis. Councillors did not in practice vote *en bloc* but engaged in often heated debate over the issues raised by individual applications.

The scenario outlined above is persuasive in a number of respects. Decision making (and non-decision) behaviour as observed in practice appears to indicate councillors acting as representatives of their particular parishes rather than as members of party groups. Independence of judgement is exercised with decisions being made on individual applications for agricultural dwellings irrespective of any political influence or objectives of party cohesion. Young and Davies (1990) comment that such a spirit or quality of independence is distinctively rural. The notion ties in neatly with the profile of the rural councillor previously noted.

Thus, irrespective of the political control potentially exercised during meetings the 'policy outcomes' did not reflect the impact of party politics. In contrast, a parochial and professional alliance manifested itself, members with similar interests as applicants overtly demonstrating support for the development against the officer recommendation in a substantial proportion of cases.

It may be noted, however, that the observer participation exercise demonstrated that the shared interests did not derive solely from an economic rationale driving the restructuring of a farm holding or attempts to add value to that holding. The interests extended to a recognition of other factors, embracing social and cultural dimensions and included the origins of the applicant as a local landowner and farmer, the wish of the applicant to remain resident on the holding and a shared understanding of the difficulties experienced by farmers.

The adoption of different strategies by members has also been highlighted by Fleming and Short (1984). The development control committee is identified by the latter commentators as the last opportunity for members to influence specific developments. In their examination of the role of councillors in development control decisions Fleming and Short comment on the refusal of applications contrary to officer recommendations of approval ('blocking' strategies) and the approval of applications contrary to officer recommendations of refusal ('facilitating' strategies). Whilst the dominant trend was found to be one of consensus between officers and members, the authors also identified a tendency for the committee to block applications for new dwellings. It will be appreciated that such an inclination contrasts with that identified from the present research in respect of new agricultural dwellings. Interestingly, Fleming and Short comment that in circumstances of restraint, such as in those cases which require an agricultural justification, "such a need is not lightly acknowledged by officers and their official consultees, but the committee has been more generous in its assessment".

Fleming and Short also identify but do not detail the influence of personal circumstances and the 'parish factor'. There is also the contribution of 'bargaining' towards policy outcomes. When bargaining takes place the development control function of councillors is viewed as less constrained by policy than by officers. Thus, as noted in preceding paragraphs, approval of applications against policy may be viewed by members as a special case which need not set a precedent and may indeed bring about positive benefits to the local community for example, as a result of the bargaining process having achieved 'planning gain'.

Conclusion

It is emphasised that the participation exercise presents only a partial insight into decision making on applications of a particular nature over a limited period of time. There remains a need to temper any findings with caution as, notwithstanding the sensitivity of the methodology and the range of primary data derived from the exercise, the findings nonetheless do not portray a definitive picture but only an approximation of the reality of decision making. The motivations and intentions of individual participants were rarely explicitly revealed and consequently needed to be inferred from the participation exercise: decision making behaviour demonstrated inconsistencies as well as consistencies and in all likelihood changed between (or even during the course of) each application for reasons of which the actors may or may not have been consciously aware. Thus, it was not possible directly and with certainty to pinpoint what motivated the actions of particular individuals at any specific point. However, the exercise did allow us to draw the following conclusions to the three issues raised at the outset of the chapter.

First, decision making was in practice biased in favour of the agricultural sector, largely because of the actions of a few key councillors who employed a variety of tactics to achieve their aims. Second, local human agency can subvert the aims of national legislation and policy guidance even when this has been confirmed by local policies. Third, the observed implementation gap in planning is probably due to the effect of sectoral factors rather than any consistent grouping of factors along, for example, class lines, although class issues, notably middle class values, are important in setting the overall agenda within which the debate is set. The study thus provides an important cautionary lesson for those who would infer an all powerful state acting in the interests only of international capital and confirms the observations made by Pincetl (1994) at the outset of the paper concerning the diversity still inherent in planning policy implementation:

"... to understand the state, we must understand the locality, what goes on within it, and how local practices vary from one locality to another ... This point of view validates what planners already know: human action is important, and a proliferation of different social practices in different localities exists, even though there may be strong homogenizing influences at the level of both the state and of the economy. Thus, as Kirby points out, legislation, even that at the highest levels, must still be implemented in place, and implementation depends on the particular circumstances of a particular place. The struggles that emerge within the local state are cast within the histories and experiences of its residents; and despite their universality, neither the struggles nor the outcomes are uniform".

References

Blacksell, M and Gilg, A, (1981), *The Countryside: Planning and Change,* George Allen & Unwin, London.

Cloke, P (Ed.), (1987), *Rural Planning: Policy into Action?* Harper & Row, London.

Council for the Protection of Rural England, (1990), *A Place in the Country,* CPRE, London.

Fleming, S C and Short, J R, (1984) Committee Rules OK? An examination of Planning Committee Action on Officer Recommendation, *Environment and Planning A,* 16, 965-973.

Gilg, A W and Kelly, M P, (forthcoming) The Analysis of Development Control Decisions: a position statement and some new insights from recent research in south-west England, *Town Planning Review.*

Kelly, M P and Gilg, A W, (forthcoming) The delivery of planning policy: an account of decision making in a rural planning authority, *Policy and Politics.*

Lees, A M (1993) *Enquiry into the Planning System in North Cornwall District,* Department of the Environment, HMSO, London.

Murdoch, J and Marsden, T (1994) *Reconstituting Rurality,* UCL Press, London.

Pincetl, S (1994), Review of Kirby, A, 'Power Resistance: Local Politics and the Chaotic State', *Journal of the American Planning Association,* 60, 420.

Short, J R, Fleming, S and Witt, S (1986) *Housebuilding, Planning and Community Action: The production and negotiation of the built environment,* Routledge & Kegan Paul, London.

Young, K and Davies, M (1990) *The Politics of Local Government since Widdicombe,* Joseph Rowntree Foundation, London.

CHAPTER 9

Environmental Reform of the CAP:
An Analysis of the Short and Long Range Opportunities
Clive Potter

It was inevitable that agricultural policy would attract the attention of environmentalists eventually. There is surely no other public policy for rural areas which baulks quite as large in terms of spending power or institutional reach, and once the connection had been made between the environmental transformation of Western Europe's countryside over the last thirty years and the operation of the Common Agricultural Policy (CAP), the scene was set for a sustained campaign to bring about reform. The first specifically environmentalist critiques of the CAP began to appear in Britain in the early 1980s when commentators like Bowers and Cheshire (1983) pointed to the link between agricultural subsidies and landscape change. Their central argument is that "the problem is not one of ill-will and ignorance, but of a system (the CAP) which systematically establishes financial inducements to erode the countryside, offers no rewards to offset market failures, and increases the penalties imposed on farmers who may wish to farm in a way which enhances the rural environment" (Cheshire 1990, p17). It was a powerful thesis, promoting the agriculture and environment debate from a discussion about individual farmers and their separate acts of environmental destruction to one concerned with policy and the need for reform. As Newby (1993) comments, the perception grew that there was nothing immutable or haphazard about post-war countryside change - rather, it was the product of policy decisions quite consciously pursued within a large and complex network of institutions created for just this purpose.

The first proposals to 'green the CAP' were, nonetheless, modest in scope, concerning themselves chiefly with improving the incentives for conservation on farms by switching small amounts of national expenditure from farm support into conservation grant schemes (MacEwan and Sinclair, 1983; Potter, 1983). As a House of Lords enquiry put it at the time: "there is nothing immutable about the present system of agricultural support...and a case can be made for putting the environment at its heart rather than on the fringes" (House of Lords, 1984, p10).

These ideas bore fruit with surprising speed when the UK Ministry of Agriculture set up a pilot scheme on the Norfolk Broads and agreed to lobby for inclusion of an environmental scheme in the EC Structures Regulations that were being renegotiated at the time. With the support of other member states, particularly the Netherlands and Denmark, Britain was successful in obtaining an article on Environmentally Sensitive Areas under Regulation 2078/85. This allowed all member states to set up agri-environmental schemes which offered contracts to farmers on a wide front. By the early 1990s the new field of agri-environmental policy was claiming a small but significant share of agricultural spending, and environmentalists were beginning to speak more ambitiously about the need to pull some of the bigger levers of price support in order to achieve their goals (see, for example, Jenkins, 1990; Dixon and Taylor, 1990). Today, many look back on these events, culminating in an EU-wide agri-environmental programme agreed under the MacSharry reform package of 1992, as markers on the first leg of a longer journey. They point to the opportunities for further 'decoupling' the subsidies farmers receive from decisions about production and to the need to extract the greatest possible 'conservation dividend' from future liberalisation of agricultural trade in the context of GATT. This is the long game of agri-environmental policy reform, played for high stakes but with an, as yet, uncertain outcome. Some commentators, for instance, can envisage a time when the *only* politically sustainable form of support to agriculture will be for the production of public environmental goods. Others anticipate a more pragmatic mix of social and environmental subsidies.

What is clear is that the greening process is far from complete and that it is increasingly bound up with questions of international farm policy reform and the renegotiation of policy entitlements which this implies. Around it gather important questions about the willingness of citizens to pay for environmental protection through government programmes, and the ability of farmers to become private producers of public goods by responding to the incentives being offered to them. By seeking to reform the CAP, environmentalists were challenging the operation of a policy which, in its basic design, encoded deep assumptions about the European countryside and the best way to manage it. They were also implicitly challenging a set of policy entitlements which historically had been fiercely defended by a farm lobby renowned for its political agility and entrenched institutional links. In reviewing what has been achieved to date and speculating about the future, this chapter sets out to assess the broader significance of the greening process. It begins with the 'short game' which led to the setting up of the EU's current agri-environmental programmes, and argues that its successful conclusion was largely the result of a bargain struck between conservationists and farm groups at a time of impending policy retrenchment. Turning to speculate about the future course of the 'long game', the chapter identifies two alternative scenarios, the first centred on the idea of 'conservation compliance', the second brought about by full decoupling of CAP support from production. It concludes with a discussion of their relative merits from an environmental point of view.

The Pressures for Reform

It is tempting to view the early agri-environmental reforms of the mid-1980s as the predictable outcomes of adroit environmental campaigning. Certainly, if policy change requires consensus about the problem at hand and its causes, then by 1985 the conditions were ripe for doing something about the environmental effects of the CAP. Commentators could point to the steady depletion of semi-natural habitats across the European Community - of wetland, moorland, woodland and grassland in the Northern States and rough pastures, vineyards, orchards and dry grasslands in the South - and to mounting problems of water pollution, entrophication and the erosion of soils (see, for instance, Baldock, 1990). Behind the intensification, specialisation and marginalisation of agricultural production which were giving rise to these effects stood the CAP, and the technological revolution of post-war agriculture. It required only a little reflection to work out that the 'coupled' system of farm support offered to farmers through the CAP (whereby farmers who produced most received more) had been an important driving force. Basic economic theory suggests a positive relationship between product prices and output which operates in the short run by encouraging a greater use of variable inputs like fertilisers and pesticides; in other words, intensification. In the longer run it is the interaction of the price support system with technical progress which has brought about changes in the structure, pattern and practice of farming that has had such profound environmental results. It would appear that once they became convinced that price support was likely to continue, farmers (aided by national investment subsidies) used the short run profits from higher prices to re-equip their farms and refashion their farming systems, bringing about changes in farm layout and land use on a very broad front. Meanwhile, however, the capitalisation of farm support into land values and rents which was one of the second-round effects of high price guarantees, increased the opportunity cost of uncultivated or unimproved land, giving a further spur to land improvement, reclamation and the progressive loss of semi-natural vegetation and landscape features which this involves.

Environmentalists quickly made these connections, linking their critique to broader criticism of the CAP as an expensive and socially wasteful policy (see, for instance, Bowers and Cheshire, 1983). At this stage, though, the main motive for action flowed from an uncomplicated, if profound, recognition of the need to correct a basic failure of policy which resulted in farmers being offered powerful incentives to intensify production and abandon traditional farming practices, coupled with a wish to improve the incentives for conservation management on farms. The British story has been told elsewhere (see Whitby, 1994), but in its early stages revolved around finding a solution to the problem of conserving larger tracts of countryside outside key sites. Environmentally Sensitive Areas (ESAs) were invented to subsidise environmentally sensitive farming practices and systems within certain ring fenced areas. As Felton (1993) observed, a growing sense of retreat by wild nature across wide stretches of the countryside and a recognition that site protection was ill-equipped to defend 90% of the conservation resource that was located there, pushed conservationists into campaigning for the first agri-environmental schemes and a redeployment of farm support in favour of the environment. Mechanisms were needed which would provide an incentive for environmental management in the wider countryside and ESAs appeared to serve the purpose. For the farm lobby, meanwhile, MAFF's ESA programme was to mean a welcome new source of subsidy and, more important at this politically fraught moment, a chance to demonstrate the environmental credentials of its members and the workability of the voluntary approach. It was in this pragmatic vein that an EC Regulation was agreed in 1985, permitting other member states' agriculture departments to set up similar schemes. This was followed by an amending Regulation which allowed them to claim partial funding from the EC.

Not until the early 1990s, however, were agri-environmental policy questions swept into the wider debate about CAP reform. A coincidence of events was opening up a space in the policy machine and it was only now that 'greening the CAP' could actually begin. In reality, of course, the appearance of more substantial green reforms at this point in the policy cycle, when policy makers were coming under pressure from other quarters to do something about agricultural support (and not only in the EU but in the US and Scandinavia too), suggests that the greening process was more fortuitous than many would like to think. From his survey of agricultural policy making over the last twenty years in the EU and US, for instance, Petit (1985) has concluded that the reform of a public policy as politically embedded and culturally entrenched as the CAP is rarely, if ever, a straightforward result of its own contradictions, obvious though these were by 1992, the year of the MacSharry agreements. Rather it requires a convergence of 'domestic' and international pressures to bring about change.

Domestically, this took the form of a mounting budgetary crisis and a dawning recognition that the CAP, as well as being environmentally damaging, was failing in its own terms to meet the primary goal of supporting the income of the average farmer and his family. In effect, the CAP suffers from a basic design fault. By attempting to solve the income problem through price support, the policy had bid up input costs and land prices, squeezing the incomes of many small and medium sized farms, even while it gave a profit bonanza to larger producers who managed to control production costs by getting ahead on the technological treadmill. This critical flaw was acknowledged by the EC when it identified "a contrast between, on the one hand such a rapidly growing budget and on the other agricultural incomes growing very slowly and an agricultural population in decline (which) shows clearly that the mechanisms of the CAP as currently applied are no longer in a position to attain objectives laid down for agriculture in the Treaty of Rome" (CEC, 1985, p65). At the same time further water was building up behind the dam of agricultural protectionism on the international scene. The effect of having subsidised exports of surplus production and the erection of non-tariff barriers at the borders of the EU had long exercised third parties and, with the convening of a new GATT round in 1989, the issue of agricultural trade liberalisation took centre-stage. A neo-liberal agenda for radical reform now began to emerge which advocated dismantling price supports to move farmers closer to world markets and pursuing income objectives through direct and transparent income aids instead - in other words, 'decoupling' the subsidies farmers receive from their decisions about production by abandoning the idea that farmers can be made better off by being encouraged to produce more in a protected market. It is a policy option that has long had the support of academic economists (see, for example, Koester and Tangermann, 1977), for whom the present construction of the CAP has always been something of an intellectual puzzle. They approve because it obeys the cardinal rule of efficient policy design, which is to match policy instruments to policy objectives, something the CAP has signally failed to do by trying to use the price instrument to achieve both market and income support objectives. Once decoupled, so the argument goes, the way would be clear to redeploy CAP subsidies for specific purposes, social or environmental.

The Short Game

Now the prospect of decoupling suited environmentalists well, up to a point. Cutting output prices promises some lessening of the economic incentives to intensify production, and the consensus amongst economists who have looked at the question of farmers' supply response, is that a steady, sustained reduction in price guarantees should bring about an extensification of production on a broad front. But it was also widely agreed that in a managed countryside like Western Europe's some sort of green recoupling of the money released by price reform would be necessary if environmental assets were to be managed to maintain their conservation interest. This chimed well with the interests of the farm lobby which, by this date, was increasingly exercised by the problem of how to retain public support for income transfers that, with decoupling, were becoming ever more visible and 'transparent'. Money transferred through agri-environmental programmes was likely to be considerably more politically defensible, particularly in the long-run, than income support justified as compensation for policy change. As the British Minister of Agriculture, John Gummer, put it at the time: "it is a difficult concept that you can give income support to a farmer simply because he is a farmer. The support you are giving him has to be because he is looking after the land".

Agriculturalists and conservationists were thus increasingly able to find common cause as the decade wore on. In the UK this was aided by the apparent success and popularity of the ESA programme, now MAFF's flagship environmental scheme (Waters, 1994). Far from challenging their traditional policy entitlements, arguments in favour of an expanded system of green payments offered a means of defence, provided environmental reform could be presented as requiring a redirection rather than a net withdrawal of farm support. The immediate result of this coincidence of interest was the Agri-Environmental Package (AEP) agreed by farm ministers in 1992 as part of the MacSharry CAP reform agreement, itself the first step towards decoupling the CAP. Under the new Regulation, member states' agriculture departments are now required to set up AEPs through which farmers can receive payments for the purposes of environmental protection. Scheme objectives range from reducing fertiliser and pesticide use to improving the upkeep of abandoned farmland or neglected woodland.

Supporters point to the significance of these developments, widely regarded as the culmination of the green reforms of the 1980s, not only in terms of the injection of 'new money' into the conservation of the EU's countryside which the AEP represents (the Commission expects to spend over 2 billion ECUs on the AEP during its initial five years), but also as a first step towards the larger goal of a 'green CAP' and a renegotiated social contract between farmers and the state. The advent of AEP, they argue, paves the way to a pan-European approach to the protection of the countryside, and, taken together with the Habitats Directive, has the capacity to contribute substantially towards meeting the obligations of member states under the Biodiversity Convention. It brings about a shift in emphasis from conservation sites to farms that was long overdue. Critics, on the other hand, reflect on the fact that total projected EC expenditure under the AEP is still dwarfed by the much larger sums still being absorbed by the price support arm of the CAP and by the direct compensation schemes that, in apparent contradiction of Gummer's earlier hypothesis, were also set up under MacSharry. On current estimates, AEP expenditure will account for little more than 2% of total agricultural support spending by 1996/97 (MAFF, 1993). Indeed, they note that, even compared to the other 'Accompanying Measures', the AEP does not dominate: projected expenditure under the early retirement scheme that will operate in other member states will itself cost the Commission as much as all AEP measures put together. For them, the AEP is at best a side benefit of incomplete CAP reform, at worst a series of disguised income transfers masquerading as environmental schemes. They point to the spatially limited coverage of existing schemes and the difficulties of reaching a sensible judgement about the real effects of environmental contracts, such as those operating in British ESAs, which, in many cases, subsidise the continuation of existing practices rather than the adoption of new ones.

Inevitably perhaps, the truth probably lies somewhere between these two extremes. There are many features of the AEP that are innovative in straightforward policy design terms and to have secured, as the MacSharry agreement has managed to do, the funding of environmental schemes, not through the guidance fund but from the *guarantee* fund of the CAP, is regarded by many lobbyists as an important concession with implications for future funding. Meanwhile, the wider use of environmental contracts made possible by the AEP means that it is now one of the largest scale experiments in the use of quasi-market incentives to influence and reward behaviour and encourage innovation in the production of public goods (comparable in scale to the soil conservation payments made to US farmers under the Conservation Reserve Programme). What is less clear is how effective the contracts will be in bringing about real and enduring changes in environmental management on the many (several thousand now, but several tens of thousands by the end of the first five year programme) farms concerned. An expanding budget suggests closer and more critical public scrutiny and there is now a sense in which the debate about the design and implementation of the EU's AEP needs to enter a new phase.

To begin with, the much wider deployment of AEP schemes in member states, particularly in Southern member states where institutional structures and delivery systems may be much less well developed, raises questions about the overall allocation of the AEP budget between member states and the ability of some states to implement and deliver schemes to farmers in an efficient and cost-effective way. For those member states such as the United Kingdom, Holland and Germany with a longer history of involvement in AEP-type programmes, a distinction will increasingly need to be made between agriculture departments' ability to bring about a change in *policy outcomes* - setting up the schemes themselves and enrolling sufficient farmers to make a difference - and *policy results*: the short and long run environmental benefits that are actually produced on farms and in fields. Questions are already being asked about the extent and quality of the environmental protection and improvement which 'conservation by contract' is able to bring about. A particularly important aspect of this will be the durability of the benefits that are produced. As Moore (1989) reminds us, the lapse of time is a vital element in all conservation and a long term range perspective is essential, particularly where habitat restoration is concerned. Yet AEP scheme contracts currently available in the UK finance farmers for only a few years at a stretch and little consideration has been given to protecting any environmental gains once agreements expire. The length of agreements is obviously determined by the almost certain reluctance of farmers to enrol for long periods and a calculation has been made which balances agreement length against participation rates. There is also the possibility that farmers will be able to re-enter schemes after their agreements expire, an event that is more likely if current schemes are farmer-friendly and still in existence in ten or more years time. But there is also a profounder issue at stake here, namely the effectiveness of green payments in bringing about enduring changes in attitudes and knowledge about countryside management which will outlast the schemes themselves. Colman, *et al* (1992, p69) hint at this when they argue that "policy measures which encourage positive attitudes to conservation will in the long-term be more effective than those that do not, since a positive shift in attitudes will increase the output of conservation goods at any specified level of budgetary cost". Indeed it could be argued that *unless* they exert such an influence, AEP measures will inevitably be seen as temporary bribes, shallow in operation and transitory in impact.

The Long Game

Meanwhile, the reluctance of policy makers to decouple the commodity programmes which continue to absorb the lion's share of agricultural spending, means that strong intensification incentives remain securely in place for years ahead. In this sense, the long term effectiveness of the AEP depends critically on further reforms to the commodity regimes themselves as well as the 'self-improvements' mentioned above. Ostensibly, the MacSharry reforms were the first step in this 'long game' of moving to a fully decoupled CAP but, in practice, farm ministers could agree only modest price cuts and have been preoccupied with ensuring that farmers are compensated for these. Now there is nothing surprising about the appearance of the compensation schemes themselves: as Rausser and Irwin (1989) argue, in periods of radical policy change a case can be made for payments which buy-off the losers if the prize is a more socially efficient policy arrangement. In the agricultural policy case there is an argument that legitimate policy entitlements have been created by a policy as long-standing as the CAP and that farmers have restructured their farms and invested in capital to take advantage of these. Any change might, therefore, be seen as a breach of contract, for which compensation is due. The critical point is that compensation schemes must be partial, transitional and fully decoupled from production, otherwise they create as much social waste as the policies they replace. MacSharry fails to meet these conditions. Not only is there no time limit on the new payment schemes offered to arable and livestock farmers, but also many of them are far from production-neutral. All of which vastly complicates the policy scene for environmental reformers, with policy makers apparently readier to recouple the new income aid schemes to environmental objectives through the expedient of 'cross compliance' than contemplate their removal altogether.

Payments to sheep and beef producers, for instance, continue to be paid on a headage basis and while the requirement on beef producers to observe stocking rate limits implies decoupling of sorts, it is unlikely that these will bring appreciable environmental benefits. In fact, Crabtree (1993) has pointed out that the linkage of beef premium payments to stocking rates is quite weak. Payments are not dependent on maintaining the specified stocking rate - merely that animals in excess of these limits cannot be claimed for. In the sheep sector, ewe premium payments are calculated on the basis of a farm's 'performance flock': the number of ewes present in 1991. This means that farms receive a quota which puts a ceiling on the number of ewes eligible for subsidy. Again, decoupling of sorts, through the ability to purchase quota from other farms, suggests that premiums will inevitably be subsidising increases in flock sizes on some farms. Conservationists are looking anxiously at the way this trading system operates in practice and at how well the national reserve works to prevent a drift in production away from the hills and uplands.

But it is probably the system of compensatory payouts offered to arable producers, and the set-aside scheme to which these are linked, that has attracted particular criticism. Under the 'Arable Area Payments Scheme', farmers producing 92 tonnes of arable crops or more a year are required to set-aside between 12 and 15% of their 'base' acreage in order to qualify for area compensation payments (a simplified scheme, not entailing set-aside, is available to smaller producers). Many environmental groups remain deeply critical of the set-aside idea - CPRE (1993) for instance, deplores the landscape impact of large areas of fallow land - and there is concern that the incentive to intensify production on the land that is still cropped will be irresistible to most farmers. In Britain, MAFF's determination to apply a 'green gloss' to what is undisguisedly a rather crude instrument of supply control, has meant that farmers can chose to set-aside the same blocks of land for up to six years and apply for additional payments in return for managing the retired land in more environmentally sensitive ways than simply fallowing it. The fact that land under permanent grass at the time the scheme was introduced (December 1991) is ineligible for payment may also reduce the incentive to plough in subsequent years. Nonetheless, concern remains that the set-aside scheme will 'crowd out' existing AEP measures, both in a financial sense and in the way it operates on the ground. Farmers required to comply with the 12-15% set-aside condition are going to be increasingly reluctant to find more land for agri-environmental schemes, or if they do, they will require higher payouts, by way of compensation (though in Britain a derogation now allows agriculture departments to count land enrolled in the farm woodland and some other agri-environmental schemes towards a farmer's set-aside requirement). Most conservationists agree that, even with conditions attached to a non-rotated set-aside, a longer term land diversion scheme, expressly designed for the purpose, would be far preferable. Under the existing system, policy makers, in Britain, at least, are torn between ensuring that set-aside is efficient in controlling production (hence the rotational element, designed to reduce slippage) and securing environmental benefits from such a large scale land use change (hence the concession on a non-rotational option). Winters' comment that in the agricultural policy field there is always a greater tendency towards 'doing something' than towards 'undoing something', with resulting "costly tangle of potentially inconsistent instruments" (Winters, 1987, p300) appears well confirmed here.

The pragmatic reaction to this state of affairs has been to press for a fuller application of conservation compliance, effectively making a virtue out of the increased leverage over individual farmers which the introduction of direct payments has brought about. Environmental groups like the UK's Royal Society for the Protection of Birds (RSPB), particularly enthusiastic promoters of this concept, propose that farmers should be required to enter land into a suite of agri-environmental schemes in order to qualify for production premiums or compensation of any sort (Dixon and Taylor, 1990). More likely is further refinement of the 'green ticket' approach implied by recent amendments to the livestock schemes, whereby farmers have to agree to abide by environmental standards and limits in order to retain eligibility (though a 'red ticket' system under which a farmer may actually be disqualified for direct aids after transgressing these standards is also implied by the introduction of guidelines for 'environmental over-grazing' linked to livestock premium payments). Conservation groups are pressing for a tightening of these conditions and the introduction of new ones related to the management as well as simply the stocking or destocking of upland vegetation. In the arable sector, advocates of conservation compliance are aiming for further derogations to allow even stricter conditions to be attached to what farmers must do with their set-aside land.

Conservation compliance is an attractive idea because it sorts well with the goal laid down by the Single European Act of ensuring that "environmental protection requirements shall be a component of the Community's other policies". With set-aside now widespread on arable farms and livestock premium payouts an essential income support for many hill and upland farmers, its impact is potentially much more widespread than that of agri-environmental payments, which have to be applied for and taken up by a farming community still wary of countryside management role that is being prepared for them. Philosophically, conservation compliance is also very much in tune with the shift towards protecting the fabric of the wider countryside outside key sites and protected areas. It promotes the idea that agricultural production and conservation are joint products, particularly in the livestock sector where production aids, long accepted by farmers as legitimate forms of state support, are efficient ways of keeping existing producers on the land and maintaining the farming mix. That it should so quickly have gained favour with the farm lobby is a reflection of its additional merits as a solution to the legitimation problems which partial decoupling creates - how to justify the increasingly visible transfers that are being made through compensation schemes and direct producer aids?

Nevertheless, conservation compliance must be seen for what it is: an expedient rather than a genuine reform of the agricultural support system. Indeed, by apparently legitimising their use as instruments of policy, conservation compliance may keep in place compensation schemes that would otherwise be politically unsustainable over the long term. Far from speeding up the decoupling process, compliance could slow it down, preventing the reallocation of resources in favour of strictly decoupled agri-environmental schemes and perpetuating the economically inefficient practice of using single instruments to achieve more than one policy objective, the problem decoupling is designed to correct. Such criticism is a little disingenuous because full decoupling is probably irresistible in the long term anyway due to pressures bearing down on the CAP from outside (see below). More valid is the objection that conservation compliance risks tying agri-environmental policies to a system of income aids and compensation schemes with a limited shelf-life. Any retrenchment or more careful targeting of such payments (itself increasingly likely as time passes) reduces the effectiveness of conservation compliance by limiting coverage and reducing the scope for killing two policy birds with one stone. There is no guarantee, for instance, that the marginal or disadvantaged farmers who will be the last to receive income aids under a much more decoupled CAP, will necessarily farm land of greatest environmental need or potential. Of course, it could be argued that producer aids eventually become agri-environmental payments anyway as the environmental conditions attached to getting a ewe premium or arable compensation become tighter. Proposals have been made to accelerate this transmutation by making all headage payouts on a hectarage basis. The sticking point is that even these payments would retain a link with production, albeit one now related to an input (land) rather than an output (stock) (Egdell, 1995). It is hard not to concur with Jenkins (1990), who argues that a politically cleaner course, and one more in step with the longer-term realities of the longer agricultural policy situation, is to move rapidly towards paying farmers directly for their environmental services through a recoupled system of environmental payments. In the United States there is already discussion of green payment programmes which would substitute for some, if not all, existing commodity programme payments and in the EU it has long been recognised that environmental incentives would operate more freely and cost-effectively if they did not have to work against the grain of larger subsidies.

But this green recoupling strategy also raises difficult questions. The environmental repercussions of a substantial and sudden cut in price guarantees that would be necessary to release funds for widespread agri-environmental payments are still poorly understood, especially in a managed countryside like Western Europe's, which relies heavily on regular human intervention to maintain biodiversity and landscape interest. Radical decoupling would also signal a retreat from the idea of joint production which underpins conservation compliance, entailing a more selective allocation of monies, possibly on a quasi-market basis. Targeting would be inevitable given the continuing budgetary pressures to reduce aggregate spending on agriculture, but methodologies to prescribe and evaluate environmental management on farms are still poorly developed and we are some way from the system of paying by results that would arguably be necessary for agri-environmental payments on a large scale to be politically defensible. RSPB's approach recommends itself here, which is to promote a strong version of conservation compliance as a bridge to stand-alone environmental support. By requiring enrolment in discrete agri-environmental schemes as a condition of any government payment, farmers become familiar with the environmental contracts and may be less reluctant to enrol when given the chance. As an approach to greening the CAP it has the advantage of being both pragmatic and far-sighted because it exploits the current situation while also preparing for the day when the compensation schemes fall away and payments are channelled exclusively through the agri-environmental schemes.

Future Prospects

As we have seen, policy makers have temporarily driven a wedge between decoupling support from production and recoupling it to environmental objectives by introducing the MacSharry compensation schemes and beginning to recouple these to green concerns. At present, measures such as the arable areas payment scheme and the various beef and ewe premiums are allowed by GATT rules because they are notionally 'green box' instruments, having no, or at most minimal, trade distortion effects. But they are unlikely to enjoy this immunity indefinitely. Haynes, *et al* (1992) believe it is no coincidence that the recent GATT negotiations first stalled because of the EC's determination to press on with the arable areas payment scheme and policy which, by definition, maintains the link with production by calculating payments on a cropped area basis. Their comment is that as long as this connection remains, the cereals regime will continue to distort EU production and world trade. The next GATT Round, scheduled for the end of the century, will once again act as a catalyst for reform, while enlargement of the EU to embrace Hungary, Poland and the Czech and Slovak Republics in 2003-2005 can only add to the 'domestic' pressures for change. As Newby (1993 p11) remarks, the indications are "that wholesale reform of the CAP can now safely be placed in the 'sooner or later' category". Evidently, the long game to bring about a 'European Rural Policy' which is decoupled from agricultural production and recoupled to environmental and other social goals has barely begun.

Winning the short game to make it possible for some of the farm budget to be redirected into environmental protection has demanded a number of compromises and in the medium term it will be interesting to see how far the mixed income support and environmental protection of existing agri-environmental schemes separate out as pressure grows to target and tighten their design. According to Bonnen and Browne (1992), environmental groups have certainly become participants in the agricultural policy making process, members of the farm policy club, for the first time, but possibly as more than a minor presence, presenting hurdles for the long empowered farm lobby to jump over rather than challenging the essentials of policy. Not all agri-environmental spending is strictly for environmental purposes and too many schemes are little more than mechanisms for making disguised income transfers. Winning the long game will require a fundamental re-examination of what agricultural support is for and who deserves to receive it. It may take some time to work out the terms of this new social contract between farmers and the state, but the need for it is now widely recognised. Importantly, there are signs of growing international convergence towards similar solutions. GATT in particular is likely to be critical in supplying and codifying the rules of the new contract and will become an increasingly important institution for the environmental reform of farm policy.

Meanwhile, a Europe-wide debate about farmers and their role in the future countryside is needed. To date, the core assumptions or 'programmatic doctrines' of the CAP have largely escaped scrutiny - most obviously the assumption that governments have a duty to intervene to maintain or improve farm income and the related view, until recently very widely held, that conservation is best produced jointly with food by maintaining family farmers on the land in large numbers. Yet as Majone (1989) has pointed out, policy reform is as much an intellectual as a political process and there is a sense in which more radical options may have been closed off by the constrained nature of the agricultural policy debate itself. One very plausible hypothesis which deserves further exploration is that long established policies like those for agriculture become immunised against reform by having a 'core' of key assumptions surrounded by a 'protective belt' of more peripheral assumptions and hypotheses which can, if necessary, be challenged or refuted without requiring a fundamental reorientation of policy. In treating habitat loss and agricultural pollution as essentially policy failures and criticising the way farm policies were being operated rather than their longer-term purpose, environmentalists and reform-minded commentators may have been engaged in refuting peripheral hypotheses about their design and effectiveness and were deflected from a deeper re-examination of the underlying rationale for continuing with agricultural support in the late 20th century. It may be time to plan for what Batie (1986) pointedly calls 'non-incremental policy reform' in the agricultural field.

References

Baldock, D (1990) *Agriculture and Habitat Loss in Europe*, Discussion Paper 3, World Wildlife Fund, London.

Batie, S, Shabman, L, Kramer, R A (1986) US Agricultural and Natural Resource Policy: Past and Future in Rungie, C F (Ed), *The Future of the North American Granary: Politics, Economics and Resource Constraints in North American Agriculture*, Iowa State Press.

Bowers J and Cheshire P (1983) *Agriculture, the Countryside and Land Use*, Methuen, London.

Bonnen, J and Browne, W (1989) Why is agricultural policy so difficult to reform? in Kramer, C (Ed) *The Political Economy of US Agriculture*, Resources for the Future, Washington DC., 7-33.

Cheshire, P (1990) The environmental implications of European agricultural support policies, in Baldock and Conder (Eds) *Can the CAP Fit the Environment?* IEEP/CPRE/WWF, London, 10-17.

Colman, D, Crabtree, B, Froud, J and O'Carroll, L (1992) *Comparative Effectiveness of Conservation Mechanisms*, Department of Agricultural Economics, Manchester University, Manchester.

Commission of the European Communities (1985) *Perspectives for the Common Agricultural Policy*, Comnd 85, 258, Brussels.

Crabtree, B (1992) A more environmental CAP? Paper presented to Agricultural Economics Society Special Conference, December 1992.

Dixon, J and Taylor, J (1990) *Agriculture and Environment: towards integration*, RSPB, Sandy.

Egdell, J (1995) Switching CAP livestock support from headage to area payments: the implications for the environment and farm incomes, Paper to Agricultural Economics Society Annual Conference 1995, Cambridge.

Felton, M (1993) Achieving nature conservation objectives: problems and opportunities with economics, *Journal of Environmental Planning and Management*, 36, 23-31.

Haynes, J, Buckwell, A, Tangermann, S and Mahe, L (1992) *Making a Virtue Out of Idleness*, CEAS Consultants Ltd, Wye College, Kent.

House of Lords (1984) *Agriculture and the Environment*, 20th report, 1983-84 session, HMSO, London.

Jenkins, N (1990) *Future Harvests: the economics of farming and the environment*, CPRE/WWF, London.

Koester, U and Tangermann, S (1977) Supplementing farm price policy by direct income payments, *European Review of Agricultural Economics*, 4, 7-31.

MacEwan, M and Sinclair, G (1983) *New Life for the Hills,* CNP, London.

Ministry of Agriculture Fisheries and Food (1993) *Agriculture and England's Environment : a consultation document on environmental schemes under the CAP,* MAFF, London.

Majone, G (1989) *Evidence, Argument and Persuasion in the Policy Process,* Yale University Press, London.

Moore, N (1987) *The Bird of Time : the science and politics of nature conservation,* Cambridge University Press, Cambridge.

Newby, H (1993) The social shaping of agriculture : where do we go from here? *Journal of Royal Society of Arts,* 154, 9-18.

Petit, M (1985) *Determinants of Agricultural Policies in the US and EC,* International Food Institute, Research Report 51, London.

Potter, C (1983) *Investing in Rural Harmony,* WWF, London.

Rausser, G and Irwin, D (1989) The political economy of agricultural policy reform, *European Review of Agricultural Economics,* 15, 349-366.

Tangermann, S (1992) *Reforming the CAP? In for a Penny, In for a Pound,* IEA Inquiry 28, Institute of Economic Affairs, London.

Waters, G (1994) Government policies for the countryside, *Land Use Policy,* 11, 88-93.

Whitby, M (1994) *Incentives for Countryside Management,* CABI, Wallingford.

Winters, L (1987) The political economy of the agricultural policy of industrial countries, *European Review of Agricultural Economics,* 14, 285-304.

CHAPTER 10

Farm Diversification and the Environment*
Bill Slee

This paper considers the policy context in relation to farm diversification and reviews the extent to which farm diversification has generated, and is likely to generate, effects on the environment. The focus is principally on the UK, but reference is also made to the situation in other developed economies. Given the growth of academic interest in both farm diversification, pluriactivity and related subjects on one hand, and agri-environmental questions on the other, it is surprising how few attempts have been made to explore the interactions between these two areas of concern. This absence of detailed investigation is all the more surprising when the prevalence of farm households with diversified income sources is considered (Gasson, 1988).

There is a significant body of work on styles of farming (van der Ploeg, 1994) which focuses on the heterogeneity of responses of farmers to market developments. A relationship is suggested between environmentally beneficial land management and styles of farming activity which are less locked into market relationships. Van der Ploeg argues (1994 p15) that "the interlinkages, fusion and synergy of agricultural and 'extra-agricultural' activities within one and the same economic unit (currently the family) are central to our understanding". This assertion provides support for the study of the relationship between diversified farm households and the environment, not only in the marginal areas which are the focus of his study, but also in other circumstances where the fusion of agricultural and extra-agricultural activities impacts on the quality of the rural environment.

Interest in farm diversification and pluriactivity can be dated back to two distinct areas of study: the first, exploring part-time farming, is reflected in the work of Gasson (1986;1988); the second, examining the potential of farms as the location for new forms of business activity, is reflected in the work of Slee (1987;1989) and Haines and Davies (1987) in the UK, and of Brunåker (1993) in Sweden. These two strands have tended to merge in more recent

* The helpful comments of Dr Simon Davies and Professor Ken Thomson are much appreciated. Helen Farr is thanked for delivering the paper.

work (see especially, Arkleton Trust, 1992). Prior to the mid 1980s the extent of agency interest in farm diversification had been very limited, and policy development had been restricted to modest support from the EC for certain forms of diversification in Less Favoured Areas (LFAs) and a general desire to create larger farm businesses, usually employing at least one full-time equivalent, through such national schemes as the Small Farm Business Management Scheme (a UK scheme) and the Farm and Horticultural Development Scheme and its successor schemes, which were EC-funded.

In the late 1980s, the UK Ministry of Agriculture began to look more favourably on farm diversification, as evidenced in the ALURE package which introduced the Farm Woodland Scheme, Farm Diversification Grants and a slackening of the notification procedures relating to development control on farmland. Although the Farm Diversification Grant Scheme has ceased, there is now, at both UK and EC level levels, a recognition of the importance of diversified income sources for farm households.

Interest in the relationships between farming and environmental issues dates from the late 1960s and 1970s when the connections between agricultural intensification and the ecological environment were highlighted, for example by Moore (1966). From these beginnings, concern about the environmental effects of agricultural change broadened to embrace landscape change (Westmacott and Worthington, 1974), ecological change, fertiliser- and pesticide-related pollution, and access. Connections were increasingly made between adverse environmental effects and agricultural policy measures (Shoard, 1980; Bowers and Cheshire, 1983; Knickel, 1990), thus initiating the debate which has led eventually to the development of a wide-ranging set of EC and national agri-environmental policy instruments. The support for agri-environmental measures remains a small, but increasing, proportion of total EC agricultural policy support costs.

The academic study of farm diversification and the study of agri-environment relationships have rarely tended to overlap. However, the adverse response of a number of amenity societies to the ALURE proposals led them to sponsor a number of studies, notably by Watkins and Winter (1988), who explored the effects of barn conversions on visual amenity and the built heritage, and more recently, Clark *et al* (1994) who examined the impact of leisure-related development on the visual and cultural environment of the countryside. Other studies (e.g. Gasson, 1988) have made passing reference to the relationship between farm diversification, as part-time farming, and the environment.

Defining Farm Diversification

Many authors have struggled to find an unambiguous definition of farm diversification and attempts to classify diversification are fraught with difficulty. Different and sometimes confusing terms have been used to describe the various economic activities taking place within farm households which are not mainstream farming operations. The terminology includes the following.

Part-time farming: Gasson (1988) opts for the term to denote "the combination of farming with other paid work". Gasson also uses the term 'Other Gainful Activities' to describe non-agricultural income sources to farm households. These can include unconventional[1] on-farm activities as well as off-farm income. It is likely that certain unconventional agricultural activities would be excluded from this definition, such as certain forms of alternative livestock and crop enterprises, as would payments for environmental goods.

Alternative farm enterprises: Slee (1987;1990) and Brannigan (Ed) (1994) use this term to denote on-farm diversification and include within their definition unconventional agricultural enterprises as well as non-farming activities that are based on a farm.   .

Farm diversification: Haines and Davies (1987) use this term to describe the broadening range of business activities of farmers, and this term has received institutional benediction as it became the label for government grants to farmers in 1987. It is, inevitably, the preferred term used in UK government-sponsored inquiries (McInerney *et al*, 1989; Dalton and Wilson, 1989).

Pluriactivity: Shucksmith *et al* (1989) use the term 'pluriactivity' to embrace the use of farm household labour on and off the farm in non-agricultural activity, noting the neglect of the study of off-farm income sources of farm households in the UK. Fuller (1990) includes within his definition of pluriactivity employment on other farms, para-agricultural activity such as food processing, other non-agricultural activities on the farm and off-farm wage labour. Arkleton Trust (1992) summarises the evolution of the concept of pluriactivity from its origins in part-time farming, but add little to Gasson's (1988) definition other than to move away from the ambiguities (see Lund, 1991) surrounding the term 'part-time farming'.

These varied definitions are a major source of concern to the study of relationships between diversification and the environment, insofar as some of the definitions exclude economic activities that are likely to affect the environment in various ways. What is needed for this purpose is a working definition that embraces the broadest possible range of non-conventional sources of well-being of farm households. For example, Hill (1989) has asserted that the farming share of the sum of farmers' incomes in the UK varied from 51 to 64 per cent of their taxable income over the period 1980 to 1987. Given that on-farm diversified enterprises are likely to be included in the farming element, this suggests that the average farmer may be drawing only about half of his taxable income from farming. This emphasises the need for a broad definition of diversification.

Gasson (1991) has argued that "it is surely relevant to take account of all contributions to a common housekeeping fund, whether made by husband or wife or other household members and/or business partners". This assertion raises the question about the role of unearned income derived from non-farm assets and the broad definition used by Slee (1989), which recognises both changes in the stock of farm assets as well as in the income stream derived from that stock, recognises this point. It accommodates both off-farm and on-farm diversification and revenue from asset sales and off-farm investments (see figure 10.1).

The choice of a definition is guided by a recognition that if any potentially significant economic factor affecting household well-being is excluded, then the potential for that factor impacting on the environment

Figure 10.1 A Working Definition of Diversification

	ON-FARM	OFF-FARM
INCOME STREAM	e.g. snail farming pick-your-own	e.g. agricultural contracting agriculturally unrelated work
ASSET REALISATION	e.g. barn sale	e.g. sale of shares

Source: derived from Slee (1989)

will be ignored. For example, unearned income may be a vital factor in enabling environmentally beneficial extensive farming practices to be maintained, when farm households without such income sources may intensify their farming operations in an attempt to maintain income levels. Only one of the above definitions embraces unearned income. A further important example is whether or not environmental payments from the EC and central or local government constitute forms of diversification. Slee (1989) includes these in his definition, whereas Shucksmith *et al*, 1989) exclude them. A final example of where definitional differences can include or exclude potentially significant environmental problems is barn conversions. Pluriactivity excludes activities such as selling barns for alternative use, but includes them if they remain in the control of the farm household as rented premises. Given that the majority of barn conversions occur after they have been sold by the farm household, they could not be considered as diversification if a restrictive definition were adopted. However, the scope for using capital created by barn sales to relieve indebtedness or to generate investment income from such sales may be important in determining the intended or unintended environmental consequences of this particular household adjustment strategy.

All of the above definitions treat the farm as a unit of production and the farm asset base as comprising the land, labour and capital resources. The analytical closure around the farm has been criticised for ignoring off-farm work, which is a more common form of diversification of the set of resources including the farm and the farm household than on-farm diversification (Shucksmith *et al*, 1989). However, all of these definitions exclude from consideration the farm as a unit of consumption. Given the predilection of many to see land not as a productive asset but as a positional good (Hirsch, 1976), and to acquire and retain land not as a source of income but as a source and store of wealth and leisure opportunity, it is surprising that the social theorists of diversification should have largely neglected this fact. For example, Marsden *et al* (1987) focus on the continual attempts of outside capital to penetrate farming, treating land as a potentially lucrative destination for capital rather than as a source of private leisure benefit. Although hobby farming has long been recognised as a phenomenon, these farms frequently occupy an apparently anomalous role in the hands of capitalist accumulation strategists, and are often retained not so much as mechanisms of accumulation but as outlets for their leisure spending. Almost certainly, Paul Getty junior did not buy an estate in the Chiltern Hills as a profit maximising venture, any more than did Victorian industrialists who bought farming and sporting estates.

This use of the farm as a consumption good rather than as a productive asset is likely to be of critical concern in the examination of the environmental effects of diversification. Owners of such land are more likely to enhance its environmental qualities than those who are treating farming as purely a business activity. These 20th century amenity landowners are the natural successors of the owners of the great 18th century landscaped parks. The Farm Woodland Grant Scheme and its successors and related schemes for amenity enhancement can be seen as no more than a government-sponsored scheme to deliver a contemporary version of the work of Repton, Brown and others. Consequently, it is important to consider not just the sources of income of farm households but also whether or not farm households are using farms and farmland as a destination for leisure-related spending.

Types of Diversified Activity

In addition to there being different definitions of diversification, a number of different classifications of types of diversification have been offered. Given that the environmental consequences of different forms of diversification are likely to vary, these attempts to classify may be helpful in highlighting the potential environmental effects. A selection of these is summarised in figure 10.2.

Figure 10.2 Alternative Classifications of Diversified Enterprises.

McInerney *et al* (1989) Services Contracting Processing and sales Miscellaneous	Speciality products
Brannigan (1994) Diversification of retailing processing Diversification of on-farm services Extensification of woodland Farming extensification	Conversion
Slee (1989) Tourism and recreation Value-adding enterprises Ancillary resources Public goods	Unconventional agricultural enterprises
Arkleton Trust (1992) Stability Disengagement	Professionalisation

Although some of the classifications above are for somewhat different purposes, there is sufficient comparability for them to be potentially useful in providing a framework in which to examine potential environmental effects. Of the classifications, that of Arkleton Trust (1992) is least similar to the others, in that its focus is the adjustment strategy rather than the type of diversification.

The Environmental Effects of Diversification

The environmental effects of diversification are generally thought to be negative. This perception is fuelled by both a general resistance to change and specific examples of diversification with known undesirable side effects (e.g. fish farming and water pollution). This image is reinforced by the outcry from organisations such as the Council for the Protection of Rural England

(CPRE) about leisure-related developments (Clark *et al*, 1994). However, it is also possible to identify positive environmental effects that might arise from diversification, as in farm woodland planting, or making use of public money to maintain or enhance environmental assets. It is thus important to consider the range of environmental effects that can arise. These can be considered to fall into four main groups (figure 10.3)

Figure 10.3 Potential Environmental Effects of Farm Diversification.

POSITIVE EFFECTS	NEGATIVE EFFECTS
Landscape enhancement	Landscape deterioration
Habitat enhancement	Habitat destruction
Pollution reduction	Pollution increase
Access enhancement	Access reduction

The potential visual intrusiveness of certain forms of diversification is especially apparent in view of the tendency for modern farming to produce a simpler landscape from which many detailed elements have been removed by modern agricultural practice (Westmacott and Worthington, 1974). The incongruity between the appearance of modern golf courses and the farmed landscape of lowland England illustrates the visual tensions that can arise with the conversion of land to alternative use. Horse enterprises in an urban fringe setting can intrude in an already blighted rural landscape. Caravan sites rarely blend well into the landscape of rural Britain. Whatever criteria are used to assess landscape deterioration, whether quantitative or qualitative, it is evident that diversification has the capacity to reduce landscape quality. However, other forms of diversification, such as farm woodland planting or Stewardship-funded land management practices, may generate landscape-enhancing effects. Building conversions may result in the sensitive re-use of vernacular buildings in ways which enhance the rural landscape.

Some forms of diversification can threaten habitat and wildlife quality. For example, scarce semi-natural habitat may be replaced by exotic conifers when farm woodland is planted. Physical disturbance may arise in relatively sensitive habitats as a result of tourist enterprises. Quarries may be turned into landfill sites. It is relatively easy to produce a catalogue of diversification-induced environmental damage of wildlife and habitat quality. However, habitat enhancement can arise from various forms of diversification, including game management and woodland planting, and by the uptake of public incentives for habitat provision in Environmentally Sensitive Areas (ESAs) or via Stewardship and other schemes. The habitat-enhancing effects of some types of game management have been amply illustrated in the work of the Gamebirds and Cereals Research Project (Game Conservancy, 1985). Unsprayed headlands have proved beneficial to butterflies and songbirds as well as grey partridges.[2] In an upland situation, heather management is more likely to occur where there is sporting use of moorland for red grouse. Such ecosystems also favour a number of rare species such as the merlin and hen harrier.

The third type of environmental effect to consider is pollution. Pollution can arise from diversification as a result of value-adding activities generating waste products, from traffic associated with farm visitor enterprises, and in many other ways. However, there is likely to be a trade-off between diversification-induced and agriculturally-induced pollution. Agricultural pollution is broadly correlated with the intensity of farming. Any form of diversification which leads to extensification of farming practices is likely to reduce the polluting effects of conventional farming practices. Thus, the relationship between diversification and pollution is by no means straightforward.

Access opportunities have been impeded by the modernisation of farming, particularly by field enlargement, which has led to closure or diversion of footpaths. In addition, hobby farmers who purchase their land for their amenity may be reluctant to share access to land with others. Thus the two forces of intensification and engrossment on full-time farms and the growth of part-time farming can be seen to have a generally negative effect on access opportunities. However, under the Stewardship Scheme and the

Figure 10.4 A Synopsis of the Environmental Consequences of Diversification.

TYPE OF DIVERSIFICATION	ENVIRONMENTAL EFFECT
(A) ON-FARM	
Unconventional crops and livestock	Generally no more environmentally threatening than conventional agriculture; may be less so, especially if production system is less intensive.
Tourism and recreation	Scope for major environmental effects with some types such as visual intrusion of caravan sites; physical wear and tear of sensitive sites possible; increased pollution. However, environmental enhancement may accompany developments.
Ancillary resources	Building conversions can be positive or negative. Woodland and wetland creation normally, but not universally, beneficial.
Value-adding enterprises	Possible waste products from processing. Increased traffic on roads (PYO).
Payments by government for public goods	Exclusively environmentally beneficial.
(B) OFF-FARM	
Off-farm work of farmer	Likely to be associated with de-intensification of farming, thus benefiting the environment. Hobby farmers likely to spend significant sums on enhancing environmental quality.
Off-farm work of other member(s) of family	Environmental effects uncertain: may increase household income and result in cross-subsidy to agricultural enterprise thus maintaining or increasing adverse environmental effects; alternatively, may result in environmental spending on holding.

earlier 1949 Access Agreements, it has been possible to compensate providers of access.

The potential environmental consequences of different types of diversification are summarised in figure10.4 A brief examination of this table reveals that it is impossible to assert the existence of a simple relationship between increased farm diversification and increased environmental damage.

Only a modest amount of attention has been given to the environmental consequences of diversification. Gasson (1990) notes that concern over the rural environment may favour part-time farming as "the farmer who does not depend wholly on farming for a living can afford to follow farming practices which are more 'friendly' to the environment." Elsewhere, Gasson (1986) has pointed to the lower intensity of land use where there are diversified income sources, and notes that, although labour input per unit output may be high, this may reflect farming for leisure rather than farming for profit. Knickel (1990) notes that there appears to be a general relationship between small-scale mixed farming and landscape quality, but stresses that the relation is not always a simple one. However, he emphasises the creation of new policy instruments (polluter ·pays principle and provider paid principle for negative and positive externalities respectively) rather than an increase in part-time farming as a solution to the current ecological problems. This approach appears to deny the scope for non policy-led, endogenous adaptation towards more environmentally friendly land management.

The most serious recent attempt to review the relationship between diversification and the environment (Davies and Dalton, 1994) offers evidence that farm households with diversified income sources manage their land less intensively than full-time farmers. It should be stressed that their data relate only to three regions of Scotland. In the north-east of Scotland, Ellis and Heal (1993) found diversified farm households to have a greater species diversity on their land than farm households devoted to farming full-time. In other situations it is conceivable that a reduction in the intensity of agricultural activity could have negative consequences on the environment.

Although in a UK context it may be hard to contemplate how environmental quality could be enhanced by intensification there are widespread fears of *desertification* in other parts of Europe. On calcareous grassland, the removal of grazing ruminants has been found to lead to reductions in species diversity, and in Germany Knickel (1990) has noted that 50 per cent of Red List plants depend on low-input, land-use systems. Thus, if there is a possibility of these extensive farming systems disappearing, there is a case for supporting them for environmental reasons.

A major omission from many studies of diversified farm households is the extent of transfer from diversified sources of income into environmental expenditure, for example into farm woodland. Appleton and Crabtree (1991) found that in some regions of Scotland those taking advantage of the Farm Woodland Scheme obtained the majority of their income from outside conventional farming enterprises. In addition to the increased uptake of environmentally-related grants, such households may well be more predisposed to invest in new habitat creation, and to invest in the restoration of traditional buildings and field boundaries.

A further example of non-farm income sources feeding into environmentally beneficial behaviour may arise in situations where elderly farmers have no successor and continue to farm with the help of off-farm income sources which may include pensions and welfare payments. The environment-benefiting behaviour may be a result of the general tendency of such households to farm less intensively, and, although not conscious and intended efforts at environmental enhancement, may nonetheless represent a real, if potentially short-term, environmental gain.

Discussion

The evidence of a link between environmental quality and farmland owned or managed by households with diversified income sources can be established. The types of environmental benefits are likely to vary greatly and are likely to be associated with a number of key factors, including:

- intensity of land management;
- availability of funds to invest in environmental enhancement;
- environmental values; and
- recreation and amenity seeking behaviour.

In different regions, the relative importance of these factors is likely to be highly variable. For example, in remote rural areas, the extent of hobby farming is likely to be limited, but low-intensity farming may be conditioned by poor quality land and traditions of off-farm work, as in the crofting regions. In areas of attractive countryside close to built-up areas, hobby farming may generate high levels of environmental investment.

The failure of the academic community to explore the connections between environment and the activities of diversified farm households is surprising in view of the existence of such initiatives as the ESRC Countryside Change Initiative. Those people who are "seeking their place in the country" (Centre for Rural Economy, 1993) are seen as an entirely different group from those who are seeking new development opportunities in the countryside. The polarisation into an amenity-seeking and an entrepreneurial group may be analytically convenient but may not truly represent the situation in many rural regions. In fact, these groups overlap, with many newcomers seeking to develop land in various ways, sometimes for financial profit and sometimes to pursue private amenity, and many farmers combining amenity consumption activities with commercially oriented food production. There is nothing new about these competing functions or their occurrence within individual households, as well as between different social groups. However, the contemporary farm household with multiple income sources is often the setting in which this conflict and competition occurs. The resolution of these competing demands, and the balance of amenity-related demands and commercially-motivated demands, will be a significant influence on the future quality of the rural environment.

To date, the general response of amenity societies to diversification has been one of suspicion and concern. Rather than seeing the potential environmental merit of a more diversified rural economy, such institutions seem to be locked into a retrospective Arcadian vision. Newby has argued that incomers to rural areas have often sought a 'village of the mind'. Amenity societies have long shown a tendency to seek a countryside of their mind, as is evidenced in the nostalgic sentiments of the Scott Committee in the 1940s, and the outpourings of proliferating pressure groups since that time.

Given the relatively recent recognition of the extent of farm households with multiple income sources and the belated recognition by academics and public sector agencies that such economic units are not anachronisms but units with the scope to devise flexible adjustment strategies, there is a strong case for more detailed investigation of the environmental consequences of different forms of diversification of household activity. It is likely that there will be very significant regional variations in the extent and type of diversification, with the possibility of significant environmental damage in some areas and significant environmental gains in others.

The recognition that the well-being of both rural communities and the environment are core concerns of a reformed CAP makes the need to explore the environmental implications of diversification all the more urgent. The pressures of policy reforms which reduce support to conventional farm enterprises and public and institutional demands for a better quality rural environment can potentially be interwoven in a new and dynamic vision of rural development.

Notes

1. The question of what is unconventional inevitably raises difficulties. These are fully discussed in Brannigan (1994).

2. It is recognised that there are potential moral objections to the desirability of using the joint product argument (i.e. the game management creates opportunities for other forms of environmental gain) as a justification for hunting and shooting. The only implication above is that there are environmental joint products arising from game management.

References

Appleton Z and Crabtree J R (1991) *The Farm Woodland Scheme in Scotland: An Economic Appraisal*, SAC Economics Report 29.

Arkleton Trust Research Ltd (1992) *Farm Household Adjustment in Western Europe 1987-1991*, EC, Brussels.

Bowers J and Cheshire P (1983) *Agriculture, the Countryside and Land Use: An Economic Critique*, Methuen, London.

Brannigan J (Ed) (1994) *Alternative Farming Systems in Lagging Regions of the EC*, Working Paper 13 Regional Report for the Highlands and Islands of Scotland, SAC, Aberdeen.

Brunåker S (1993) *Farm Diversification - New Enterprises on Competitive Markets*, Uppsala University, Uppsala.

Centre for Rural Economy (1993) *Countryside Change: A Synopsis*, CRE, Newcastle.

Clark G *et al* (1994) *Leisure Landscapes: Leisure, Culture and the English Countryside, Challenges and Conflicts*, Centre for Environmental Change, Lancaster.

Dalton G E and Wilson C (1989) Farm Diversification in Scotland, *SAC Economics Report No. 12*, SAC, Aberdeen.

Davies A S and Dalton G E (1994) *Pluriactivity: A Way of Protecting the Natural and Social Environments of Rural Areas Whilst Reducing Agricultural Support*, unpublished typescript.

Ellis N E and Heal W O (1993) *Differences in Farmland Ecology Associated with Pluriactivity: Grampian Region*, JAEP Report, Institute of Terrestrial Ecology, Edinburgh.

Fuller A M (1990) From Part-time Farming to Pluriactivity: a Decade of Change in Rural Europe, *Journal of Rural Studies* 6, 361-373.

Game Conservancy (1985) *Gamebirds and Cereals Research Project: Third Newsletter* Game Conservancy, Fordingbridge.

Gasson R (1986) *Farm Families with Other Gainful Activities*, Department of Agricultural Economics, Wye College, Wye.

Gasson R (1988) *The Economics of Part-time Farming*, Longman, London.

Gasson R (1990) Part-time Farming and Pluriactivity, in Britton D (Ed) *Agriculture in Britain: Changing Pressures and Policies*, CAB, Wallingford.

Gasson R (1991) Part-time Farming: a Note on Definitions-Comment, *Journal of Agricultural Economics*, 42, 200-202.

Haines M and Davies R (1987) *Diversifying the Farm Business*, BSP Professional, Oxford.

Hill B (1989) *Farm Incomes, Wealth and Agricultural Policy*, Avebury, Aldershot.

Hirsch F (1976) *Social Limits to Growth*, Harvard University Press, Cambridge.

Knickel K (1990) Agricultural Structural Change: Impact on the Rural Environment, *Journal of Rural Studies*, 6, 383-393.

Lund P J (1991) Part-time Farming: a Note on Definitions. *Journal of Agricultural Economics*, 42 ,196-199.

Marsden T, Whatmore S J and Munton R J C (1987) Uneven Development and the Restructuring of British Agriculture: a Preliminary Exploration, *Journal of Rural Studies*, 3, 297-308.

McInerney J, Turner M and Hollingham M (1989) *Diversification in the Use of Farm Resources*, Report No. 232, Agricultural Economics Unit, University of Exeter, Exeter.

Moore N Ed (1966) Pesticides in the Environment and Their Effect on Wildlife, *Journal of Applied Ecology*, 3, special supplement.

Shoard M (1980) *The Theft of the Countryside*, Temple Smith, London.

Shucksmith D M, Bryden J, Rosenthal P, Short C and Winter M (1989) Farm Household Strategies and Pluriactivity: A Review, *Journal of Agricultural Economics*, 40, 144-160.

Slee W (1987) *Alternative Farm Enterprises 1st Ed*, Farming Press, Ipswich.

Slee W (1989) *Alternative Farm Enterprises 2nd Ed*, Farming Press, Ipswich.

Van der Ploeg J D (1994) Styles of Farming: an Introductory Note on Concepts and Methodology, in Van der Ploeg J D and Long A, (Eds) *Born from Within: Practice and Perspectives of Endogenous Rural Development*, Van Gorcum, Assen.

Watkins C and Winter M (1988) *Superb Conversions? Farm Diversification: the Farm Building Experience,* Centre for Rural Studies and CPRE, London.

Westmacott R and Worthington T (1974) *New Agricultural Landscapes*, Countryside Commission, Cheltenham.

CHAPTER 11

Environment-Friendly Farming in Southwest England:
An Exploration and Analysis

Martin R. J. Battershill and Andrew W. Gilg

The increasing importance of agri-environment problems in politics and society has led to changes in agricultural and conservation policies and to new structures in the wider food industry. Central to agricultural policy reform has been the notion of environmental incentive payments. With the Environmentally Sensitive Area (ESA) scheme as a model, the 1992 European Common Agricultural Policy (CAP) reform created an obligation on member states to offer incentive payments to farmers in return for them providing environmental protection or improvement. Whilst totally dwarfed by price support and Set-Aside payments, the new agri-environment schemes are a precedent in terms of their being funded by the same guarantee sector of the CAP. The principle of simple and standardised environmental payments is increasingly replacing the old Management Agreement system of protecting wildlife sites, a system characterised by complex and expensive individual agreements and by more than a hint of blackmail from farmers with their hands on the plough.

Equally the growth and formalization of food marketing structures which promote standards of production practices have given consumers in the market place an opportunity to support organic or low-input farming systems. People can, and do, pay premium prices for food produced using environment-friendly husbandry techniques.

However, understanding of the farm circumstances that lie behind participation in these new schemes and initiatives is still only partial. Research has tended to focus on two distinct branches of environment-friendly activity, namely creative conservation work and incentive scheme participation. Enquiries have pursued economic and attitudinal influences on farm behaviour, and often suggested that freedom from economic constraint, i.e. circumstances associated with expansionist, accumulator or wealthy farmers, creates both a greater ability and willingness to undertake conservation work, and to take advantage of incentive payments which encourage this work (see Potter, 1986; Potter and Gasson, 1988; Clark and

O'Riordan, 1989; Marsden and Munton, 1991). Equally in some areas, and particularly in ESAs, farmers have been seen to be receiving money for nothing as conservation incentive schemes have supported their existing traditional farming and have not obliged farmers to make changes to their farming practices (see Baldock *et al*, 1991; Whitby, 1994).

It was against this policy and research background that an investigation was undertaken into farms and farming activity in fourteen agri-environment schemes and initiatives in Devon, Cornwall and west Somerset. These initiatives comprised: incentive schemes; management agreements; conservation advice; food marketing standards; and landlord/tenant arrangements. A full list of the schemes and a brief outline of their main attributes is provided in figure 11.1. Between May 1992 and August 1993 122 scheme participants were visited. The research sought to illuminate how geographical, attitudinal, socio-economic and farm system circumstances influenced the nature of environment-friendly farming or activity and, in particular, which circumstances were most influential on that activity. Against this circumstantial background, scheme impact could then also be assessed. The research specifically sought to develop the understanding of these influences on farms from the full and diverse spectrum of existing agri-environment schemes: this afforded an examination of common influences as well as the influences which moved farms towards different types of scheme or activity.

The main findings of the research are presented below. The chapter is divided into four parts: the first part discusses the objectives of the research; the second part summarises the most important impacts of the schemes; the third part presents the main conclusions about the influence of farm circumstances; and the final part offers a brief summary of the academic and policy implications of the research findings.

Research Objectives and Methodology

The primary research objective was to better understand how individual farm circumstances led to or influenced different types of environment-friendly farming activity, since as Lowe *et al* (1989, p66) have stated:

"an ability to comprehend change at these scales (ie. at the level of individual farm businesss) is increasingly demanded by shifts in public policy which cast farmers as managers of countryside change and require regulation and support to be precisely targeted".

A second objective of the research was then to investigate the impact of the schemes and initiatives on the farms themselves, given the known circumstances of the farms.

Different types of environment-friendly activity could be identified. However, these activities were mostly independent from any scheme-based influences. Instead environment-friendly activity was strongly influenced by geographical and especially attitudinal circumstances, and also at times by the legacy of traditional farming.

The sample was dominated by farms where the whole farming system could be defined as environment-friendly, including some farms which also contained specific areas of uniquely high conservation value. A smaller number of farms were involved with grant-aided creative conservation or public access work, in an otherwise less environment-friendly system. Others were engaged in the single-minded pursuit of premium food prices.

The Impact of the Schemes

Most of the schemes had had very little substantial impact on the environment-friendly activities of the farms. As is shown in part 3, this activity was largely a result of existing farm circumstances. However, any impact that was noted was always positive in either conservation or social terms. In addition, many farms needed financial help from the schemes if their most valuable conservation and farm management practices were to continue.

Practical impact: The incentive schemes and Wildlife Enhancement Scheme had had an important influence on some farms. The financial assistance which these schemes offered had helped to encourage or fund

Figure 11.1 Outline of the schemes studied

1. Countryside Stewardship scheme: a Countryside Commission scheme offering standard rate acreage and capital works payments for conservation and public access work in certain landscapes. The majority of Southwest participants were in the Coastal or Riverside options.

2. ELMS: a Devon County Council scheme offering ten year agreements for conservation management (especially of Culm grassland) and public access work.

3. and 4. ESAs: the Somerset Levels & Moors and West Penwith ESAs were visited, the former protecting a distinct landscape of wetland and drainage dykes, the latter a landscape of Celtic fields and coastal moorland.

5. Exmoor Farm Conservation Scheme: an Exmoor National Park scheme offering shared costs between the Park, the Farm and Conservation Grant Scheme and the farmer for landscape, hedging and conservation work.

6. Dartmoor National Park Management Agreements: agreement holders were visited with agreements for moorland and wetland conservation and for public access work.

7. Wildlife Enhancement Scheme: a pilot scheme run by English Nature to fund conservation improvement work on SSSI status areas of the rare and fragmented Culm grassland habitat.

8. FWAG: offering conservation advice to farmers who request it.

9. Royal Association of British Dairy Farmers Conservation Prize: a national prize scheme with the award based on the successful incorporation of conservation work into commercial farming.

10. Conservation Grade: a food marketing standard encouraging lower-input practices and the use of benign agro-chemicals.

11. Soil Association: the largest verification scheme for organic produce.

12. West Country Lamb: a food marketing scheme encouraging extensive and traditional husbandry in sheep farming.

13. and 14. Duchy of Cornwall and the National Trust: promotion or support of conservation work in a landlord/tenant context.

conservation work on certain farms where the farmers would otherwise not have been willing or able to do the work. In particular the schemes had helped to support very important traditional hedge and boundary management. On some farms the schemes had also helped improve the management of Culm moorland. The schemes had also helped to prevent the abandonment of important conservation practices, either offering work and financial assistance to farms with larger, family-based workforces, or paid for conservation work by contractors when the farm labour force was small.

Financial impact: Often the scheme help was greatest on 'traditional' farms which were seriously constrained by low incomes and often poor farming conditions. Whilst the farmers' interest in conservation may have been at best minimal, the scheme payments helped to keep the farms working and at times even to keep them viable. There may have been a selectivity effect on many farms, with only 50% of farmers saying they had changed any practices as a result of the scheme. However, on the poorer, traditional farms this effect was financially essential, and also justified in terms of equity.

Attitudinal impact: Nevertheless, few farmers stated that the schemes were important on the farm. Many farmers believed that their farming system had created the conservation value of the farms, and that the scheme was peripheral and of little influence. Often the schemes' only contribution was seen as financial. However, there was evidence that the schemes could build on a basic sympathy for conservation to educate and enthuse farmers towards more informed or willing conservation activity. Many of the incentive scheme farmers said the scheme had had a positive effect on their attitude to conservation. In the existing and new ESA areas there was also evidence that the scheme was encouraging a farming confidence in the future, even when farmers said the payments levels were too low or were insecure.

Other observations on impact: There was evidence that the schemes were being well targeted. Many incentive scheme farms and Wildlife Enhancement Scheme farms had farm landscapes of higher conservation value than their neighbours. However, in several incentive schemes there were also individual examples of intensive or agribusiness farms, indicating that participation was quite possible on farms which were not already low-input or traditional. There was, however, no evidence of scheme payments being abused through being reinvested on the farm in an environmentally harmful way.

The Influence of Farm Circumstances

As stated above, three different circumstances were observed to be a dominant influence on the type and extent of environment-friendly activity on farms in the sample, namely the geography of the farms, the farmers' attitudes, and the characteristics of traditional farming. The influence of these circumstances is shown in the three sections below.

Geographical influences

Previous research has suggested that geography and farm land factors would be a basic and fundamental influence on farming activity (for example Tarrant and Cobb, 1991; Potter, 1990) . This was observed to be true in the examination of influences on environment-friendly farming activity. It was evident that much of this activity was associated with poor farmland.

Many of the farms were agriculturally disadvantaged, as would be expected from a sample of Southwest farms: 40% of farms were in Less Favoured Areas, often having steep fields, poor soils and high rainfall. This inhibited commercial cereal production and meant that most of the farms were stocked at extensive rates. Nitrogen applications were sometimes limited by the lack of response in output.

However, these agricultural disadvantages created conservation advantages. Most of the farms had at least moderate-to-high farm landscape conservation values, especially farms in the incentive and management agreement schemes. The farms were often in localities characterised by areas of rough land, woodland and other semi-natural habitat. Many of the farms contained semi-natural habitat, some of which such as moorland was also farmed. On average each farm contained two landscape or conservation designations, with only the small, lowland organic farms largely undesignated.

There was a strong relationship between the quality of the farm land, the conservation value of the farms, the intensity of the farming system, and the type of farm. The poorest farms were almost all low-input beef and sheep farms, and often contained farm landscapes of the highest conservation value. These were often also farms which included certain areas of uniquely high conservation value. The incentive and management agreement schemes had often specifically targeted these areas.

It was also often the case that farms in poor farming areas were in need of the financial support which scheme payments could offer. Many of the farmers in the poorest areas said that their farming system was not viable, despite their seemingly genuine attempts at profit maximisation. Intensification to a level where profits could increase was often not an agriculturally viable option. Although the farmers' interest in conservation might be low, such natural constraints meant that scheme participation was nevertheless logical. For example, scheme payments could help with the continuous process of repairing hedges.

Farmers' attitudes

Farmers' attitudes were also a major influence on the nature of environment-friendly activity, and were seen to dominate most other circumstances.

Common attitudes: Many farmers in the sample had attitudes which were compatible if not fully supportive of environment-friendly farming. 'Intrinsic' aspects of farming were most valued, for instance the independence and the natural world, and almost all farmers showed aesthetic rather than economic preferences when discussing landscapes. Nearly 80% of farmers also thought that environment-friendly farming was good husbandry, whilst over 60% were concerned about the impact of agro-chemicals on the environment or human health. Most farmers were also opposed to speculative borrowing. It was noted that even when it was possible, many farmers were not prepared to intensify their farming practices to ease financial constraint or to accumulate wealth.

Many farmers were also interested or knowledgeable about wildlife conservation. Sixty per cent of farmers had taken conservation advice, half of which was from FWAG. Fifty per cent of farmers said they had never damaged the conservation value of their farms. Rather, many farmers had created new wildlife habitats, with on average two new habitats per farm, including 50% of farmers who had planted woodland. Thirty five per cent of farmers also spent regular tangible sums of time or money on conservation activity. A large number of farmers were also planning future conservation work.

Much of this conservation work was attributed to a family attitude or sympathy for conservation. Such an attitude was associated with almost all types of environment-friendly activity. Thirty per cent of farmers also had holiday and visitor enterprises on the farm, and although few specifically said this was an influence on their conservation work, this was speculated to be the case.

Many farmers showed support for more environmental controls over the farming industry, in particular for quotas on nitrogen applications which were specifically mentioned by 30% of farmers. Conservation incentive schemes such as ESAs or the Countryside Stewardship scheme were also popular.

Fifty per cent of farmers had other off-farm activities, including 30% of farmers engaged in agricultural contracting. This activity sometimes provided a conscious or unconscious source of income to offset against reduced income, environment-friendly, farming activities. Off-farm work was also a source of social influence on some farmers' attitudes, especially when farmers mixed with non-farmers.

Seventy five per cent of farmers also regarded scheme payments as a windfall. This included farmers who said the scheme left them better off, but also farmers who believed that the scheme practices made them worse off. The crucial factor was that many farmers would, in the short-term, have done almost the same practices anyway through necessity or inertia.

Relationships between farmers and scheme administrators were generally very good. This was particularly the case when a closer relationship was established, based on regular, easy and informal contact. Farmers often liked the administrators to have a farming background. They also emphasised the importance of initial impressions, and the personality of the administrator in encouraging uptake and participation. It was very important that farmers' attitudes to the scheme and scheme administration were good, as many farmers stated that the schemes could easily be cheated and were thus heavily dependent on trust in enforcement.

Other common attitudes included a universal belief that farmers were in a difficult position when selling and marketing their produce, in particular losing out to the middle-men in the marketing process. It was also evident that the farmers generally had a positive attitude to public access, with only the most remote or the most tormented farmers indicating any resistance.

Definitions of conservation by farmers: Although farmers in the sample were seen to have a positive attitude to conservation, definitions were an important influence on those attitudes. Farmers often defined conservation as sympathetic countryside management practices, rather than the more sophisticated or subtle needs of wildlife and ecology. Using their definition, 32% of farmers said that the costs of conservation on their farm were held within farm management practices. Over 60% of farmers also said conservation activities on the farm were well-established, whilst 70% said that the conservation initiative on the farm was their own rather than from the scheme.

When discussing the question of 'whole farm' conservation, it was evident that farmers with a reasonable grasp of the definition often had poorer whole farm practices than farmers whose definitional understanding was poor. In general these definitional differences did not create a conflict with conservation and, indeed, often provided a basic attitude that could readily be enhanced by sensitive conservation policy. However, farmers' commonly stated preference for tidy farming did indicate one potential conflict, with farmers often disliking some of the untidy or semi-neglecting practices which at times created high conservation value.

Factors which did not influence attitudes : It was evident that a number of structural factors which were hypothesized to be an influence on farmers' attitudes to environment-friendly farming were not in fact of influence. Attitudes generally dominated over structural factors.

It was apparent that the degree of economic constraint on the farm had no effect on the farmers environment-friendly activities or attitudes. A variety of environment-friendly activities, some of them radical, were practised under comparatively severe economic constraint. Indeed, some of the farmers under the greatest constraint did not acknowledge the constraint at all.

Nor was the stage in the family lifecycle a dominant influence. Farmers with similar family pressures or freedoms were seen to have very different farming activities and attitudes. This included the effect of having an agricultural successor, which was hypothesized to be of influence on farming intensity, on practices and on conservation value; in fact, it was of much less influence than geographical or attitudinal influences.

It was even apparent that attitudes could be a dominant influence over geographical circumstances, with farmers with similar geographical constraints or freedoms responding in quite different ways to those circumstances.

It was at first thought that farmers who practised a creative conservation approach might be the same farmers whose business attitudes had already driven them to expand their farms and damage the conservation interest. This was shown not to be the case. Farmers from a variety of very different business circumstances were found to be equally interested in creative conservation. This included some very unprofitable farms and organic farms, where the farmers used other income to fund creative conservation.

Finally, farmers' responses to other issues and influences were equally determined by their attitude as by structural factors. This included their belief about the impact of other policies and pressures on environment-friendly farming activities, and even farmers' experiences of doing paperwork.

Influences on attitudes: However, some structural factors were noted at times to be an influence on farmers' attitudes.

Farmers' ages were sometimes important. There were particular differences between middle-aged farmers who had farmed through the 1960s and 1970s and often been influenced by this most productivist period of British agriculture, older farmers who had been too old to be strongly influenced by the production drive and were now sometimes also the most resistant to any conservation drive, and younger farmers who were often more influenced by the contemporary problems and circumstances of modern farming. Interestingly, these younger farmers seemed more interested in food marketing issues than conservation issues, especially those who had trained at national agricultural colleges.

There were some differences in the attitudes of 'new' farmers. New farmers were sometimes the most willing and prepared to apply for, and enter, incentive schemes. Several had also pursued interests and beliefs developed outside agriculture and become organic farmers. Interestingly, many of the farmers whose families grew and ate much of their own produce were new farmers, rather than traditional farmers as might be expected.

At times farm size was an influence on attitudes, with some smaller, more constrained farmers often alone in arguing that payment levels were too small.

Finally, it was noted that professional advisors or neighbours rarely provided a significant source of influence. There was no evidence of a negative influence on environment-friendly farming attitudes. Rather, it was noted that farmers who had moved their own practices away from the conventional practices of their neighbours often became openly critical of their neighbours' farming.

Attitudes to the schemes: Some differences were evident in farmers' attitudes to the schemes Some of the farmers who were most interested in environment-friendly activity had approached the schemes of their own volition, whilst many of the farmers initially had been themselves approached by the scheme administrators. Equally, farmers' reasons for entering the schemes varied, with farmers often having entered the voluntary conservation and food marketing schemes because they were interested in the schemes' objectives, whilst most farmers in the incentive and management agreement schemes had entered primarily because of the financial incentives available. These initial motivations were also evident in farmers' attitudes to who should pay for conservation, with voluntary conservation and food marketing scheme farmers much more likely to say that farmers themselves should have at least some financial responsibility.

However, the schemes had often had a legitimizing effect on farmers' attitudes to agri-environment policy. Farmers evidently become more supportive of the methods they were used to, even when they had initially been coerced or resistant to the scheme.

The example of organic farmers: Organic farmers can be used as a good example of how farmers' attitudes dominated over most structural factors in influencing environment-friendly farming activity.

Organic farming was the most radical form of environment-friendly farming in the sample. Soil Association farms had a uniquely high level of most environment-friendly farm practices and management activities. Organic farmers unanimously rejected the idea of farming some areas organically and some areas using chemicals. As well as obviously not using any chemicals in their farm husbandry, organic farms often had very mixed and inter-related farming enterprises. They also undertook positive wildlife conservation: Soil Association farmers commonly believed that unfarmed areas of the farm had a detrimental effect on farm production, but nevertheless tolerated, and even encouraged, such habitats because of their wildlife benefits. They were even very concerned about finding environment-friendly methods for disposing of waste plastics.

However, despite this thorough and radical approach to environment-friendly farming, organic farms were often under high structural constraint. The farms were often initially constrained by being small. Many of them were also of only marginal profitability. Some of the farms had been bought with borrowed money. A number of organic farms also had young families to support. Where the family had another income it was often only small despite being essential. Because of the extensive nature of the farming system, some organic farmers also had to rent extra land.

Nevertheless, almost all organic farmers said that their financial constraints did not constrain their organic activities. However, it was observed that several organic farmers or their spouses had reluctantly had to go out to work because of the financial pressure. It was apparent that organic farmers were often 'survivors' (after Marsden *et al*, 1986), struggling to maintain an income and viability, but nevertheless practising the most low-input and radical environment-friendly farming. This refusal to intensify or abandon any environment-friendly practices was based simply on the organic farmers' profound wish to practise organic methods. This represented a triumph of attitudes over structural constraint.

The persistence and tolerance of organic farmers was even more remarkable given the often poor relationship between the farmers and the Soil Association administrators, and the high number of demands placed on the farmers which were considered difficult or unreasonable. In addition, organic farmers had been the most imaginative and resourceful in their marketing strategies, being active in local and direct marketing and pursuing premium prices that almost all of them believed would not exist in the future.

Traditional farming

Characteristics of traditional farming: A number of farms in the incentive and management agreement schemes could be described as 'traditional' farms. Traditional farming was another radical environment-friendly farming system, containing many of the most valuable aspects of such a system. However, traditional farming was not necessarily influenced by geographical circumstances and rarely, if ever, influenced by the farmers' attitudes to environment-friendly farming. Instead, it had its own unique circumstances and self-contained influences. Traditional farms often urgently needed financial support; such support was provided by a number of the schemes, targeted at the environment-friendly features of the traditional system.

There were a number of environment-friendly characteristics of traditional farming. Many traditional farms had low intensity, simple stock or mixed stock farming systems. They were often observed on poor farm land, but this was not a dominant influence. Many traditional farms were almost fully organic, often using no sprays and only very small amounts of fertilizer. This was the case even when the farms were mixed and growing cereals for home feed. Traditional mixed stock farms often had good manure for use as fertilizer. Interestingly the mixed system on traditional farms had not been inhibited by poor or wet farming conditions, unlike modern or commercial mixed farming.

Like organic farms, these traditional, simple stock and mixed stock farms had the highest levels of environment-friendly farm management practices and soil and field husbandry practices. They often also farmed semi-natural habitats, protecting them through traditional, low-intensity grazing and swaling (burning) of moorland fields. The farmers had often never damaged the conservation interest of the farms, and had some of the highest conservation value farm landscapes in the sample. Overall conservation value was particularly high when the farm also contained certain areas of uniquely high value. However, because of geographical influences not all traditional farms will contain such areas.

A long history of environment-friendly practices meant that traditional farms had the smallest fields in the sample, yet the many hedges were often in the best condition. The farmers often routinely managed hedges with traditional practices such as cutting and laying. Many traditional farms reported having quiet spells for doing such traditional management. Where hedges were cut by machine, the farmers often only used a labour-intensive trimmer, preferring to pick up the cuttings rather than smash the hedge with a flail.

Like organic farmers, traditional farmers nearly all went out onto their farms every day on foot to inspect stock and manage the farm.

The attitudes of traditional farmers: The attitudes of traditional farmers were often compatible with environment-friendly farming. Many thought that their areas of semi-natural habitat such as hedges and moorland were of benefit to livestock, providing shelter but also medicinal and nutritious herbs and grasses. Several traditional farmers used such observations to argue that the traditional farming system was both environment-friendly and good husbandry. Some traditional farmers also identified their practices specifically with conservation, although for others the subject of conservation was too foreign to mention. In areas of wider countryside, traditional farmers were often quite critical of neighbouring farmers who had intensified their farming and damaged the conservation interest of their own farms.

However, other traditional attitudes were less compatible with environment-friendly farming. Traditional farmers' interest in wildlife conservation was often low, with very few ever having done any creative conservation work. Their poor understanding of conservation definitions was indicated well when the majority of traditional farmers said they only practised conservation in the areas of the farm designated by the scheme, whilst in reality traditional farms often had the best whole farm approach in the sample.

Unlike organic farmers, traditional farmers were not always interested in farming self sufficiency. Although they often consumed a lot of home grown feed and used their own manure, like many farmers, traditional farmers also bought in extra feed and fertilizer. Traditional farmers also often showed little interest in fuel conservation, typically because they were very low users. Nor were they likely to be at all interested in alternative agricultural technology, or even environment-friendly methods of disposing of waste plastics. Very sadly a cavalier attitude to dangerous substances had left several traditional farmers badly affected by organophosphates in sheep dip.

Traditional farmers often tended to have the most short-term farm planning, especially on simple stock farms uncertain about changes to the livestock support system. However, it was noted that the ESA schemes had injected a more long-term business confidence into some traditionally-farmed areas.

The fact that traditional farmers had very environment-friendly systems alongside poor attitudes to conservation illustrated Morris's (1993) observation that farmers actions ultimately count more than their attitudes.

The constraints of traditional farming: Many traditional farms were under comparatively severe financial constraint. This was particularly the case when the farms were small and had large families to support. In several cases extended families living on the farm appeared to be indicative of a traditional farm, although the pressure of having to support or even find work for several dependents placed a severe and often excessive strain on the farm. In such circumstances, and with the farmers unwilling and often unable to intensify, extra income and work from conservation incentive schemes was obviously very welcome.

Nor did the issue of succession on traditional farms alter the farming system. Often traditional farming families would want children to succeed, although the difficulties and pressures did not always make this an attractive option for the children. However, the farming system was unlikely to be altered much as a result of succession, especially if older family members retained an influence.

Traditional farms often made only small profits, despite the farmers' efforts to profit maximise within the traditional system. The squeeze on profitability, especially on poor farm land, meant that traditional farmers were sometimes the only farmers not making any farming investments.

As indicated above, incentive scheme payments were often very welcome for these farms under economic constraint. Indeed the most constrained farms often argued that they needed larger payments. On traditional farms with labour shortages the payments also helped pay for contractors to do conservation jobs. Hedging and scrub clearing were particularly difficult for farms with no workforce. Payments were often a double benefit to the farm, as the hedging and fencing work often also helped farm production. Interestingly the farmers were not always vocal in their appreciation. However, having maintained farm landscapes of high conservation value in the years when other farmers were cashing in on improvement grants and increased price support, the fact that these farms now received a windfall to help continue with their traditional practices seemed entirely justified in terms of conservation and in terms of equity.

In spite of the obvious benefit of conservation incentive payments, many traditional farmers said they would prefer financial assistance to come through price support.

Scheme participation of traditional farms: Traditional farmers were often only likely to join schemes if they were directly approached and invited to join. Often face-to-face contact with the scheme administrator was most effective at encouraging participation. With no major changes to farm practice required, as was likely with a traditional system, the farmers would be eventually be likely to sign up. However, their caution was indicated by the fact that several traditional ELMS and Wildlife Enhancement Scheme farmers had taken legal or financial advice in the nearby town before agreeing to join the schemes. The fact that Wildlife Enhancement Scheme farms had been subject to SSSI designation provided an extra, and often final, justification for joining the scheme.

In some traditionally-farmed areas such as the ESAs and National Parks, most neighbouring farmers were in the scheme creating an element of peer pressure on participation. The ESAs were also seen to have enhanced the attitudes of some traditional farmers to conservation.

Other farmers' attitudes to traditional farming: It was apparent that many other farmers had a sympathy and often nostalgic enthusiasm for traditional farming. Several non-traditional farmers said their favourite landscape was a traditionally-farmed landscape. Other farmers reported, and regretted, the decline of traditional farming in their locality.

Implications of the Research Findings

There were a number of academic and policy implications in the research findings which are summarised in figure 11.2.

Figure 11.2 : Two key findings and ten detailed findings

First key finding: *Environmentally friendly farmers are not distinguished by their socio-economic status and business characteristics but by behavioural or attitudinal traits rooted in their personal histories and circumstances: most are either practically committed to traditional farming or have strong pro-conservation attitudes. This finding undermines a tradition of structural analysis in this field.*

Second key finding: *Most conservation schemes have only a marginal impact on farming practices and environmental outcomes compared with what the participants would have been doing in any case.*

Ten detailed findings

1) There was no relationship between farmers' attitudes to, or participation in, environment-friendly activities and the degree of economic constraint on the farm.

2) There were very few examples of 'wealthy', 'accumulator' or 'expansionist' farmers engaged specifically in grant-based or creative conservation activity. Such farms appeared more likely to be associated with the single minded pursuit of food marketing premiums.

3) There was no apparent relationship between elderly farmers without successors and high farm landscape conservation value.

4) There was no apparent relationship between the presence of an agricultural successor and the type of environment-friendly activity.

5) 'Occupancy events', in particular the purchase of a new farm, appeared more likely to lead directly to new conservation work rather than adverse landscape change.

6) Many 'survivors' and part-time farms were organic farms, which retained high levels of environment-friendly activity despite their marginal profitability.

7) Most small farms were less intensive in terms of agro-chemical use than were larger farms.

8) In high value landscapes there was some evidence that larger farms had higher conservation value farm landscapes because of their size.

9) Mixed tenure farms were often extensive, with the extensive system creating a greater need for more farmland.

10) Sixty per cent of farmers thought that environment-friendly farming was also good husbandry.

The contribution to established research observations

A large number of questions, hypotheses and ideas had been borrowed or adapted from previous research projects to be employed in the research. It was apparent from the findings presented above that, beyond some areas of consistency, there were many important differences between the observations in the sample and the observations of the earlier research projects. Whilst some aspects of these differences can be accounted for through differences in the nature of the samples, in total they illustrate a more profound conclusion about farm and farmer behaviour.

Certain findings from the Southwest sample were broadly consistent with observations contained in previous work. Examples included the fact that most farmers in the sample shared 'intrinsic' farming values (after Gasson, 1973); that most of the environment-friendly farming activity and many of the farms of highest conservation value were associated with poorer quality farm land or areas (after Copper *et al*, 1989; Tarrant and Cobb, 1991); and that selectivity was more commonly associated with traditional rather than expansionist farmers (after Lobley, 1989; Whitby, 1994). Such observations offered some evidence that, despite the particular characteristics of the sample described below, it could still be usefully compared to the many samples of farms drawn distinctly elsewhere.

However, other observations from the Southwest sample differed from those that had inspired the initial investigation, drawing varying degrees of doubt about the applicability or continued validity of the earlier findings. Examples of slight differences included the observations that occupancy events, especially new farm purchase, seemed more likely to stimulate conservation than landscape damage (contrasting with Marsden and Munton, 1991); that whilst very few scheme participants had high economic constraint, few were highly enabled either (contrasting with Potter and Gasson, 1988); and that whilst farmers' definitions of 'conservation' were often different from the more sophisticated definitions employed by conservationists, there was no real conflict inherent in the differences (contrasting with Carr and Tait, 1991).

Other findings showed more marked and significant differences. These included the observations that high economic constraint, or 'survivor' circumstances, did not appear to inhibit environment-friendly farming or scheme participation (contrasting with Marsden *et al*, 1986; Munton *et al*, 1989); that the presence or otherwise of a farming successor was not a major influence on farming activity or conservation value (contrasting with Potter and Lobley, 1992; Ward and Lowe, 1994); and that there were few examples of 'programmer' or expansionist farmers engaged in creative conservation work having already damaged the conservation interest of their farm (contrasting with Westmacott and Worthington, 1984; Potter, 1986; Clark and O'Riordan, 1989; Munton and Marsden, 1991).

It seems likely that aspects of these differences stemmed from the fact that the sample was different in its construction and its character from many of those on which previous research observations had been based. Firstly, the sample was not drawn as a random and stratified sample of ordinary farms, but was constructed purposively to examine environment-friendly farms in schemes; despite the wide range of circumstances ultimately contained in the sample, and compelling evidence of the sample's representativeness in terms of such farms, this association with environment-friendly practices or schemes clearly gives the sample a colour and a bias in its activities and dispositions. This may have particularly influenced differences in the responses of farms to economic constraint and family pressures.

Secondly, the sample was drawn entirely from the southwest of England, whereas most of the literature is based on research conducted in central, southern and eastern England. Geographical differences between the Southwest and much of lowland England must account for some differences in farming possibilities, practices and even attitudes, in particular placing natural limits on the potential size, intensity and productivity of average farm land or farm businesses. Nevertheless, in its profile of land quality, farm type, farm size structure, farmers' ages etc. the sample was very typical of the agricultural profile of the Southwest as a whole, and it can be speculated that many of the farmers in the sample were similar, even in their attitudes, to many Southwest farmers on poorer land or with traditional or semi-traditional farming systems; the findings could be said to reveal a regional bias, suggesting that many Southwest farms would, or do, farm in equally environment-friendly ways under similarly constrained circumstances.

Thirdly, a significant amount of time has passed since many of the research projects referred to, during which the direction of agricultural policy and the nature of farming culture and values has shifted away from production and towards a greater awareness and consideration of environmental needs and objectives. Such changes will have had a particular relevance to differences in the studies of farmers' attitudes to or definitions of agri-environment issues. The closer comparisons with more recent research (for example, Whitby, 1994) suggests that such considerations might be important.

However, beyond such considerations, the many differences, when *compounded*, also point to and describe a situation of altogether more profound significance for attempts and approaches at understanding farm and farmer behaviour. The research findings often suggested that amongst farms in the sample the nature and style of environment-friendly farming systems had more complex origins than those anticipated by the review of previous research work; in particular, numerous examples existed of farmers practising environment-friendly farming in circumstances where previous research would have predicted they would not. The whole issue of environment-friendly farming was seen persuasively and consistently to manifest one crucial claim: that socio-economic and even geographical indicators could not alone determine or explain farm and farmer behaviour in a consistent and predictable way. Throughout a uniquely wide-ranging investigation, similar structural constraints or stimuli were seen to produce very different behavioural responses, responses which resulted time and again from individual farmer's attitudes and intentions. The final conclusion drawn was that no simple rules or statistical tests could be said to exist which could accurately anticipate how farmers respond to socio-economic pressures or policy mechanisms, as it was *only* at the level of *individual* attitudes and values that behaviour could be fully comprehended. If our knowledge of the farming world is to be further developed and applied, this is one vital field to which future research approaches and methods should be directed.

Implications for future research.

Two questions could be posed by a follow up study.

Firstly, to examine whether the circumstantial influences remained dominant elsewhere, it would be valuable to apply some of the questions to a study of a different set of farmers. This set could include a sample of scheme participants from a contrasting area of Britain, or indeed another country. It would also be interesting to examine a comparable sample of non-scheme farmers in the Southwest (or a similar region), to test whether the circumstances of the farms were regionally-based or unique to the fact that the farms were participants in agri-environment schemes.

Secondly, the importance of traditional farming has been emphasised. However, more information is needed about traditional farmers.

a) Given that traditional farmers have not responded to structural influences such as economic or family constraint, what are the attitudinal, sociological and psychological influences which have influenced their decision making, their behaviour and their continued status as traditional farmers?

b) Identifying traditionally-farmed areas such as ESAs is straightforward. However, there was clearly evidence that in the Southwest there are many traditional farmers dispersed in the wider countryside. Their identity was often concealed by the fact that the farms do not contain any areas of uniquely high value semi-natural habitat. More information is therefore needed about the characteristics and features by which traditional farmers can be identified, and how they can be most effectively recruited into agri-environment schemes.

Policy recommendations

Based on the personal observations made in undertaking the research, the authors suggest the following policy changes

Give more support for traditional farming. Britain is fortunate that many farmers have resisted the pressures to intensify their farming, and still manage farms and farming systems of high environmental value. The importance of supporting such traditional farming is recognised by the ESA scheme and concept.

However, many traditional farms outside existing ESAs remain unsupported and their systems still under threat. More ESAs should be designated where a high proportion of traditional farmers remain in an area. Otherwise efforts must be concentrated into identifying and supporting the traditional farming system of farmers in the wider countryside.

Financially, it will be necessary to ensure that the only farmers receiving windfall payments are those traditional farmers who have never damaged the conservation value of their whole farms nor, in effect, contributed to surpluses. Other farmers must be obliged to change their wider farming practices in order to receive incentive monies to protect specific areas or features. Other than on the most traditional farms, financial assistance for creative conservation work or improvements to farm infrastructure should be on a shared cost basis.

The latent fertility, smaller sizes and strong hedges of traditional farms make them ideally suitable for conversion to organic farms. Traditional farms being sold could be saved from improvement by acquiring them for a national estate of organic farms whose low-input, benign systems would help protect the features of conservation value. The farms could be let to new entrants, as the landlord/tenant system offers sufficient mechanisms and flexibility for supporting such arrangements.

Concentrate more efforts into educating farmers. There is evidence that many farmers have a basic sympathy for conservation, and some a keen interest in creative conservation. Thus in the short-term more conservation and general environment-friendly farm management could be achieved simply with strong policy statements and commands, for example using farming colleges, the agricultural media and agricultural advisors. The productivist drive demonstrates clearly that many farmers can be influenced.

MAFF's Codes of Good Agricultural Practice (eg. MAFF, 1991) represent a good model for the exhortation approach. However, a code is now required to address unequivocally conservation practices and farm management activities. After a reasonably short period of education and exhortation more planning or regulatory controls can be placed on agricultural practices and landscape features. Such a move will come as no surprise to the farmers who have observed the new policy messages.

Push European agriculture towards organic farming. Ultimately agriculture will not be environmentally sustainable until it returns to the essentially organic practices from which all conventional practices have been derived. Guiding such a change can be the only logical long-term objective for agricultural policy.

At the European level the first stage of such a change would be to limit nitrogen applications on individual farms by using nitrogen quotas. This will inevitably promote a return to non-chemical based husbandry practices. This process can be assisted by high taxes on sprays and independently funded and disseminated research into organic methods. Nitrogen quotas can be gradually increased as farmers improve their organic skills and food markets stabilize to the changing food supply. This is clearly a radical proposal: for example it would be necessary to contravene the GATT agreement by restricting imports into Europe from countries whose agriculture used more nitrogen than the European limit. However, the grave implications of contemporary agri-environment problems require a response of this nature.

A radical policy response must inevitably include a complete rejection of the most harmful practices which have developed in conventional agriculture. Many of the farms visited in this research had shown such a rejection to be entirely practical.

References

Baldock, D, Cox, G, Lowe, P and Winter, M (1990), Environmentally Sensitive Areas: incrementalism or reform?, *Journal of Rural Studies,* 6 ,143-162.

Carr, S and Tait, J (1991) Farmers' attitudes to conservation, *Built Environment,*16, 218-231.

Clark, A. and O'Riordan, T (1989) *ESRC project on conservation investment and advice on farms,* University of East Anglia.

Copper, A., Murray, R and Warnock, S (1989) Agriculture and the environment in the Mourne AONB, *Applied Geography,* 9, 35-56.

Gasson, R (1973) Goals and values of farmers, *Journal of Agricultural Economics ,* 24, 521-542.

Hill, B and Gasson, R (1985) Farm tenure and farming practice, *Journal of Agricultural Economics,* 36, 187-9.

Lobley, M (1989) A role for ESAs?, *Ecos,* 10(2), 27-29.

Lowe, P, Cox, G, Goodman, D, Munton, R and Winter, M (1990) Technological change, farm management and pollution regulation: the example of Britain, in Lowe, P, Marsden, T and Whatmore, S (Eds), *Technological change and rural environment,* David Fulton, London.

MAFF (1991) *Code of good agricultural practice for the protection of water,* MAFF, London.

Marden, T, Whatmore, S, Munton, R and Little, J (1986) The restructuring process and economic centrality in capitalist agriculture, *Journal of Rural Studies,* 2, 271-280.

Marsden, T and Munton, R (1991) The farmed landscape and the occupancy change process, *Environment and Planning A,* 23, 663-676.

Morris, C (1993) *Recruiting farmers into conservation: an analysis of farmer participation in agri-environmental schemes in lowland England,* unpublished Ph.D. Thesis, Wye College, University of London.

Munton, R, Whatmore, S and Marsden, T (1989) Part-time farming and its implications for the *rural* landscape: a preliminary analysis, *Environment and Planning* A , 21, 523-536.

Munton, R and Marsden, T (1991) Occupancy change and the farmed landscape, *Environment and Planning A ,* 23, 499-510.

Potter, C (1986) Processes of countryside change in lowland England, *Journal of Rural Studies,* 2, 187-195.

Potter, C and Gasson, R (1988) Farm participation in voluntary land diversion schemes, *Journal of Rural Studies,* 4, 365-375.

Potter, C (1990) Conservation under a European farm survival policy, *Journal of Rural Studies,* 6,1-7.

Potter, C and Lobley, M (1992a) *Small farming and the environment,* RSPB, The Lodge, Sandy.

Potter, C and Lobley, M (1992b) The conservation status and potential of elderly farmers: results from a survey of England and Wales, *Journal of Rural Studies,* 8, 133-143.

Tarrant, J and Cobb, R (1991) The Convergence of Agricultural and Environmental Policies: The case of Extensification in Eastern England, In Bowler, I, Bryant, C and Nellis, M (Eds), *Contemporary Rural Systems in Transition I, CAB international,* Wallingford, 153-65.

Ward, N and Lowe, P (1994) Shifting value in agriculture: the farm family and pollution regulation, *Journal of Rural Studies,* 10, 173-184.

Westmacott, R and Worthington,T (1984), *Agricultural landscapes: a second look,* Countryside Commission CCP 168, Cheltenham.

Whitby, M (1994) What future for ESAs? In Whitby, M (Ed) *Incentives for countryside_ management: the case of Environmentally Sensitive Areas,* CAB International, Wallingford, 253-72.

CHAPTER 12

Understanding Farmers' Perceptions of Changing Agriculture: Some Implications for Agri-environmental Schemes*
Helen McHenry

Agriculture is undergoing a process of change which must be accommodated by farmers. Previously the productive orientation of agriculture fitted well with the beliefs and interpretations of farming, but changes now occurring, particularly the increased importance of direct support and the emphasis on conservation are proving to be difficult for some farmers to accommodate. To understand the negotiation of this process of change, it is important to examine how farmers interpret the current situation. In this study the aim was an in-depth understanding of the way in which farmers perceived conservation issues.

The focus of the research was, therefore, to understand how farmers perceive agri-environmental policy and to understand why they behave as they do towards the environment. There are a number of general problems which occur when attempting to explain people's behaviour towards the environment. Brennan (1992) suggested that one of these was the difficulty that occurs in any examination of human behaviour: people know what is good and desire it, but do not necessarily behave in ways consistent with achieving it. This is pertinent to general questions of conservation, but in practice other issues arise when considering farmers. For example, some of them may not know what is good for conservation, while others may have no desire to practise it. A further consideration was also highlighted by O'Riordan (1973; 1976) and Tuan (1968; 1970) in their works on the relationship between behaviour towards the environment, and attitudes and beliefs about the environment. In separate studies they found many inconsistencies between what people say and what they actually do in regard to nature and the physical environment.

Nature, the environment and conservation are all social constructions, to which people attach different meanings, therefore it is important to try to establish these meanings before any effort can be made to relate them to

* This research was funded by the Scottish Office Agriculture and Fisheries Department (SOAFD) through the Macaulay Land Use Research Institute.

behaviour towards the environment. The question of why farmers either undertake conservation or reject environmentally beneficial practices is complex. In this study it was felt to be important to avoid the problems of 'shallow analysis' (Brennan, 1992) where issues are oversimplified so that an answer or solution can be found. As Cary *et al* (1993, p49) pointed out:

"Simplistic assessments of what are in fact complex and interrelated belief systems often produce naive and confounded ideas that changing a single belief or an attitude 'to the environment', will result in more appropriate environmental behaviour".

By using an in depth, qualitative approach, it was hoped to avoid this problem.

Background to the Study

Attitudinal studies of farmers are common, but attitudes do not always correspond to behaviour (O'Riordan, 1973; Tuan, 1968; 1970). Additionally, whatever the farmer's attitudes, it must be remembered that the farm enterprise does not exist in a social vacuum (Lowe *et al*, 1992), but is caught in a complex 'web of relations' (Cox *et al*, 1986). Agri-environmental schemes cannot be viewed separately from other changes in agricultural policies. Any decision a farmer makes about allocating land to various uses, including agri-environmental schemes, is made with reference to support policy and payments (Froud, 1994) and relates to beliefs about future policies and situations. The economic situation of the farm is also important (Munton *et al*, 1990), it may be an enabling or constraining factor in the farmer's behaviour, while the social and cultural context of the farmer can also affect involvement in conservation and agri-environmental schemes. For example, in the Scottish Highlands, Mather (1993) found that the controversy between environment and development, and views of conservationists as outsiders, were critical in the reception of conservation policies.

It is apparent that many factors influence the farmer's decisions about environmental schemes, so it is important to try to understand the meanings of the various factors for farmers and to examine how individuals conceptualise or organise their world, rather than trying to measure what farmers' attitudes actually are (O'Riordan, 1973). Therefore, the focus of research is on trying to understand how farmers interpret their world and how this might affect what they do as farmers. Studying ideas about environment and conservation in isolation from general farming beliefs is not necessarily helpful. It is more important to examine the factors which combine together to give rise to behaviour relevant to the environment. As Ward *et al* (1990) commented, alterations in the landscape are not distinctive phenomena from the point of view of farmers, they are the result of, and integrated, into farm management strategies and practices "which are usually still geared to productivist notions of farm 'improvement'" (Ward *et al*, 1990, p299). It is also necessary to understand how farmers see conservation. Green (1986), among others, suggested that many farmers see themselves as good conservationists who care for their land. However, what these farmers view as conservation may not be the same as conservationists' interpretations (Zinn and Blodgett, 1989). Thus rather than assuming that everyone understands conservation in the same way, it is necessary to try to find out what it is that farmers understand by the concept (Ramsay, 1993).

In this study an 'actor oriented' approach (Long, 1989) was used. The perspective taken was essentially that, to understand why farmers do conservation or enter agri-environmental schemes, it was necessary to look at the issues from their point of view (for more detail on the theoretical perspective used, see McHenry, 1994). The farmer was seen as a knowing and active subject "who problematises situations, processes information and strategises when dealing with others" (Long, 1989).

In practice, therefore, the *meanings* that an individual applied to the world were important in this study, while at the same time it is argued that external factors, like policies, were taken into account. The way the farmer interpreted these factors determined their influence. For example, it is the farmer's interpretation of the meaning of price changes, new policy incentives and changing markets which dictate how he or she responds or acts. Of course, interpretations of these factors were also affected by the farmer's past, education, stage in the family life cycle as well as farm characteristics like type or tenure. However, the effect of these factors was again influenced by the farmer's view of the world. When trying to improve our understanding of farmers, it is important to be cautious about generalising. There is no single set of goals which all farmers entering a particular scheme want to achieve. The decision to enter a scheme is dependent on a very individual mix of factors which is different on each farm (Hill *et al*, 1992). To understand the changes caused by farmers we need to understand the current opportunities facing them and how they perceive their long term interest (Agriculture EDC, 1987). Ideally, therefore, research into farmers' involvement in conservation should focus on how the individual understands and interprets the issues including the macro forces which influence behaviour, while at the same time recognising the variation among farmers.

Characteristics of the area and the Southern Uplands ESA

The study was carried out in the Southern Uplands of Scotland where an Environmentally Sensitive Area Scheme was designated in 1993. The Southern Uplands are a range of mountains and hills stretching from the West to the East coast of Southern Scotland, through three regions (fig.12.1). In the context of the UK it is sparsely populated, especially in the central section. Farms are located in the numerous valleys, with their land ranging from the 'in bye' at low levels to the high hills. Tenant farms are common and the area has a number of large estates with both farming and sporting interests. There are great contrasts between the farms, in terms of business size, area and income, but in comparison with most other UK farming they are extensive low input operations. Black face sheep dominate and there is a strong tradition of pedigree breeding. Afforestation provides one of the few alternatives to hill livestock farming, and the west of the area in particular is the site of many large sitka spruce plantations.

The Southern Uplands ESA was introduced with the preservation and expansion of heather as its primary objective. Somewhat controversially, SOAFD attributed some of the loss of heather moorland to overgrazing in

Figure 12.1 The Study Area: Southern Scotland

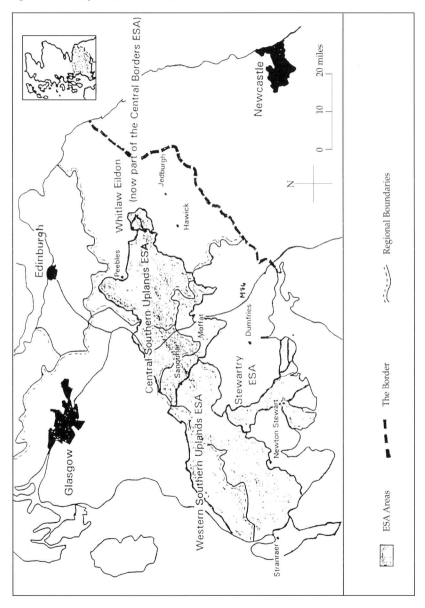

the area; many of the farmers had different views. This ESA, unlike the early Scottish ESAs, includes a number of management incentives where the farmer may either produce a grazing plan for better management of the heather at existing stock levels or reduce absolute numbers. As an incentive for farmers to join, there are generous dyking grants, but only for hill dykes (stone walls). A farmer joining must prepare a conservation plan and also agree to comply with certain basic restrictions on land drainage, reseeding and herbicide applications.

Data sources

As the aim of the study was to understand the farmer's view, a qualitative approach was appropriate. The main sources of data in this study were farmer interviews. These were semi-structured; the interview was in the form of a conversation, but there was an interview guideline of topics to be covered. The farmer could bring up what he or she thought was relevant or particularly wanted to talk about, but similar issues were covered with all farmers interviewed. The interviews were tape recorded unless the farmer objected. Six of the forty interviews were not taped. In these cases notes were taken and dictated later.

Most of the interviews were conducted in the area of the Southern Uplands ESA which was designated in May 1993. The interviews in this area were done in the Spring of 1993 (before the designation of the scheme), and in the Summer (after the designation) when farmers were considering whether to get involved. The Southern Uplands ESA adjoins the Whitlaw Eildon ESA, where a number of interviews were undertaken. This ESA was of interest as it had a considerably poorer uptake than the other first round Scottish ESAs

Various people responsible for the implementation of the ESA scheme were also interviewed (Agriculture department officials, Scottish Natural Heritage (SNH) staff, agricultural and Farm and Wildlife Advisory Group (FWAG) officials). The public meetings for the launch of the Southern Uplands ESA were observed both to record farmers' reactions and to note how the schemes were being promoted. In addition the written responses to the consultative documents for the ESA were examined.

Findings and their Implications

This study aimed to uncover what farmers saw as the issues, and so in the interviews the farmers spoke freely on the topics that were of interest to them. This chapter thus gives a picture of the farmers' view and allows us to understand better how the targets of agri-environmental policy perceive the issue. The following section provides an overview of the farmers' perspectives. As has been discussed above, reaction to, and participation in, agri-environmental schemes is the result of a combination of different factors. These may be grouped loosely into four main areas: the way the farmer views the current situation; what is seen as the role of the farmer; perceptions of conservation; and reactions to the particular ESA scheme. These all affect the farmers' ideas about agri-environmental policy and ESAs in particular. Quotations from interviews are used here for illustration purposes. All names are pseudonyms and have no connection with any farmer interviewed.

The current situation

The farmers' interpretations of their situation were an important influence on their views of agri-environmental schemes. It was evident that the most important questions for farmers related to the CAP and the changes in support as well as the market situation. These issues dominated many of the interviews and were, for the farmers studied, of vital importance. By contrast the questions of conservation and agri-environmental policy were for many of little significance and, for some, appeared to be irrelevant. Agri-environmental policy is usually seen by academics and policy makers as very significant and tends to be considered an inevitable element of future policy. This is in contrast to many of the farmers' interpretations and it is important that this difference is recognised; it is not assumed that farmers will perceive agricultural policy in the same way as other groups.

The main concerns of farmers related to the uncertainty in agricultural policy, whether the CAP reform would continue or change, and the practical implications of livestock quotas. This, combined with the uncertainty normally prevalent in farming (concerning the weather and the markets), meant many farmers interviewed were finding their situation very stressful.

"It's a total uncertainty that costs real money, bearing in mind from you produce an animal until it's a piece of steak, or still, it's conceived as steak that is three years so you know a farmer is making a policy for three years ahead." (Mr Angus B108)

However, as Lemon and Park (1993) found, there was a general acceptance of the variability of natural systems as inherent to the practice of farming. This tolerance was not extended to the unpredictability of the policy framework. Uncertainty is accentuated by the need to respond to policy instruments which do not take account of the long natural cycles on which practical farming decisions are based. Previously support policies encouraged a sense of security and protection and modified the risks facing farmers. Combined with the uncertainty there was a feeling that farmers did not have control over their situation and that, instead, they were dependent on the government. This feeling of dependency was enhanced by the shift to more direct payments in the MacSharry reforms. In order to receive these payments, farmers were having to fill in more forms, which added to the feeling that farmers were becoming more controlled by the government.

"My feeling at the moment is a feeling of acute frustration in farming I'm sitting at my desk day after day after day filling up forms and I've got five men on the farm and I'm making more money sitting at my desk than they are looking after the stock outside, the whole thing is ridiculous ... It's acute frustration I can't get on with my interest of farming." (Mr Cooper D310)

Farmers disliked the paperwork associated with the CAP but felt they had no choice but to participate in the support system. This was another symptom of their lack of control over their situation. Therefore when the farmers were asked about their future many looked for situations where farmers would regain some control, either through the removal of subsidy or the need for more food production.

The farmers' role in society

These views of the situation have implications for the role of the farmer. As agriculture changes, farmers must come to terms with this and adjust or negotiate their view of themselves to account of it. This seemed to be proving difficult, as attributes which had previously been important, like self sufficiency, independence and food production, were felt to be becoming less so. At the same time, even in what was a remote area, farmers were aware that they were becoming less significant in the rural community. One element of the farmers' role comes from the way it is believed others see them (McHenry, 1994), and farmers were very conscious of their public image. They felt attacked by the media, and that their role was being undermined because of their success in increasing food production.

"Farmers were good guys, they were working very hard and they were doing a very worth while job and they supplying commodity you know that people had to have it a reasonable price and it was only when we had a sort of surplus situation with a lot of commodities ... stories about farmers being paid an arm and a leg to dump stuff and keep stuff in intervention stores eh ... it's quite to be disillusioned just now as a producer of food." (Mr Aldridge B102)

One of the most important issues to emerge in this research was the way that the farmers interviewed remained very strongly attached to their role as food producers.

"I mean the life of a real farmer if you look at it, is producing food as cheaply utilising the land to it's best of it's abilities. Well to some farmers that is, just growing animals growing crops, nothing else no frills." (Mr Angus B108)

"There's bound to be a future for agriculture I mean there must be a, I mean when all said and done folks got to eat" (Mr Cheyne, D308)

It was felt by some farmers that the existence of food surpluses and food security enabled the public to become concerned about 'luxury' issues such as the environment. Although some farmers were prepared to become involved in conservation, they often maintained that, in the future, farmers would again be required to increase their food production, and so looking after the environment would become less significant. Farmers' pride in the success of the agricultural sector was affected by criticisms of agriculture especially about the impact of modern farming methods and habitat destruction. Farmers interviewed were often defensive about this but at the same time maintained that, as they had created the countryside, they were the best people to be responsible for it.

"there's no better keepers of the land as farmers, and especially owner occupiers or farmers that are proud of their work. What better way to keep the land? This is what I can't understand, is that farmers have always kept it.. and especially British farmers, I think they have kept it as well as anybody could be expected to, and if somebody has pride in their work pride in their farm.. what more do you want? they'll keep the farm no matter what, in good repair ..." (Mr Barret B207)

Awareness of their public image combined with the recognition of dependence on the taxpayer seemed to be making some farmers feel they would have to make an effort to provide what the public wanted. This was happening slowly and for many there was difficulty in adjusting. However, in the future if more and more support relates to agri-environmental measures most will, perhaps, feel they have little choice but to participate. Nevertheless efforts are likely to be made by both farming organisations and individuals to shape the new policy in a way which is compatible with their new beliefs.

At the same time, farmers thought that they were losing status: that the esteem in which they were held, and their access to rights and privileges as an occupational group, was in decline. But, despite this feeling of a loss of control and a declining role in society, farmers still have considerable power. Many policies, especially agri-environmental schemes, seek to entice farmers to behave in a desired manner rather than to coerce them. The ESA has allowed farmers to negotiate the policy, and to choose many of the aspects which suited them.

Views of conservation

The majority of farmers saw conservation as very instrumental. It was either associated with aspects of farming like dyking or shelter belts, or conservation was expected to be productive in some other way, for example enhancing tourism, or providing sporting benefits. There was very little consideration of the idea of 'existence' or an intrinsic value in the environment; it was expected to be productive. For this reason perhaps, some farmers welcomed electricity pylons and the idea of windmills on their land. These fitted in with their concept of a productive countryside. The farmers' views of nature, which was sometimes seen as something to be controlled, exploited, or appeased were related to this. Interestingly, these views of nature related mainly to situations where nature and farming were in competition. Where there was no conflict between farming and elements of nature, such as in relation to wildlife (excluding 'vermin'), farmers seemed more likely to consider an 'existence' value, particularly for charismatic species. At the same time, however, what had previously been considered good farming could be adapted to be seen as an element of conservation. For example, Mr Bain considered that maintaining walls and gates, and improving land constituted looking after the environment. He therefore associated them with conservation, although they also fitted with what he meant by 'good farming'. This is an example of what Cary (1993) called 'symbolic' conservation.

"I like every gate to be swinging I like every dyke to be built, we tiled drained and re-seeded a lot of ground on my original farm and fenced it off. We planted a lot of trees and eh in many many ways tried to improve the environment." (Mr Bain B201)

It has been suggested that there is a fundamental conflict between food production and conservation (Buckwell, 1989; Green, 1986). This, therefore, has implications for the relationship between farmers and conservationists. In many ways their interpretations of conservation are incompatible, and although this is not always apparent or an obvious factor in their differences, it certainly plays a significant role.

"I mean what do conservationists think they are achieving by letting it grow wild like that, like this up here [points] I mean that's basically it, what do they think they are achieving, because would they want to go and walk through it? no, you know, would they like to look at it?" (Mrs Dawson D502)

The question then remains whether in the future the two groups will gain more understanding of each other. Conservationists seem at present to have public opinion on their side (against farmers) in relation to conservation of the countryside. But farmers remain a powerful interest group which receives considerable financial support while agri-environmental policy remains voluntary.

Environmentally Sensitive Area Schemes

Conservation, however, was often accepted where it was felt to be the same as, or compatible with, agriculture. This was clear in the farmers' responses to the ESA which was designed to take advantage of this. Even farmers who strongly opposed the idea of agri-environmental policy, and doing conservation on their farm, were tempted to join. They were interested in having their dykes rebuilt at little cost, and being paid to continue as before, while at the same time accepting some minor restrictions on their behaviour. It seemed that while the policy remains very much in line with the farmers present farming activities, many join despite other reservations. The ESA scheme has accommodated this, containing many agricultural benefits. These were emphasised in the promotion of the schemes and attracted farmers to an 'environmental' scheme which they might otherwise have found incompatible with their constructions of farming. Dyking provides a simple example of this.

The importance of the dyking grants in the ESAs in Scotland was mentioned earlier. Dykes were the major attraction of the scheme, but although they provide a landscape feature, their other conservation benefits are minimal while their agricultural benefits are significant. Dykes were very symbolic for farmers, providing evidence of the impact of farming on the landscape and the taming of nature.

"I'm fond of stone dykes and I think a lot of them, they give shelter, a fence gives no shelter and also I like to see them, a good stone dyke is... I'm very proud of some of the ones here I've got one I call it my Waterloo Dyke it was built in 1815, and it is nearly six feet high, I can't see over it. I'm very proud of that dyke I haven't... there is not a stone missing of it, what shelter it gives from the north is marvellous." (Mr Cooper D310)

It is ironic that dykes, which farmers associate with agriculture and 'real' farming, are now funded by agri-environmental schemes and so are becoming associated with conservation. Nonetheless, some farmers who were farming in an extensive and traditional manner and who were concerned to 'work with nature' were very strongly against the idea of conservation. They seemed to associate it with outside interference and a loss of control over the farm and the freedom to do as they wished. At the same time they often continued to farm in what might be considered an 'environmentally friendly' manner. As their way of farming seemed unlikely to change, it could be argued that there was no need to attract these farmers into agri-environmental schemes, even though these were often the poorest farmers. In contrast some of the farmers who were most interested in joining the ESA were the ones who had previously taken advantage of other grant aid. They were businesslike and very keen to remain in farming and pass their farm on to the next generation. Aiding these farmers, who seemed to be the ablest negotiators, to farm in an agri-environmental manner has its ironies. They are the ones who responded most ably to productivist policies and so are likely to have less conservation interest on their farms than those described above.

Consequences for Agri-Environmental Schemes

The way farmers understood their situation was found to be important. Feelings of dependence on the government and control by the government were powerful and were closely connected to their uncertainty about the future and objections to regulations and bureaucracy. It was found that farmers were interested in the agri-environmental schemes for the most part because they felt it would benefit their farming activity. While this was, in part, an aim of the ESA scheme, the more conservation oriented elements of the scheme remained unpopular and were only accepted to achieve other gains. So while the farmers' reactions to agri-environmental policy were often favourable, this was apparently because the ESA did not require much change in farming practice and farmers could receive reasonable payment. It is important to remember that in the minds of farmers and in practice, economic pressures continue to dominate. The needs of the farm, security and the family income have to be met before other questions can be addressed (Marsden and Munton, 1991). Understanding how farmers perceive their situation gives an important basis for interpreting how this affects their ideas about their role and their feelings about conservation. It is an essential element in their reaction to agri-environmental policies.

Farmers have always faced uncertainty but although the weather, other physical factors and the markets have always been considered unpredictable, farmers had become used to a reasonably stable agricultural policy scenario. At present, however, the agricultural policy direction was no longer felt to be predictable. This was mainly the result of the uncertainty about the consequences of the CAP reform and the potential effect of the GATT agreement. These were combined with a recognition of the changing position of farmers in society and a rise in the importance of conservation as an agricultural issue. It is recognised that conservation has long been an issue in relation to agriculture, but for farmers in this study it was a relatively new consideration. It is not clear how the perception of uncertainty affects involvement in ESA schemes. Wilson (1992) suggested that it would increase interest as the ESA would provide a guaranteed payment, but in this study many farmers expressed fears about being tied into a scheme which might restrict their choices if the policy situation were to change.

The increase in bureaucracy required to claim support payments also affected reactions to the ESA. Although a common characteristic of the ESA schemes is that the application procedure is relatively straight forward (Baldock et al, 1990) the schemes were inevitably felt to be adding to the bureaucratisation of farming[1]. From this point of view, the launch of the Southern Uplands ESA was unfortunately timed coming just after farmers had filled out their first IACS forms. Related to this hesitation regarding paperwork was the suspicion that the scheme would also tie them further into the regulatory systems evolving in farming and the feeling that they would become more subject to interference and restriction. Thomas (1993), in her study of the Llyn Peninsula ESA, also noted that farmers distrusted bureaucratic interference as well as the conservation basis of the ESA initiative. Because of the farmers' wariness about being 'told what to do', the decision to get involved in agri-environmental schemes is a process of balancing restrictions against the benefits of the scheme. It should be noted, however, that farmers have always faced bureaucracy in regard to grant applications. Farm plans were often required, and farmers were also subject to inspections of the grant aided work. For many farmers it is likely that the increased paperwork will become an accepted part of the scheme, provided that it is attractive in other ways.

Connected to the notion that farmers are becoming ever more a part of a bureaucratic system, which exposes them to more outside interference, is the idea that they are subject to more control. Control may be related to financial considerations: in order to receive money farmers are forced to behave in a particular way. This is a factor to be taken into account in considering of the ESA schemes; they involve agreement to behave in a specific manner in exchange for financial reward. The feeling that the ESA was involving farmers in further subsidies, restrictions and interference was quite strong, and in some cases was the reason for not joining the ESA scheme. There was also a worry that the restrictions might become compulsory at a later date. This feeling of unease that schemes which are voluntary today could be obligatory tomorrow was also found by Hill et al (1992). The restrictions in the Southern Uplands ESA were not strong , but even so they were an important factor in farmers' consideration of the ESA. But it was not necessarily the detail of the restrictions which was critical, sometimes it was simply the idea of voluntarily agreeing to more control. As Mather (1993) found in regard to SSSIs in Northern Scotland, there was resentment at the restrictions in the farmers' freedom to use and manage land. Although the restrictions may be minor, they are nevertheless real, even if they have little practical effect. Despite reservations, however, farmers were still prepared to join if other conditions were felt to be right. The fact that farmers may have many objections and fears about environmental schemes and yet join them is a key point. Although much of this chapter has focused on the concerns expressed by farmers about the scheme, for many these could be compensated for by the belief that the payments made it worthwhile or the conditions were not too restrictive.

The farmers' perception of their role was also found to influence their reaction to the ESA scheme. The traditional aspects of being a farmer remained strong, and there was little enthusiasm for changing this. Food production was an important element of the farmers self image and the ESA and similar schemes do not fit in with this view. This meant farmers had some difficulty in adjusting to them but also in understanding why they had been introduced. The idea that such schemes are acceptable as long as they do not interfere with farming is significant. If one of the reasons behind such schemes is to change farmers' behaviour (Morris, 1993) and to ensure that conservation is more integrated into farming, then this belief reflects the difficulties faced by those who are trying to do this. Farmers did not want to have to change their farming practices. This is linked to their perceptions of their role, which they generally saw as 'doing farming'. As Herrmann (1992) noted, new social requirements such as landscape protection and wildlife preservation do not allow farmers to act purposefully. Environmental tasks may not be regarded as alternatives to food production, but may be seen as a by-product of other work. It was suggested by farmers in this study that the schemes which had not 'interfered' with farming were the ones which would be popular, and those which required changes in farming practices would find it more difficult to attract farmers.

This coincided with the belief that conservation should not cost the farmer in any way and that they should be compensated for any restrictions which might be imposed on their 'real' farming practices. Hence, the restrictions in the scheme were a key consideration. Farmers disliked any semblance of interference in their farming, or the thought that they might be constrained in what they do. Thus their reactions to the scheme were very dependent on how they perceived the scheme's prescriptions would affect their farming. But because of their interest in the scheme from an 'agricultural' point of view, many farmers had accommodated the ESA. They had negotiated their ideas about conservation work. For them it had come to mean many of the activities which they would have previously considered to be a part of their farming. Dyking is an obvious example of this. Thus farmers in the ESAs are often engaged in 'symbolic' conservation, joining an environmental scheme for farming purposes. The farming goals are what are paramount and it is these which influence reactions to the ESAs.

This highlights the dilemma facing policy makers who seek to direct agricultural support to environmental goals. Do they introduce 'soft' policies which are popular with farmers and achieve good uptake and at the same time provide the Agriculture Departments (SOAFD, MAFF, etc.) with favourable publicity? Or do they introduce policies with a more overt conservation benefit, which might achieve a poorer uptake, and at the same time threaten to alienate farmers? There seems no simple response to this, especially while the goals of policy makers are not very clear and conflict between conservation and farming over the representation of the countryside continues.

Notes

1. In Scottish ESAs, where farm conservation plans are obligatory, the application procedure is more complex than some other ESAs, but efforts have been made to keep the schemes as 'user friendly' as possible.

References

Agriculture EDC (1987) *Directions for Change: Land Use in the 1990s*, National Economic Development Office, London.

Baldock, D, Cox, G, Lowe, P and Winter, M (1990) Environmentally Sensitive Areas: Incrementalism or Reform? *Journal of Rural Studies*, 6, 143-162.

Brennan, A A (1992) Environmental Decision Making, in Berry, R J (Ed) *Environmental Dilemmas: Ethics and Decisions*, Chapman and Hall, London.

Buckwell, A (1989) Economic Signals, Farmers' Responses and Environmental Change, *Journal of Rural Studies*, 5, 149-160.

Cary, J (1993) The Nature of Symbolic Beliefs and Environmental Behaviour in a Rural Setting, *Environment and Behaviour*, 25, 555-576.

Cary, J, Wilkinson, R, Barr, N and Milne, G (1993) Establishing the basis for effective care of rural land: Exploring the relationships between revegetation and salinity, salinity control and landcare in North Central Victoria, *Australian Journal of Soil and Water Conservation*, 6, 44-49.

Cox, G, Lowe, P and Winter, M (1986) The State and the Farmer: Perspectives on Agricultural Policy, in Cox, G, Lowe, P and Winter, M (Eds) *Agriculture: People And Policies*, Allen & Unwin, London.

Froud, J (1994) The impact of ESAs on Lowland Farming, *Land Use Policy*, 11, 107-118.

Green, B I I (1986) Agriculture and the Environment: A review of the major issues in the UK, *Land Use Policy*, 3, 193-204.

Herrmann,V (1992) Behaviour Patterns of Farm Families in Response to Social Change in Agriculture. Integrated Panel Report: Rural Change in Europe: Research Programme on Farm Structures and Pluriactivity, Forschungsgesellschaft Fur Agrarpolitik und Agrarsoziologie.

Hill, P, Green, B H and Edwards, A (1992) *The Cost of Care: the costs and benefits of environmentally friendly farming practices*, Royal Institute of Chartered Surveyors: Paper No.15.

Lemon, M and Park, J (1993) Elicitation of Farming Agendas in a Complex Environment, *Journal of Rural Studies*, 9, 405-410.

Long, N (1989) Conclusion: Theoretical Reflections on Actor, Structure and Interface, in Long, N (Ed) *Encounters at the Interface: A Perspective on social discontinuities in rural development*, Studies in Sociology: 27: Agricultural University, Wageningen.

Lowe, P, Ward, N and Munton, R J C (1992) Social Analysis of Land Use Change: the Role of the Farmer, in Whitby, M (Ed) *Land Use Change: Causes and Consequences*, HMSO, London.

Marsden, T and Munton, R (1991) The Farmed Landscape and the Occupancy Change Process, *Environment and Planning A*, 23, 663-676.

Mather, A.S (1993) Protected Areas in the Periphery: Conservation and Controversy in Northern Scotland, *Journal of Rural Studies*, 9, 371-384.

McHenry, H L (1994) Understanding the Farmer's View: Perceptions of Changing Agriculture and the move to Agri-Environmental Policies in Southern Scotland, *unpublished Ph.D Thesis*, The University of Aberdeen.

Morris, C (1993) *Recruiting Farmers into Conservation: an analysis of participation in agri-environmental schemes in Lowland England*, unpublished PhD Thesis: Wye College, University of London.

Munton, R. J C, Marsden, T K and Whatmore, S J (1990) Technological Change in a Period of Agricultural Adjustment, in Lowe, P, Marsden, T K and Whatmore, S J (Eds) *Technological Change and the Rural Environment*, Fulton, London: .

O'Riordan, T (1973) Some Reflections on Environmental Attitudes and Behaviour, *Area*, 5, 17-21.

O'Riordan, T (1976) Attitudes, Behavior and Environmental Policy Issues, in Altman, I and Wohlwill, J F (Eds) *Human Behavior and Environment*, Plenum Press, New York.

Ramsay, P (1993) Land-owners and Conservation, in Goldsmith, F B and Warren, A. (Eds) *Conservation in Progress*, John Wiley and Sons, London.

Thomas, E E (1993) *The Socio-Economic Context of Agricultural and Ecological Change in the*

Llyn Peninsula, unpublished PhD Thesis, University of Liverpool.

Tuan, Y (1968) Discrepancies between environmental attitude and behaviour: Examples from Europe and China, *Canadian Geographer*, 12, 176-181.

Tuan, Y (1970) Our Treatment of the Environment in Ideal and Actuality, *American Scientist*, 58, 244-249.

Ward, N, Marsden, T K and Munton, R J C (1990) Farm Landscape Change: Trends in Upland and Lowland England, *Land Use Policy*, 7, 291-302.

Wilson, O (1992) Landownership and Rural Development in the North Pennines: a case study, *Journal of Rural Studies*, 8, 145-158.

Zinn, J A and Blodgett, J E (1989) Agriculture versus the Environment, *Journal of Soil and Water Conservation*, 44, 184-187.

CHAPTER 13

Farmers' Attitudes to Woodland Planting Grants and the Potential Effects of New Forestry Incentives

Tim Lloyd, Charles Watkins and Daniel Williams

The conversion of agricultural land to woodland is not a recent aspect of British rural land use change. From the seventeenth century onwards, plantations have been made on former agricultural land for a wide range of reasons including commercial timber production, game preservation, hunting and landscape improvement. In the twentieth century the process of afforestation has been encouraged by a wide range of government schemes including the provision of grants and tax concessions to farmers and landowners, and the state purchase and planting of substantial areas of woodland. The types of woodland planted vary from small amenity plantings and hunting cover on high quality agricultural land, to extensive plantations of commercial crops on what, at the time of planting, were considered to be poor agricultural soils. Much woodland was established on the sands of Breckland (East Anglia) and Sherwood Forest (Nottinghamshire) during periods of agricultural depression, such as the inter-war period.

In recent years the surplus of agricultural land resulting from the overproduction of food within the EU has resulted in further pressure for the conversion of agricultural land to woodland. Such woodland is seen as providing potential nature conservation, recreation and commercial benefits (Grayson, 1993; Watkins, 1991). This policy shift has been accompanied by changes to the incentives available to existing and potential private woodland owners, particularly farmers. Various surveys have indicated that many farmers are unsympathetic towards woodland planting (Watkins, 1983; 1984; Scambler, 1989 and Bishop, 1990; 1992) Their research clearly shows this lack of interest in woodland planting:

"....enthusiasm for trees was not true for the majority (64%) of the farmers". (Watkins, 1983)

" The most important conclusion is that farmers in the study showed little interest in forestry". (Scambler, 1989)

"The vast majority of respondents interviewed (over 90%) were not interested in new woodland planting". (Bishop, 1992)

Unless there is a very significant shift in government policy towards state afforestation, the majority of the new woodland required to take up the excess agricultural land will have to be established by farmers and landowners. Indeed, various new schemes have been introduced since 1990 to encourage such planting. In this chapter we explore recent changes in forestry incentives and report on a personal interview survey of 30 farmers in the Sherwood Forest area. We assess the extent to which recent developments in forestry incentives are likely to encourage farm woodland planting.

Policies Affecting British Woodland

Grants for forestry have been available from the early years of the twentieth century (Watkins, 1984). Despite the varying nature of the grant schemes over this period, it was not until the late 1980s that farmland became a major target of national policy for tree planting. The apparent excess of agricultural land within the European Union has been a contributory factor in this change, resulting in the proposed establishment of 12 new lowland forests adjacent to large urban areas in England called Community Forests and one New National Forest. The purpose of these forest designations is to create well wooded landscapes for wildlife, work, recreation and education, and provide major environmental improvements both for the local people and others who choose to visit them from further away (Countryside Commission, 1994a).

Until 1988 farm woodland planting was at a fairly small scale, there being negligible pressure for farmers to plant on all but the poorest land. Various farm woodland planting grants were available including the initial Farm Woodland Scheme (MAFF, 1988) and the Woodland Grant Scheme with its two supplements (the Community Woodland Supplement and the Better Land Supplement (Blyth *et al*, 1991). Although these are essentially the same grants that are in use today, they have undergone several revisions since 1988. The Farm Woodland Premium Scheme (MAFF, 1994) was introduced in

April 1992 as a successor to the Farm Woodland Scheme. It, too, was administered by MAFF and offered annual payments to compensate farmers for the loss of farming income where woodlands were established on agricultural land. However, to qualify for this, the proposed woods required approval by the Forestry Commission and must attract establishment grants under the Woodland Grant Scheme (Nix, 1993). This scheme and its supplements have also changed since their introduction, as have the additional management grants.

The designation by the Countryside Commission of 12 Community Forests in England marked a new development in forestry policy (figure 13.1). The areas were chosen because they were close to urban areas and contained significant areas of reclaimable disused industrial land which had the potential for afforestation and the creation of recreational areas. Farmers living within these areas have the opportunity to receive guidance from the Community Forest teams and obtain several forms of financial assistance. The New National Forest Scheme, on the borders of Staffordshire, Derbyshire and Leicestershire, is a similar scheme to the Community Forests, although it is jointly supported by the Countryside Commission and the Forestry Commission. Another scheme is the Forestry Commission's Sherwood Initiative which aims to stimulate farmers to establish new woodland, and improve their management of existing woodland, through the establishment of a Trust. All of these schemes can be seen as part of the general move to `bring forestry down the hill' and encourage the afforestation of lowland agricultural land (Watkins, 1991).

Two more general policies also need to be considered. Uncertainty over changes to the Common Agricultural Policy (CAP) has meant that here has been a tendency for long term decisions, such as the conversion of agricultural land to woodland, to be delayed. The major reform of the CAP in 1992 is likely to lead to a period of relative agricultural stability. This has already been partly borne out by the current stability and, in some areas, increase in agricultural land values during 1994 and 1995. This relative stability might give some farmers the confidence to plant new areas of

Figure 13.1   Community Forests and the National Forest

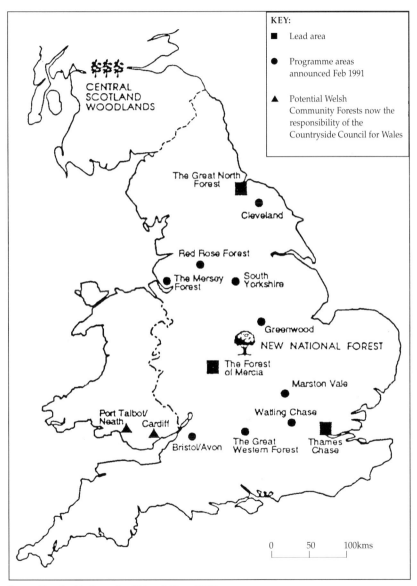

Source: Countryside Recreation Network News (1993)

247

woodland. Other farmers, however, might be tempted to leave well alone and see how high agricultural land values rise. More specifically, the designation of Nitrate Sensitive Areas also has an impact on farmers' attitudes to woodland planting. Under the NSA scheme significant payments are given within designated areas of between £65-£590 per hectare to farmers who reduce nitrate inputs to, and outflow from, agricultural land (MAFF, 1994b). This is a voluntary scheme aimed at improving the quality of drinking water. On some farms it could compete with farm woodland grant schemes as a form of government subsidy.

Nottinghamshire Farm Woodland Survey

In order to examine contemporary attitudes to planting grants, a personal interview survey of farmers in West Nottinghamshire was undertaken in the spring and summer of 1994. The survey area was chosen as it is was influenced by two of the new forestry schemes: the Greenwood Community Forest (Countryside Commission, 1993) and the Sherwood Initiative (Forestry Commission, 1993). These schemes both aim to increase the area of farm woodland to some degree. Two Nitrate Sensitive Areas are also included within the study area (figure 13.2).

The area is physically uniform, located upon highly permeable Bunter Sandstone, creating a landscape of low, undulating hills, dry valleys and poor, light pebbly soils (Brady, 1992; Seymour, 1988). Modern agricultural technology allows the production of high quality cereals and root crops and the study area is therefore currently characterised by intensive and profitable farms. Historically the area is a classic example of poor sand land agriculture (Makings, 1944). In the inter-war period extensive plantations were made by the Forestry Commission (Watkins, 1981).

All 51 farms in the Yellow Pages and within the study area were contacted, producing 30 interviewees (Williams, Lloyd and Watkins, 1994). A standard questionnaire was used though the opportunity was also taken to explore the issues of farm woodland in a wide ranging interview. Themes discussed included general attitudes to woodland, agricultural change,

Figure 13.2   Characteristics of the study area and the locations of farms visited

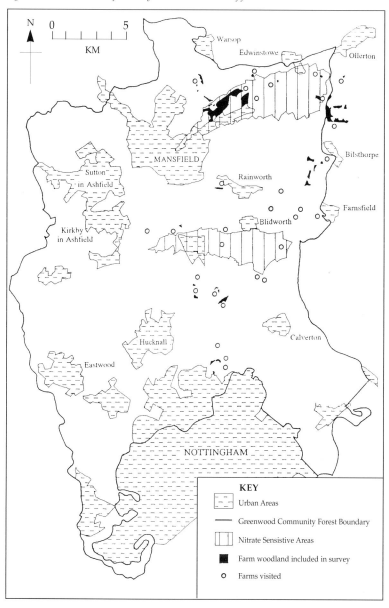

thoughts about the new Community Forests and Sherwood Initiative and the changing grant system under consideration. The average farm size, excluding one anomalously large holding, was 197ha. The total area of farmland occupied by those interviewed was 9,775ha of which 320ha was woodland. A variety of forms of tenure was found, though all but one consisted of some freehold land. The main crops were cereals, root crops and legumes. Irrigation is very important in this area due to the naturally unretentive nature of the land (Makings, 1944) and farmers required licences to exploit the aquifer, the absence of which would make agriculture more difficult and forestry theoretically more attractive.

Farmers' Attitudes to Woodland Planting

The survey revealed that farmers had a wide variety of attitudes to woodland. Most liked to see woodland and trees in the landscape and those who had planted using Forestry Commission grants suggested that plantations enhanced the countryside, though only a small minority were actively managing their woodland. Farm woodlands were generally most used for recreation, amenity, wildlife and sport. Distinct from major Forestry Commission funded plantings, several farmers had planted on a very small scale around the farm house, in hedgerows and field corners. Occasionally this was carried out with trees provided by the Farming and Wildlife Advisory Group or the County Council and was done for amenity reasons. None of the farmers possessing woodland wished to reduce its area.

Regardless of their disposition to existing woodlands, farmers do still have a negative attitude to woodland planting. It is one thing to have a little woodland scattered around the farm in field corners and along boundaries, it is quite another to be investing time, energy and money into expanding that area by planting agricultural land or indeed carefully managing existing woodland. The primary reason for this lack of interest is the poor return from woodland compared with agricultural crops. Thus, it is generally only the largest, wealthiest farm businesses that can forego some income make plantations. Ilbery (1992) stated that the farmers most likely to plant using

Forestry Commission grants often had the following personal characteristics: larger farms, younger in age, higher educational attainment and formal agricultural training. Furthermore, the possibility of being compensated slightly by increased personal utility from woodlands was seen as a remote possibility, particularly by older farmers.

Farmers in the survey expressed concerns about the long term nature of woodland. They believed that the unstable grant system could change at almost any time, therefore causing them to miss out on more favourable rates. Similar worries were expressed about the potential changes to the CAP and the various ways in which it affected their farms. Other worries based on future uncertainty were the perceived irreversibility and reduced flexibility of wooded land, affecting the farmer's ability to adapt to future conditions or opportunities (Lloyd, Watkins and Williams, 1995).

Additionally, woodland tends to exacerbate the already difficult problem of public access and associated vandalism. This is especially relevant given the existence of the Greenwood Community Forest which suggested to some farmers that public access to their woods may become practically compulsory. However, farmers' awareness of local woodland policy initiatives proved to be varied. The Greenwood Community Forest was known of by all respondents; about 25% having been directly involved with its planning and consultation phase. About half had only a limited knowledge of exactly what the scheme entailed and none thought they would plant woodland because of it. Generally it was perceived in a rather negative light, particularly with regard to public access.

Views were also obtained on schemes which involved the planning and management of woodland being temporarily taken over by independent organisations such as English Woodlands (1994) and the Woodland Trust (1994). Eighteen farmers said they would use these schemes should they ever plant woodland, though concern was voiced over the loss of farmer independence and how such schemes could possibly be operated profitably.

Farmers' Attitudes to the Woodland Planting Grants

Only five of the 30 farmers interviewed had obtained one of the planting grants available. However not all of the grants being used are still available. Four farmers had used the Woodland Grant Scheme and one of these had also used the Farm Woodland Premium Scheme and the Better Land Supplement. The now defunct Forestry Grant scheme was still in use on two farms, and the Broadleaved Woodland Grant Scheme on one. Effectively, therefore, the take up of existing grants was very low indeed. Moreover, only two of the grants were used to establish new woodland, the remainder were used to replant existing woods.

As the range of planting grants is large, this section of the survey was dependent on being able to display the current grant levels clearly to the farmers. Grant scenario tables were devised which clearly displayed the different grants and the levels of payment which could be received for planting a standard area of either conifers or broadleaves under optimum circumstances, along with a grand total of the level of payment. These tables were supplemented by grant cash flow tables which displayed how the grants were awarded over a period of years.

On the whole, the grants were considered to be not nearly generous enough to make up for income lost by taking land out of agricultural production. Farmers were far more concerned with claiming the money for other schemes such as Set-aside and the Nitrate Sensitive Areas. Even those farmers with a positive attitude towards trees found planting unrealistic. It was noted that if agricultural incomes dropped in the future, the grants might then become more attractive. To this end three farmers expressed the belief that the present CAP system of support should be removed and a free market reinstalled. This would remove much of the unnatural value of agricultural land, thus making it more viable to plant woodland. Indeed, Crabtree (1988) argued, that unless substantial European finance is made available, farm forestry can only become more competitive as a result of reducing support to agriculture, and with it the land values and marginal agricultural returns. Generally it was believed that the grants not only fail to account for the cost of woodland establishment and maintenance, but also do not make allowances for other indirect non-pecuniary expenses such as the loss of farm flexibility, increased uncertainty and possibly increased trespass and vandalism.

Only two farmers considered the present grant rates adequate. One of these was the largest and most commercialised farm in the survey. This was perhaps the farm that could most easily spare the land and money to improve the appearance of the farm. The owner had also been rearranging the disposition of woodland on the farm by clearance and planting in order to maximize the area of good quality land. The other farm was considerably smaller and had already undertaken some planting without using the grants; on viewing the grants now available, the farmer thought he might apply for them in the future.

During the survey a hypothetical situation was proposed whereby farmers would be compensated for the expenses incurred during woodland planting and their present income would not change as a result of such planting. This concept garnered some useful reactions. Eleven farmers said they would plant woodland if this was the case, eight farmers said they would not and nine remained unsure. Positive responses were backed up by the belief that farmers will grow whatever is most profitable. Negative responses tended to be linked to the non-economic costs of woodland and the opinion that `farmers are not foresters'. Farmers from all sides expressed concerns about the capital value of the land under trees being depressed. Three farmers stated that they could foresee no level of grant that would persuade them to make plantations.

The grant system as a process was criticized by farmers largely for its complexity and the fact that the many supplementary grants were badly advertised and poorly integrated into the whole. Several farmers pointed out that the Forestry Commission should deal with all the woodland planting grants individually and MAFF should not be involved. The present form of payment was considered essentially correct but grants should be index linked and simplified. There views were similar to those of Jones (1994) who has suggested that a synthesis of the various strands and themes is needed, which can only be achieved through an integrated national strategy and by making forestry the responsibility of one government minister.

Recent Changes to Forestry Incentives

A government review of the public forestry sector was published in 1994 after the Nottinghamshire survey was carried out. This included new incentives to encourage private sector planting of commercial woodlands. Incentives were increased by 10%, with £3m in new money and an additional £1m reallocated from reduced grants for replanting (Maitland, 1994). The changes were broadly welcomed by the forestry industry, though forestry and landowner organisations and conservation groups were not wholly satisfied, believing that incentives had not been increased sufficiently.

The main changes affected the Woodland Grant Scheme. The payments available in the old scheme since 1988 are shown in figure 13.3. These payments have been simplified, with a new emphasis on making larger grants per hectare available for larger planting schemes and the separation of restocking and natural regeneration grants (figure 13.4). There are now only two size categories, though the conifer/broadleaf distinction remains. Grants for restocking are considerably reduced to £325/ha for conifers and £525/ha for broadleaves, irrespective of the size of the plantation. Grants for natural regeneration now receive a fixed rate payment equivalent to that for restocking and an additional discretionary payment of 50% of the agreed costs of work necessary.

Figure 13.3. Establishment Grants for Planting, Restocking and Natural Regeneration.

GRANT BAND	CONIFER £/ha	BROADLEAVED £/ha
less than 1.0 ha	1005	1575
1.0 - 2.9 ha	880	1375
3.0 - 9.9 ha	795	1175
10.0 ha and over	615	975

NB. Grants for native pinewoods were paid at the broadleaved rate. Source: Forestry Commission (1991).

Figure 13.4. Planting Grants Under the Woodland Grant Scheme Since September 1994.

GRANT RATES	CONIFERS £/ha	BROADLEAVES £/ha
Woods less than 10 ha	700	1350
Woods of 10 ha and over	700	1050

NB. Grants for native pinewoods are usually paid at the broadleaves rate. Source Forestry
Commission (1994).

The Community Woodland Scheme remains largely unchanged in both the value of payment and its administration. However the Better Land Supplement has been simplified to provide a standard additional £600/ha for planting on arable or improved grassland of both conifers and broadleaves; this improves conifer rates by £200/ha. The previous management grant has also been modified to provide just one standard payment of £35 per hectare to help toward some of the cost of work to maintain and improve woodlands. The Farm Woodland Planting Scheme rates have not been altered since their introduction in 1992, with up to £250/ha/pa available on arable and improved grassland outside less favoured areas (MAFF, 1994b). In addition to these changes instigated by the forestry sector review of summer 1994, forestry ministers announced in late 1994 a special flat rate supplement to the Woodland Grant Scheme of £600/ha for the 12 community forests and the Sherwood, Welsh Valleys and Central Scotland Woodlands Initiatives.

Several new and potentially interesting grant forms were created in the wake of the forestry review. These are for Short Rotation Coppice, Woodland Improvement and Livestock Exclusion.

Short Rotation Coppice

A grant is paid for planting poplar and willows on suitable sites to be worked on short rotation. Grants of £400/ha are paid if this is set-aside land and £600/ha if it is not (FC, 1994). This idea was first officially mooted in early 1994 in the changes to the arable areas payments rules (MAFF, 1994c).

Woodland Improvement Grant

This is available for woodland improvements such as coppice restoration or rhododendron clearance. It is discretionary and based on 50% of agreed costs (FC, 1994)

Livestock Exclusion Annual Premium

This is paid to compensate for the loss of revenue to the farmer from excluding agricultural stock from woodland. This applies especially to woods of high environmental value where stock might prevent regeneration of the woodland or field layer. Grants are £80/ha/pa and can run for up to 10 years (FC, 1994).

Overall the changes introduced in 1994 demonstrate a continuing commitment by the government to encourage farm woodland planting. However, although more money is available, the changes can be interpreted as tinkering with the grant schemes to simplify procedures rather than a significant increase in funding. Perhaps the most significant change is the reduction in the grant for very small plantations of less than a hectare, and the increase in grant for new woodland of 10 hectares or more. This change reflects the concern of the Forestry Commission over the future management problems associated with the large number of very small woods which the previous schemes had encouraged. The introduction of woodland improvement and livestock exclusion grants reflects general concern with the need to improve the management of existing farm woodlands rather than just concentrating on the planting of new woodland.

Discussion

This study has shown that despite the strong government support for new farm woodland, the wide range of grants available, and the existence of two new special forestry schemes, the farming community in the study area was largely uninterested in planting trees. This is true even though the area is characterised by a naturally poor soils, which require expensive inputs of fertiliser and irrigation.

The grants in operation during the survey were seen by farmers as inadequate for the task allotted to them. Even the additional incentives focused upon farmlands were unsuccessful in persuading new farmers to plant woodlands, despite some success on a national scale. Results from the study area showed a surprising level of ignorance about the existing grant structure and its organisation. Of those interviewed, 83% had not utilised grants and most knew little of them. A similar proportion (73%) was discovered in the Marston Vale Community Forest (1994) survey of farmers.

It is doubtful whether the grant system was acting as an encouragement, or as a bonus for those farmers who would have planted anyway. Our Nottinghamshire survey suggests this is true for four out the five grant users, three of whom were replanting exiting woodland. Both Bateman (1992) and Cater (1994) suggest that grants are not a motivating force for owners, but may facilitate activity under the right circumstances. Such a situation has been identified as a *selectivity effect* whereby the grant is subsidizing farmers in carrying out development schemes they would have completed anyway (Ilbery, 1992; Ilbery and Stiell, 1991; Gasson and Potter, 1988). Some commentators such as Bateman (1992) have suggested that the grant system could be an intervention failure.

The assorted woodland planting schemes therefore seem to have failed both from an economic and promotional point of view. If farmers cannot relate to the levels of grant available, how can the levels of grant incentives possibly be satisfactorily examined for effectiveness and then favourably altered? Obviously interview conditions tend to put farmers in a difficult position and some questions could not be answered without considerable thought and research by the farmer, but the future for new farm woodland plantations in the study area appears to be bleak. Ilbery (1992) suggests that much more research is required on the ways in which public and private institutions in the external environment publicise policy measures and inform farmers. Certainly the subtle changes to the grant system introduced in 1994 after the survey was carried out are hardly of a magnitude to persuade farmers in the survey to change their views on farm woodland planting.

Similarly, the Greenwood Community Forest scheme does not yet appear to have encouraged farmers to plant on their arable land. There was a very low level of enthusiasm about this scheme and a rather negative attitude, for many farmers disliked being included without their consent. The Sherwood Initiative appeared to be treated with similar apathy. Other community forests around England seem to be suffering similar problems although research commissioned by the community forests tends to avoid `talking down' the projects they are trying to promote (Watkins, Williams and Lloyd, 1996). Time and familiarity may eventually soften some of these attitudes, after all most Community Forests are only just past their public consultation phase and are producing their 3-5 year business plans setting out how the project teams are going to implement the forests in practical terms (Countryside Commission, 1994b). More effective head-on policies, stronger government support and additional funds might help to speed up this process.

The study confirms that woodland creation is unlikely to occur to any great extent on commercial farms, given the incentives available at the time of survey, because woodland is uneconomic compared to arable crops and there is a long time lag between the initial capital invested and any returns. The changes made to the grants since the Nottinghamshire survey are a step in the right direction. The increased grants for larger plantations and for new woodland in Community Forests are particularly important, the latter indicating a shift towards the targeting of woodland grants to specific designated areas as opposed to the traditional blanket approach. The introduction of grants for short rotation coppice has been anticipated by farmers for several years and in conjunction with set-aside may yet prove an incentive.

Unfortunately all the signs suggest that these new incentives will not be enough to engender significant new planting, for they do not approach compensating farmers for the loss of agricultural land at the present time. They may perhaps facilitate activity or reduce the overall financial burden for some farmers, but are unlikely to ignite much new interest. There is a development, however, which may change the future of farm woodland planting dramatically. This is the announcement that the European Union's set-aside rules are to be changed in 1996 to allow the establishment of woodland on set-aside land (Hornsby, 1995). In 1995 around 12 per cent of the arable area of Britain was set-aside. From 1996 farmers will be able to include plantations on arable land under the scheme as part of their set-aside requirement. It is difficult to estimate the effect of this change on farmers with precision. The change certainly means that farmers who make plantations will not have to add the area planted to their set-aside requirement. This will benefit planters who would otherwise have needed to take too much of their land out of arable production and should greatly assist in persuading farmers to plant more woodland. Ultimately the suspicion persists, however, that the personal attitudes of farmers to woodland remain a major obstacle to the successful establishment of substantial areas of well managed woodland in lowland Britain.

References

Bateman, I (1992) The United Kingdom, in Wibe, S and Jones, T *Forests: Market and Intervention failures*, Earthscan, London.

Bishop, K D (1990) *Multi-purpose woodlands in the countryside around towns*, unpublished PhD thesis, University of Reading.

Bishop, K D (1992) Britain's new forests: public dependence on private interest? in Gilg, A W (Ed) *Restructuring the Countryside: Environmental Policy in practice*, Avebury Studies Green Research.

Blyth, J, Evans, J, Mutch, W E S and Sidwell, C (1991) *Farm Woodland Management*, Farming Press, Ipswich.

Brady, A (1992) Forestry in Nottinghamshire, *Forestry*, 65, 103-26.

Cater, J (1994) Small Woodlands and their owners: The Silvanus Experience, *Quarterly Journal of Forestry*, 88, 128-33.

Countryside Commission (1992) *Farming in Community Forests*, Countryside Commission, Cheltenham.

Countryside Commission (1994a) *Community Forests CFDATA2*, Countryside Commission Community Forest Unit, London.

Countryside Commission (1994b) *Forests for the Community Programme,* personal correspondence from Community Forest Unit, London.

Crabtree, J R (1987) *The Role of Forestry in UK Agricultural Adjustment*, Vth European Congress of Agricultural Economists, Hungary 1987.

English Woodlands (1994) *Farm Woodland Finance Scheme*, English Woodlands Ltd, Newbury.

Forestry Commission (1991) *Woodland Grant Scheme: Applicants pack*, Forestry Commission, Edinburgh.

Forestry Commission (1993) *Sherwood Initiative*, (leaflet) Forestry Commission, Edinburgh.

Forestry Commission (1994) *Woodland Grant Scheme: Applicants pack - revised version*, Forestry Commission, Edinburgh.

Gasson, R and Potter, C (1988) Conservation through land diversion: a survey of farmers' attitudes, *Journal of Agricultural Economics*, 39, 340-51.

Grayson, A.J. (1993) *Private Forestry Policy in Western Europe*, C.A.B. International, Wallingford.

The Greenwood Community Forest (1993) *The Greenwood Community Forest Plan: Draft for consultation*, The Greenwood Community Forest, Hucknall.

Hornsby, M. (1995) Farmers win right to convert unused acres to woodland, *The Times*, 27/5/95.

Ilbery, B. (1992) State assisted farm diversification in the United Kingdom, in Bowler, I R, Bryant, C R and Nellis, M D (Eds) *Contemporary rural systems in transition Volume 1: Agriculture and Environment*, CAB International, Wallingford, 100-116.

Ilbery, B. and Stiell, B. (1991) Uptake of the Farm Diversification Grant Scheme in England, *Geography*, 76, 259-63.

Jones, R B (1994) National Forestry Strategy Required, *Land Use Policy*, 11, 124-27.

Lloyd, T, Watkins, C and Williams, C (1995) Turning farmers into foresters via market liberalisation, *Journal of Agricultural Economics*, 46 (in press).

MAFF (1988) *The Farm Woodland Scheme. A general introduction and rules booklet*, MAFF publications.

MAFF (1994a) *The Farm Woodland Premium Scheme: Rules and Procedures*, MAFF publications.

MAFF (1994b) *Nitrate Sensitive Areas scheme- information pack*, MAFF publications.

MAFF (1994c) *AR17: Changes to the Arable Area Payments Rules*, MAFF publications.

Maitland, A. (1994) Woodlands avoid sell-off, *Financial Times*, 19th July 1994, 8.

Makings, S M (1945) *The economics of poor land arable farming*, Edward Arnold, London.

Marston Vale Community Forest (1994) *Agricultural Chapter*, unpublished report.

Nix, J (1993) *Farm Management Pocketbook*, Wye College, London.

Scambler, A. (1989) Farmer's attitudes towards forestry, *Scottish Geographical Magazine*, 105, 47-49.

Seymour, S (1989) The `Spirit of Planting': Eighteenth-century parkland `improvement' on the Duke of Newcastle's north Nottinghamshire estate, *East Midland Geographer*, 12, 5-13.

Watkins, C (1981) An Historical Introduction to Woodlands of Nottinghamshire, in Watkins, C and Wheeler, P T (Eds) *The Study and Use of British Woodlands*, Department of Geography, University of Nottingham.

Watkins, C (1983) *Woodlands in Nottinghamshire since 1945: A Study of changing distribution, type and use*, unpublished PhD thesis.

Watkins, C (1984) The use of grant aid to encourage woodland planting in Great Britain, *Quarterly Journal of Forestry*, 78, 213-224.

Watkins, C (1991) *Nature Conservation and the new lowland forests*, Nature Conservancy Council, Peterborough.

Watkins, C, Williams, D J, and Lloyd, T (1996) Constraints on farm woodland planting in England: a study of Nottinghamshire farmers, *Forestry*, 69 (In press).

Williams, D J, Lloyd, T and Watkins, C (1994) *Farmers not foresters: constraints on the planting of new farm woodland*, Department of Geography, University of Nottingham, Working Paper 27.

The Woodland Trust (1994) *Licence Planting Scheme*, The Woodland Trust, Grantham.

CHAPTER 14

Environmentally Sensitive Areas and the Conservation of the Built Environment in England and Wales

Peter Gaskell and Michael Tanner

Environmentally Sensitive Areas (ESAs) were introduced in the mid-1980s as a response to growing concern about the impact of farming activities on the rural environment. The nature and extent of the changes that were taking place had been demonstrated by a series of surveys that began in the early 1970s and became more systematic in the 1980s (see for example, Westmacott and Worthington, 1974; 1984; Porchester, 1977; Parry *et al*, 1982; Barr *et al*, 1986). These surveys focused particularly on the destruction of habitats important to wildlife and on the loss of other features important to the aesthetic quality of the landscape. Evidence was collected about the loss of a limited range of landscape components, especially hedgerows, woodlands, traditionally-managed pastures, wetlands and various categories of unimproved semi-natural vegetation. Generally little attention was paid to the built environment, apart from the introduction of modern farm building and fencing materials.

This situation changed with the passage of the Agriculture Act 1986, which made provision for the establishment of ESAs. This Act attempted to make agricultural policy responsive to the needs of environmental conservation by imposing on Agricultural Ministers a general duty to balance "the conservation and enhancement of the natural beauty and amenity of the countryside" with their other duties [sec. 17(1)], but it also specified the protection of buildings and other cultural features as one of the objectives of ESA policy. The designation of ESAs therefore represented an additional policy instrument for the conservation of the built environment, which often makes a significant contribution to the distinctive character of rural areas. The purpose of this paper is to examine the extent to which the management of the built environment has been taken into account in the implementation of ESA policy, both in the original designations and in the changes that have subsequently been made in the light of experience with the early schemes.

Development of ESA Policy

The introduction of ESAs as part of the reform of the Common Agricultural Policy was very much a British policy initiative (Baldock, 1985) and British concern about agricultural impacts on the natural environment was reflected in the relevant European legislation. Article 19 of Council Regulation (EEC) No 797/85 makes provision for the designation of ESAs in "particular areas of recognised importance from an ecological and landscape point of view". Within such areas "aid may be granted to farmers who undertake to farm environmentally important areas so as to preserve or improve their environment." When it came to making statutory provision for the establishment of ESAs in Britain a rather broader view of their function was taken. Section 18(1) of the Agriculture Act 1986 gives power to Ministers to designate ESAs for one or more of three purposes, "(a) to conserve and enhance the natural beauty of an area; (b) to conserve the flora or fauna or geological or physiographical features of an area; or (c) to protect buildings or other objects of archaeological, architectural or historic interest in an area".

Unlike the more traditional 'planning' countryside conservation schemes, responsibility for the designation and administration of ESAs in England was given to the Ministry of Agriculture, Fisheries and Food (MAFF); in Wales the responsible ministry is the Welsh Office Agriculture Department (WOAD). In selecting the areas to be designated, Ministers were required to seek the advice of the Countryside Commission and English Nature; in Wales this advice is now given by the Countryside Council for Wales. English Heritage and Cadw, its equivalent body in Wales, have subsequently been added to the list of consultees and provide Ministers with advice about the built environment.

MAFF began cautiously in December 1986 by designating only five ESAs in England and one in Wales, but these quickly proved so successful in terms of farmers' response that a second round of six ESAs in England and one in Wales was announced only six months later. Subsequently the scheme has expanded rapidly, with further rounds of designations in 1993 and 1994, so

Figure 14.1 Environmentally Sensitive Areas in England and Wales

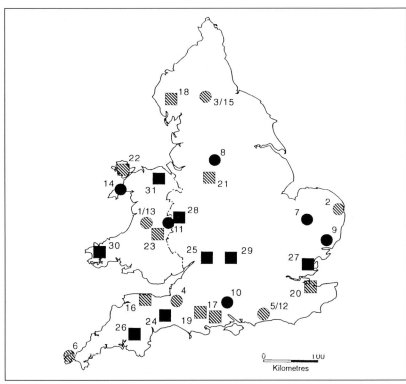

Date of Designation and Area (Ha.)

◎ **1987**

1.	Cambrian Mountains	72,800
2.	Norfolk Broads	29,870
3.	Pennine Dales	15,960
4.	Somerset Levels and Moors	26,970
5.	South Downs	26,643
6.	West Penwith	7,210

● **1988**

7.	Breckland	94,032
8.	North Peak	50,250
9.	Suffolk River Valleys	32,149
10.	Test Valley	2,690
11.	Clun 21,000	
12.	South Downs (Extension)	26,700
13.	Cambrian Mountains (Extension)	80,200
14.	Lleyn Peninsula	39,700

▧ **1992**

15.	Pennine Dales (Extension)	30,100

1993

16.	Exmoor	81,000
17.	Avon Valley	5,200
18.	Lake District	245,200
19.	South Wessex Downs	45,900
20.	North Kent Marshes	14,700
21.	South West Peak	33,900
22.	Ynys Môn	72,000
23.	Radnor	100,500

■ **1994**

24.	Blackdown Hills	39,300
25.	Cotswold Hills	84,700
26.	Dartmoor	100,800
27.	Essex Coast	27,000
28.	Shropshire Hills	38,500
29.	Upper Thames Tributaries	27,700
30.	Preseli	120,900
31.	Clwydian Range	28,000

that by the end of 1995 there were 22 ESAs in England covering 1,150,174 ha, about 10 per cent of all agricultural land. This process of expansion has been even more rapid in Wales, where the six ESAs extended to 519,800 ha by the end of 1995, about 30 per cent of agricultural land within the principality. The names, area and location of the ESAs in each of the four rounds of designations are shown in figure 14.1 below.

Although ESA policy is very much a national one, it involves the selection of areas for designation, which are then managed at the local level through a Project Officer, who plays an important role in the implementation of policy. The designation process is based on the recommendations made by the Ministers' consultees and involves the drawing of appropriate boundaries, the identification of features to be protected and the selection of the agricultural practices to be supported. Draft proposals are then published for consultation before the scheme for each ESA is finalised. Because each ESA is treated separately, with its boundary and management prescriptions specified by its own Statutory Instrument, they vary considerably, not only in size and characteristics, but also in terms of their objectives and the way in which these are to be achieved.

ESA policy is implemented by the use of voluntary management agreements by which farmers receive payment in return for following prescribed management practices. This is based on the power given to Ministers by the Agriculture Act 1986 to draw up a list of "agricultural practices, methods and operations ... which must be included in agreements" [sec 18(4)] and to specify the period which these agreements should cover and the rates of payment that should apply. In practice, lists of such management prescriptions are drawn up at the local level to reflect the unique circumstances of each ESA and to specify the management practices to be followed in some detail. Generally these prescriptions include both prohibitions on some agricultural activities and restrictions on others, while farmers may also agree to manage historic and other features in specified ways.

Objectives of ESA Policy

The broad objectives of ESA policy are clearly set down in the relevant British and European legislation, but the implementation of this policy has depended on the way in which these objectives have been interpreted by MAFF. It was always intended that ESAs would provide a mechanism by which agricultural support could be directed to farmers who agreed to farm in environmentally beneficial ways and this has influenced the way in which MAFF has conceptualised the landscapes to be included. In its explanatory leaflets for the farming community it defines and ESA "an area where traditional farming methods have helped to create an exceptionally attractive landscape and valuable habitats for wildlife" (MAFF, 1988, p1).

The logic of MAFF's approach is that ESA policy is aims to conserve a particular type of rural landscape, which may be described as the 'traditional agricultural landscape'. Such landscapes may also be important for the wildlife habitats they provide, but their defining character is the nature of the local agricultural system that created them and it is this system that should be taken into account in drawing boundaries. The effect of this, coupled with the fact that the designation of ESAs is restricted to land in agricultural use, is that the extent to which they can protect the built environment is also limited in another way. What this means is that, in theory at least, boundaries should be drawn tightly to include only those areas that are farmed in a traditional way, so that the villages and other settlements that often make a significant contribution to landscape character at the local level are normally excluded. Similarly the major archaeological sites and historic buildings which may be included within ESAs are usually covered by their own protective designations, while large estates and other areas of parkland of high amenity and landscape value included are usually subject to other forms of protection. This leads to the conclusion that the main role of ESAs is to protect what Meinig (1979) has called 'ordinary landscapes' in the countryside, which may be defined as areas largely comprised of features which individually may not have a particularly high historic or scenic value, but which collectively produce a landscape that is cherished.

The use of such a definition also raises questions about exactly what features of the built environment ESAs are intended to protect. Because MAFF has interpreted the purpose of ESA policy as being to protect areas whose environmental quality is dependent upon traditional methods of farming and land management (MAFF, 1993a), it is clear that its primary focus is on the preservation of particular kinds of landscape that are not only agricultural but also historic. As English Heritage pointed out in 1991, such landscapes comprise not only archaeological and built features but also "semi-natural features, such as historic woodland and hedgerows" (Fairclough, 1994). This point was also made by the Agricultural Development and Advisory Service (ADAS) in its advice to MAFF on monitoring in ESAs which argued that the concept of historic features "embraces the whole historic element in the countryside: the historic farm, field, wall or woodland in the man-made landscape. Thus all ESA countryside, however 'natural' in appearance is man-made, much of it being a product of past farming practices" (ADAS, 1992, p5). As far as the built environment is concerned, this means that attention should be mainly focused on traditional farm buildings of all kinds, together with stone walls and other traditionally-constructed boundaries.

In this respect, ESA policy is much more explicit than other similar policy instruments in recognising that such ordinary elements of the built environment are essential features of the countryside in terms of both landscape and historic values. This recognition derives from the authorization in the Agriculture Act 1986 to designate ESAs "to protect buildings or other objects of archaeological, architectural or historic interest", but it is the way in which this clause has been interpreted that is significant. The adoption of such a broad approach may also be regarded as part of the more general change of emphasis in countryside conservation policy, which had previously tended to focus on scenic quality and the habitat value of the land cover elements of the agricultural landscape. What seems to be happening is the adoption of a broader perspective in framing countryside policy, which is increasingly focusing on the management of the landscape as a whole rather than on its individual components. This more comprehensive approach is also reflected in MAFF's explicit recognition of the functional relationship between traditional farming methods and the wildlife, landscape or historic value of the countryside. Whether this is likely to lead to the more effective protection of the built environment depends upon the way in which ESA policy is implemented at the local level.

It is important to recognize here that the built environment comprises only one part of the complex of environmental resources that make up the countryside. In conceptual terms, the landscapes included within ESAs, like all agricultural areas, may be regarded as a combination of three groups of components, land cover, boundaries and buildings; habitats and wildlife are conventionally included under land cover, although both boundaries and buildings can also provide valuable habitats for some species. Because the traditional farming systems that create such landscapes produce locally-specific combinations of these components, the designation of ESAs involves two vital decisions. The first is the way in which the boundaries of individual ESAs are defined, for they should be drawn so as to include all land that plays a role in the local farming system. The second is the selection of the components within those boundaries at which management prescriptions are to be directed. The conservation of the built environment will be fully effective only if all the buildings and other cultural features that contribute to the value of the landscape are included. It is therefore necessary to examine both the definition of boundaries and the specification of management prescriptions for ESAs.

ESA Boundaries

It has already been suggested that one of the primary purposes of an ESA designation is to protect the landscape which is the product of a particular agricultural system and it might therefore be expected that boundaries would be drawn so as to include the whole of that system. In practice, however, the designation of ESA boundaries has not taken a systems-based approach. This is perhaps understandable in the case of lowland areas where the traditional systems of mixed farming were swept away during the post-war period and where only relict and isolated features of those systems remain. It may, indeed, be the most sensible approach where the remnants of traditional farming occupy only limited areas. Such an approach is clearly evident in the tight boundaries drawn around the floodplain pastures of the Suffolk River Valleys and Test Valley ESAs. In these cases the boundary does not cut across the local farming system because the system as a whole no longer exists and the main surviving parts are in the river valleys. In the uplands, however, the traditional farming system, with its distinctive upland profile, is still in place over quite extensive areas and this needs to be taken into account in the designation of boundaries.

In such areas, where the traditional farming system has been modified rather than replaced, the failure to take full account of this system in the drawing of ESA boundaries is less defensible. For example, Gaskell and Tanner (1991) and Webster and Felton (1993) have shown how the ESA boundary in the Pennine Dales cuts through a farming system that is still run largely on traditional lines. This has resulted in the exclusion of much of the common land and rough grazing allotments that occupy the upper valley sides and intervening moorland, even though they are an integral part of the local farming system. In such cases, making a management agreement with a farmer does not necessarily lead to the protection of the landscape as a whole, for environmental deterioration may continue to take place on those parts of the farm which lie outside the ESA. This is in addition to the fragmentary protection of the landscape that may arise because of the voluntary nature of participation in ESA management agreements.

ESA Management Prescriptions

The payments made to farmers who enter into ESA management agreements are based on a specified set of farming practices which they are obliged to follow. Such management prescriptions may be both positive and negative in that they prohibit or restrict some practices and encourage others. Payments may also be set at one or more levels or 'tiers of entry' in which higher rates are set for the adoption of more restrictive management regimes. Standard management prescriptions and levels of payment are set for each ESA, but may differ between areas because they are "tailored to suit the needs of each particular ESA" (MAFF, 1993a, p5). As a result, there was, from the beginning, a significant variation in the level of protection given to particular landscape components in different ESAs, even where this protection was clearly included as one of the purposes of the designation. It appears that this variation is more than just a reflection of varying pressures on particular components in different localities.

In order to examine the extent to which ESA designations have incorporated all the features that contribute to the character of the landscape, the management prescriptions specified for each of the 12 ESAs in England and Wales included in the first two rounds of designation were analyzed. This was done by using the Statutory Instruments issued for each ESA in 1986 and 1987, which form the legal basis for management agreements. Prescriptions were divided into the basic three groups of landscape component to which they refer, that is land cover, boundaries and buildings. They were then classified on the basis of their intended effect on the way in which farms are managed. Prescriptions were therefore divided into those which require traditional features to be managed in specified ways, those which prohibit or constrain particular types of management practice that may damage those features, and those which provide incentives for the restoration or re-creation of such features. The results of this analysis are set out in figures 14.2, 14.3 and 14.4 below. Figure 14.2 shows those prescriptions which required positive action from the farmer, figure 14.3 those which constrained farm management, and figure 14.4 those which were intended to lead to restoration or re-creation.

Figure 14.2 Prescriptions requiring active management from the farmer

ESA	Year Designated	Land Cover	Boundaries	Buildings
First Round				
The Broads	1986	Grassland, pond, and reedbed maintenance Grazing regime	Hedge maintenance	
Cambrian Mountains	1986	Grassland, pond and lake maintenance Exclusion of livestock from broad-leaved woodland		
Pennine Dales	1986	Grassland maintenance Grazing regime	Stockproof hedge and wall maintenance	Weatherproof field barn maintenance
Somerset Levels and Moors	1986	Grassland maintenance Graxing regime	Hedge, field gutter, and rhyne maintenance	
South Downs	1986	Grassland, dew pond and reedbed maintenance		Weatherproof field barn maintenance
West Penwith	1986	Grassland and pond maintenance Grazing regime	Maintain existing field pattern Stockproof wall and hedge maintenance Stream maintenance	Weatherproof traditional farm building maintenance
Second Round				
Breckland	1987	Grassland and pond maintenance Grazing regime	Hedge and ditch maintenance	
Clun (Previously Shropshire Borders)	1987	Grassland and pond maintenance	Hedge maintenance in accordance with programme agreed by Minister Maintenance of stream and riverbank vegetation	Weatherproof traditional farm building maintenance
Lleyn Penisular	1987	Grassland, pond and lake maintenance Grazing regime	Stockproof wall, hedge and bank maintenance Stream maintenance	
North Peak	1987	Grassland maintenance Grazing regime	Stockproof wall maintenance	Weatherproof traditional farm building maintenance
Suffolk River Valleys	1987	Grassland, pond and reedbed maintenance Grazing regime	Hedge maintenance Ditch and dyke maintenance	
Test Valley	1987	Grassland, pool, lake and reedbed maintenance Grazing regime	Stockproof hedge maintenance Stream and ditch maintenance	

Source: Statutory Instruments 1986 Nos. 2249, 2251, 2252, 2253, 2254, 2257; 1987 Nos. 2027, 2029, 2030, 2031, 2033, 2034.

Figure 14.3 Prescriptions constraining farm management

ESA	Land Cover	Boundaries	Buildings
First Round			
The Broads	Grassland improvement Grassland cropping Grazing regime		New construction
Cambrian Mountains	Grassland improvement Grassland cropping Grazing regime Retain broad-leaved woodland	Construction or removal of hedges, walls or fences	New construction
Pennine Dales	Grassland improvement Grassland cropping Grazing regime		New construction
Somerset Levels and Moors	Grassland improvement Grassland cropping Grazing regime		New construction
South Downs	Grassland improvement Grassland cropping Grazing regime		
West Penwith	Grassland improvement Grazing regime Removal of lynchets, boulders	Construction of permanent or temporary fencing Removal of walls, hedges and gate posts Widening of gateways	New construction
Second Round			
Breckland	Grassland improvement Grassland cropping Grazing regime Irrigation		New construction
Clun (Previously Shropshire Borders)	Grassland improvement Grassland cropping Grazing regime Retain wet areas, woodland and scrub Area of arable cultivation	Construction of new or temporary fencing	New construction
Lleyn Peninsular	Grassland improvement Grassland cropping Grazing regime Tree planting Retain broad-leaved trees and scrub	Retain field pattern Removal of hedges, walls, banks and gateposts Construction of fencing	New construction
North Peak	Grassland improvement Grassland cropping Grazing regime	Construction of fencing Written advice required from the Minister before field wall restoration	New construction
Suffolk River Valleys	Grassland improvement Grassland cropping Grazing regime	Ditch and Dyke water	New construction
Test Valley	Grassland improvement Grassland cropping Grazing regime Retain wet woodland in Fen habitats		New construction

Source: Statutory Instruments 1986 Nos. 2249, 2251, 2252, 2253, 2254, 2257; 1987 Nos. 2027, 2029, 2030, 2031, 2033, 2034.
Notes: grassland improvement includes constraints on cultivation, drainage, fertilisers, crop control chemicals.

Figure 14.4 Prescriptions which directly result in the creation or restoration of a traditional feature

ESA	Land Cover	Boundaries	Buildings
First Round			
The Broads			
Cambrian Mountains			
Pennine Dales			
Somerset Levels and Moors			
South Downs	Conversion of arable land to low intensity grassland		
West Penwith			
Second Round			
Breckland	Conversion of arable land to low intensity grassland		
Clun (Previously Shropshire Borders)			
Lleyn Peninsular			
North Peak	Regeneration of heather moorland		
Suffolk River Valleys	Conversion of arable land to low intensity grassland		
Test Valley			

Source: Statutory Instruments 1986 Nos. 2249, 2251, 2252, 2253, 2254, 2257; 1987 Nos. 2027, 2029, 2030, 2031, 2033, 2034.

Note: That is the direct creation or restoration as a result of a prescribed action. This is different from management prescriptions which it is hoped will indirectly lead to change (e.g. constraints on fertiliser use may result in greater florist diversity, the conversion of arable land into low intensity grassland will result in the establishment of low intensity grassland).

Management Prescriptions Relating to Buildings

These tables clearly demonstrate that the three main groups of landscape components were not treated equally and that all the early ESA schemes focused on the protection and enhancement of land-cover components, with management prescriptions affording rather less protection to vernacular boundaries and farm buildings. In seven of the 12 ESAs, traditional buildings were not included at all, which implies that they were not considered to be of sufficient landscape or historic importance to be designated in their own right. This suggests that the opportunity offered by the Agriculture Act 1986 to use the designation of ESAs to protect such buildings has not been fully exploited. In none of these ESAs was provision made for the restoration of buildings (figure 14.4), and even in the five where the maintenance of farm buildings was included in management prescriptions (figure 14.2), this did not necessarily mean that they would be afforded full protection. There were three main reasons for this, all of which stem from the specified criteria for inclusion in management agreements.

The first of these relates to the type of building. In two of these ESAs, the Pennine Dales and the South Downs, only field barns were specified for protection, so that other types of traditional buildings were excluded. In practice, this may be less serious than might appear at first sight, for in the Pennine Dales, at least, when it came to making agreements with farmers, MAFF took a broader view, and included all farmstead buildings which were traditionally constructed (MAFF, 1995). A more comprehensive approach was adopted in the other three ESAs, Clun, North Peak and West Penwith, where management prescriptions used the generic term 'traditional farm buildings'. The second reason concerns the structural condition of buildings. Farmers were required only to enter buildings that were in a weatherproof condition into management agreements, so that those which were far from derelict were excluded, even though they could be preserved intact with a little renovation. There was a similar problem with the management of field boundaries, where there was usually only an obligation to maintain traditional boundaries that were stockproof (figure 14.2).

The third factor which can limit the effectiveness of ESA designation in protecting the built environment revolves around the maintenance of farm buildings. Farmers entering tenanted land into agreements were only required to include those farm buildings for which they were responsible for maintenance. The Countryside Commission (1986) identified this as a problem at an early stage of ESA policy development, when it pointed out that some components of the traditional agricultural landscape, such as vernacular buildings, were often not in the control of the agricultural occupier of the land, and that this would mean that management prescriptions might be ineffective. This proved to be the case, for example, with regard to 'vernacular buildings' in the North Peak ESA, where less than one quarter of traditional farm buildings were covered by agreements (MAFF, 1993b). Similar problems were found in some other upland areas, like the Pennine Dales ESA, where a significant proportion of farms are rented from large estates (Gaskell and Tanner, 1991).

Management Prescriptions Relating to Land Cover and Boundaries

It has already been pointed out that the management prescriptions relating to boundaries, and especially land cover, were far more numerous than those relating to buildings, but there was a similar problem in that the inclusion of a component in a list of management prescriptions did not necessarily mean that it would be afforded full protection. This may be illustrated by comparing the prescriptions relating to the management of different types of land cover, which reveals considerable variation in the level of protection, both within and between ESAs. As figures 14.2 and 14.3 show, the emphasis in most of the ESAs was very much on the maintenance of low-intensity grazing regimes on different types of grassland, such as meadows, pasture and rough grazing. In general, the most detailed prescriptions concerned the management of grassland in terms of improvement, cropping and grazing regimes. For example, in the Pennine Dales ESA farmers were told exactly how their meadows should be managed, from the date of mowing to the amount of fertiliser that could be applied. Such precision was largely absent from the prescriptions relating to other types of land cover. Woodlands, for example, were given only the most cursory treatment in the Pennine Dales, where management agreements merely required that farmers should obtain written advice on the management of their woodland or scrub within two years of the start of their agreement (MAFF, 1987), but did not have to take notice of that advice. Woodlands therefore received less protection than meadows under the ESA scheme, even though the neglect of farm woodland has been an issue of concern since the 1970s in the Pennine Dales and elsewhere.

There was a similar situation in most other ESAs where management agreements also included a clause on obtaining woodland advice like that in the Pennine Dales, without any requirement to implement that advice. Only in the Cambrian Mountains ESA were farmers required to exclude livestock from their broad-leaved woodland, but even here there was no compulsion actively to manage the woodlands or to ensure that natural regeneration was able to take place. Similarly, farmers in the Clun, Lleyn Peninsula and Test Valley ESAs were required to retain various types of woodland on the land they entered into agreements but, again, there were no prescriptions requiring positive management or maintenance.

There was also significant variation between ESAs in the level of protection afforded to boundaries, with the main emphasis on the maintenance of stockproof hedges, banks and walls, together with water features in some wetland ESAs. In only five ESAs were there management prescriptions which prevented farmers from removing traditional boundaries or constructing new boundaries out of modern materials (figure 14.3). These restrictions were not, however, applied to all ESAs, which suggests that changes in such features were either not regarded as taking place on a significant scale or that they were not considered important in landscape terms. This is surprising in view of the evidence from surveys of landscape change which show the increasing replacement of traditionally-constructed boundaries by post and wire fencing in many areas (see for example, Barr *et al*, 1986; Countryside Commission, 1990). While this limited protection given to some land cover and boundary features is certainly not so obvious as it is in the case of the built environment, it again emphasises the way in which ESA policy is failing to protect the whole landscape.

Other Criticisms of Early ESA Policy

There are a number of other criticisms that may be levelled at the way in which ESA policy was implemented in the first two rounds of designations. It might be assumed, for example, that even where traditional farm buildings, together with some boundary and land cover elements, were not specifically identified as being in need of maintenance, they would be afforded at least some protection from damage or destruction as historic features. This turns on the definition of 'historic'. The advice which MAFF received from ADAS (1992) suggested that all buildings with roofs surviving from before 1900, or listed in County Council Sites and Monuments Records, should be regarded as features of historic interest. Similarly it was advised that all woodland and boundaries present on the First Edition Ordnance Survey County Series maps should included, although it was recognised that these were based on various survey dates and did not distinguish between 18th and 19th-century and earlier features.

There seems to have been some inconsistency in the extent to which this advice was followed, which has implications for the definition of 'historic' in landscape terms. For example, in the Suffolk River Valleys ESA only 17 historic buildings were identified and these consisted of medieval chapels and abbeys, post-medieval wind pumps and martello towers, while it was found that "virtually all field boundaries and all woodlands were recorded on the first edition 'County Series' maps. These included enclosure hedges and 18th-19th Century tree plantings which are not regarded as historic features." (MAFF, 1992 p17). In contrast to the Suffolk River Valleys, where enclosure after 1700 was not regarded as historic, the most notable features of historical interest identified in the Test Valley ESA were the remains of the old watermeadow systems, which date from the 18th century (MAFF, 1993c). Similarly, the late 19th-century shelter belts in the Breckland ESA were scheduled for preservation (MAFF, 1993d).

The underlying contradiction here is that, while the adoption of a components approach has meant that it could be claimed that each ESA designation reflected the unique environmental character of locality concerned, the reality was that the management prescriptions sought to protect only those features which were deemed to be of national importance, that is of significance beyond the locality concerned. This significance seems to be based more upon their perceived scenic and wildlife value than on their contribution to the landscape as a whole. An obvious example of this is seen in the Pennine Dales ESA where the perceived national importance of one feature, the field barn, meant that it was specifically identified for protection in the Statutory Instrument. It has already been suggested that in general landscape terms it would have been more appropriate to use the term 'traditional farm building' used in the Statutory Instruments designating other ESAs.

Other criticisms levelled at the first and second round ESAs include the suggestion that the way in which policy was implemented was far too cautious in terms of protecting the landscape, in particular, because the management prescriptions adopted were sufficient only to maintain the *status quo* and there was insufficient emphasis on the restoration or re-creation of traditional features (Potter 1988; Baldock *et al*, 1990). This is clearly demonstrated by figure 14.4, which shows that there were relatively few incentives to encourage positive management by farmers. The main emphasis in most ESAs seems to have been on the conversion of arable land to low-intensity grassland.

It has also been argued that over-restrictive management prescriptions in some ESAs have discouraged farmers from participating in the scheme. For example, Brotherton (1991) found that controls on meadow management in the Pennine Dales ESA were a disincentive for farmers who might have been expected to sign management agreements. He also suggested that payments had not been pitched at the right level to encourage participation. Similarly, Potter (1988) criticised the uniform payment approach adopted in some ESAs and pointed out that this fails to reward farmers for maintaining higher quality landscapes than the minimum required by the management prescriptions.

The Revision and Relaunch of First and Second Round ESAs

Management agreements in the first two rounds of ESAs ran only for five years and it was always intended that their effectiveness would be monitored with a view to modifying the way in which policy was implemented. Indeed, the Agriculture Act 1986 places an obligation upon

Ministers to keep under review "the effect on the area as a whole of the performance of the agreements" (sec. 8). In consultation with the Countryside Commission, the Nature Conservancy Council and English Heritage, MAFF therefore drew up its strategy for monitoring and evaluation. This comprised an 'environmental' element, which focused on the effect of ESA agreements on "the landscape, ecology and historic interest of the areas", and an 'economic and social' element which considered the costs of the scheme and its effects on farm businesses and farmers' attitudes (MAFF, 1989, p39). A similar monitoring strategy for Wales was drawn up by WOAD (1989).

The development of such a comprehensive monitoring programme reflected a recognition that, because the designation of ESAs represented a departure from the approach adopted in more traditional 'planning' environmental conservation schemes, there was bound to be a certain amount of experimentation in its implementation (Potter, 1988). As a result of the analysis of the information collected by this monitoring programme, all the first and second round ESAs had been evaluated, revised and relaunched by the end of 1993. This involved considerable fine tuning of the way in which ESA policy was implemented at the local level, both through the redefinition of boundaries and the modification of management prescriptions. For the purpose of this chapter, the review and evaluation procedure was important because it provided an opportunity for policy-makers to address the problems that had became apparent in the original scheme and to use the experience of the first five years, both to improve the management of existing ESAs and to inform the designation procedure of future ones. It is therefore important to consider the extent to which the initial weaknesses of ESA policy in conserving the built environment have been rectified.

Revision of Boundaries

As a result of this evaluation procedure, some ESAs had their boundaries extended in 1992. In the South Downs this involved only minor adjustments

(MAFF, 1991a), but two others had more substantial extensions, although these still did not seem to take into account the nature of the traditional farming system. In the Pennine Dales, for example, substantial enlargement was achieved simply by including the valley bottom hay meadows and pastures of adjacent dales within the designated area (MAFF, 1991b). What this meant, of course, was that the enlarged ESA did not include the whole of the traditional farming system within its boundaries, so that areas where environmental deterioration was occurring were still excluded (Gaskell and Tanner, 1991). Similarly, the relatively minor extension to the Norfolk Broads ESA involved only the addition of the flood plain areas of the upper reaches of the Rivers Waveney and Wensom, which had already undergone agricultural intensification (MAFF, 1991c). This rather limited approach has not been followed consistently in the establishment of new ESAs where the complete farming system has sometimes been designated. In Dartmoor, Exmoor and the Lake District, for example, the whole of the upland profile, from the valley-bottom meadows to the highland rough grazings, has been included.

Revised Management Prescriptions

The experience of the early ESA designations is reflected rather less in the extension of boundaries than it is in the revision of management prescriptions. These were now incorporated into 10-year management agreements, which were intended to bring more stability to the system. Two kinds of amendment were involved, the revision of existing prescriptions, sometimes involving additional tiers of payment, and the introduction of new prescriptions for additional components. As far as the built environment was concerned, the incorporation of new landscape components was rare. In the Lleyn Peninsula, for example, buildings were not included in the original management prescriptions, presumably because they were not recognised as an important component of the landscape that was at risk from agricultural change. In the revised management prescriptions, however, farmers in the Lleyn Peninsula, were given a specific responsibility to maintain traditional farm buildings that were in a weatherproof condition, even when unused (WOAD, 1994, p5). Nevertheless, the majority of changes in management prescriptions when the original ESAs were re-designated involved the fine-tuning and tightening up of prescriptions which were already in place.

This is clearly shown by figure 14.5, which summarises the changes in management prescriptions made when the first and second round ESAs were re-designated. The most striking feature of the table is that, just as in the original schemes, the revised prescriptions concentrate on the management of certain types of land cover, especially grassland. The management of low intensity grassland, in particular, continues to dominate management agreements, while the weaknesses in the prescriptions relating to woodland in the earlier designations have not been rectified. Another important change is that schemes have become more complicated as additional tiers of payment have introduced greater flexibility by compensating farmers for agreeing to follow more restrictive management prescriptions for particular types of land cover.

Various other changes were made in response to particular problems that had become apparent during the monitoring process. In some ESAs, farmers now had to enter all their eligible land into the scheme whereas previously this was not compulsory. This was intended to deal with the problem of 'halo intensification' identified by Webster and Felton (1993), which occurs when farm units have land or grazing rights both inside and outside the ESA. In such cases, farmers may decide to improve or intensify the use of immediately adjacent land to compensate for the loss of production on land covered by their ESA agreement. A particular problem here is what Webster and Felton term 'ecological overgrazing', which can damage or destroy moorland wildlife habitats. This problem was addressed in some ESAs where agreements now impose limits on stocking density. More important in terms of protecting the built environment was the introduction in a number of ESAs of tighter controls over the removal of traditional boundaries and the construction of modern fencing. One problem that was not dealt with

Figure 14.5 Major changes in management prescriptions brought about as a result of evaluation and revision of first and second round ESAs.

ESA	Land Cover	Boundaries	Buildings	Other changes
First Round				
The Broads	Grassland improvement Grassland cropping Grazing regime Tree planting Arable conversion Creation of grassland strips	Dyke maintenance and management plan		
Cambrian	Grassland improvement Grassland cropping Grazing regime Broad-leaved tree and sapling retention Woodland management and regeneration			
Pennine Dales	Grassland improvement Grassland cropping Grazing regime Tree planting Alternative grazing for managed woodland			
Somerset Levels and Moors	Grassland improvement Grassland cropping Grassland irrigation Grazing regime Tree planting	Maintenance of gates Constraints on new fencing		
South Downs	Grassland improvement Grassland cropping Grazing regime Tree planting Scrub management Conversion of temporary grassland	Ditch maintenance		
West Penwith	Tree planting			
Second Round				
Breckland	Grassland improvement Maintenance of reedbeds and sedgebeds Grazing regime Conversion of temporary grassland Bird nesting management Creation of wildlife strips and headlands	Ditch management		Written advice on features of historic or archqelogical interest Safe disposal of sheep dip
Clun (Previously Shropshire)	Grassland improvement Grassland cropping Grazing regime Tree planting Alternative grazing for managed woodland Conversion of land to less intensive use Conservation of headlands Constraints on earth movement	Retention of hedges, banks and walls Hedge and ditch miantenance Hedge restoration	Weatherproof farm building maintenance	Safe disposal of sheep

282

ESA	Land Cover	Boundaries	Buildings	Other changes
Second Round				
Lleyn Peninsular	Grassland improvement Grazing regime Wetland management Tree planting Woodland management Conversion of land to less intensive use	Field boundary restoration	Weatherproof traditional farm building maintenance	
North Peak	Restricted area of cultivated land Grassland cropping Grazing regime Heather regeneration Retain and manage ponds Tree planting Retain woodland and scrub Alternative grazing for managed woodland	Retention of walls, hedges and banks Constraints on temporary fencing Wall restoration		Management of archaeological features
Suffolk River Valleys	Grassland improvement Grazing regime Tree planting Conversion of arable or temporary grassland Water level management	Stockproof hedge maintenance Hedgerow restoration ditch and dyke maintenance programme has to be agreed with the Minister		Written advice on features of historic or archaelogical interest Safe disposal of sheep dip
Test Valley	Grassland improvement Grazing regime Maintenance of ponds and reedbeds Conversion of arable or temporary grassland	Maintenance of water courses Hedge maintenance		Safe disposal of sheep dip Management of archaeological features

Source: Statutory Instruments 1986 Nos. 2249, 2251, 2252, 2253, 2254, 2257; 1987 Nos. 2027, 2029, 2030, 2031, 2033, 2034; 1992 Nos. 51, 52, 53, 54, 55, 1359; 1993 Nos. 455, 456, 458, 459.

was the protection of farm buildings which are not the responsibility of the farmers occupying the land.

A major area of policy where there was a significant change of attitude during the re-designation process was in the encouragement of positive conservation works. There are now more incentives for the restoration and re-creation of landscape features in the revised management prescriptions, although the main emphasis remains on the encouragement of farmers to re-create wildlife habitats through the use of tiering to offer higher payment incentives. Beyond this, a number of ESAs, like the Cambrian Mountains and the North Peak, now have prescriptions requiring the compulsory restoration of such features and in some cases these extend to the built environment. For example, farmers in some ESAs may now be required to restore specified derelict boundaries on their land in return for additional payments, but it is the greater attention to buildings that seems to indicate a new attitude to the conservation of some elements of the built environment.

The greater emphasis on the maintenance of the cultural features of the landscape was also reflected in the introduction of Conservation Plans in 1992. These offer farmers an opportunity to receive additional payments for the restoration and re-creation of landscape features of all kinds, including elements of the built environment. Conservation plans are optional for farmers already participating in an ESA scheme, who are given an opportunity to receive additional payments for carrying out a schedule of approved works. The types of work that qualify for payment vary between ESAs and, like the normal ESA management prescriptions, the main emphasis is on the land cover elements of the landscape, but there is also a range of possible works relating to boundaries and buildings. For example, although farmers are not required to maintain buildings that are not in a weatherproof condition, they can be renovated under the terms of a conservation plan. Such renovation is likely to be limited by the high cost of the work and the budgetary constraints imposed on conservation plans. Improvement works relating to boundaries are also included for all these ESAs, apart from the Lleyn Peninsula. These mainly involve the restoration of hedges and drystone walls, but also include ditches and dykes, as well as the replacement of modern by vernacular materials.

Conclusions

Although the introduction of ESAs arose out of more general concerns about the impact of modern farming methods on the countryside, and upon wildlife habitats in particular, it is clear that they have considerable potential for the conservation of the built environment. Indeed, the protection of buildings and other historic features is one of the explicit aims of ESA policy, although this seems to have been given only limited weight when policy is implemented at the local level. The underlying reason for this is that the implementation of policy has been based upon a disaggregated approach to the rural landscape in which only some components are selected for protection, primarily on the basis of their role as wildlife habitats or perceived national importance in landscape terms. This, coupled with the use of different management prescriptions and tiers of payment, means that some components are afforded much higher levels of protection than others. In particular, disproportionate attention has been given to the management and maintenance of the land cover components of the landscape compared to the boundaries and buildings that comprise the built environment.

To some extent at least, this problem was recognised during the evaluation procedure for the first and second round ESAs and a number of modifications were made during their revision and re-launch, some of which were intended to give greater protection to buildings and boundaries. Nevertheless, the implementation of ESA policy remains flawed because of the continued emphasis on land cover and the inadequate attention given to the built environment. In part, this seems to stem from a failure to conceptualise the landscape as a whole, which is reflected in the continued exclusion of parts of the traditional farm system from some of the early ESAs. There is also the continuing problem of protecting features which are not under the control of the farmer, including woodlands and farm buildings. What is needed is not only for ESA boundaries to be drawn to encompass the whole of the local farming system but also for the built environment to be given similar status to land cover in the specification of management prescriptions. Without a more comprehensive approach, it is likely that the built environment will continue to decline as a result of passive neglect so that the long-term outcome of the designation of ESAs will be the preservation of a partial landscape.

References

Agricultural Development and Advisory Service (1992) *Guidelines for Monitoring Features of Historic Interest in Environmentally Sensitive Areas*, duplicated typescript.

Baldock, D (1985) Farm structures in Europe: the British initiative, *Ecos*, 6, 2-6.

Baldock, D, Cox, G, Lowe, P and Winter M (1990) Environmentally Sensitive Areas: incrementalism or reform?, *Journal of Rural Studies*, 6, 143-162

Barr, C, Benefied, C, Bunce, B, Ridsdale, H and Whittaker, M (1986) *Landscape Change in Britain*, Institute of Terrestrial Ecology, Huntingdon.

Brotherton, I (1991) What limits participation in ESAs?, *Journal of Environmental Management*, 32, 241-249.

Countryside Commission (1986) *Environmentally Sensitive Areas: Recommendations of the Countryside Commission to the Minister of Agriculture and the Secretary of State for Wales on the implementation of Article 19 of EC Regulation 797/85 in England and Wales*, CCD 8, Countryside Commission, Cheltenham.

Countryside Commission (1990) *Changes in Landscape Features in England and Wales 1947-1985*, CCD 44, Countryside Commission, Cheltenham.

Fairclough, G (1994) New landscapes of conservation, *English Heritage Conservation Bulletin*, 22, March, 16-17.

Gaskell P T and Tanner M F (1991) Agricultural change and Environmentally Sensitive Areas, *Geoforum*, 22, 81-90.

Meinig, D W (Ed) (1979) *The Interpretation of Ordinary Landscapes: Geographical Essays*, Oxford University Press, New York.

Ministry of Agriculture, Fisheries and Food (1987) *Pennine Dales ESA: Guidelines for Farmers*, PD/ESA/4, MAFF Publications, London.

Ministry of Agriculture, Fisheries and Food (1988) *North Peak Environmentally Sensitive Area: Explanatory Leaflet*, NP/ESA/1, MAFF Publications, London.

Ministry of Agriculture, Fisheries and Food (1989) *Environmentally Sensitive Areas*, HMSO, London.

Ministry of Agriculture, Fisheries and Food (1991a) *Review of the Environmentally Sensitive Areas Scheme. The South Downs: A Consultation Document*, MAFF, London.

Ministry of Agriculture, Fisheries and Food (1991b) *Review of the Environmentally Sensitive Areas Scheme. The Pennine Dales: A Consultation Document*, MAFF, London.

Ministry of Agriculture, Fisheries and Food (1991c) *Review of the Environmentally Sensitive Areas Scheme. The Norfolk Broads: A Consultation Document*, MAFF, London.

Ministry of Agriculture, Fisheries and Food (1992) *The Suffolk River Valleys Environmentally Sensitive Area: Report of Monitoring 1992*, MAFF, London.

Ministry of Agriculture, Fisheries and Food (1993a) *'Our Living Heritage': Environmentally Sensitive Areas*, MAFF Publications, London.

Ministry of Agriculture, Fisheries and Food (1993b), *The North Peak Environmentally Sensitive Area: Report of Monitring 1992*, MAFF, London.

Ministry of Agriculture, Fisheries and Food (1993c) *The Test Valley Environmentally Sensitive Area: Report of Monitoring 1992*, MAFF, London.

Ministry of Agriculture, Fisheries and Food (1993d) *Breckland Environmentally Sensitive Area: Report of Monitoring 1992,* MAFF, London.

Ministry of Agriculture, Fisheries and Food (1995) Regional Office, Northallerton, personal communication.

Parry, M L, Bruce, A and Harkness, C E (1982) *Surveys of Moorland and Roughland Change,* Series of 13 reports, Department of Geography, University of Birmingham.

Porchester, Lord (1977) *A Study of Exmoor,* HMSO, London.

Potter, C (1988) Environmentally Sensitive Areas in England and Wales: an experiment in countryside management, *Land Use Policy,* 6, 301-315.

Webster, S and Felton, M (1993) Targeting for nature conservation in agricultural policy, *Land Use Policy,* 10, 67-82.

Welsh Office Agricultural Department (1989) *Environmentally Sensitive Areas, Wales: First Report on Monitoring the Effects of the Designation of Environmentally Sensitive Areas,* WOAD, Cardiff.

Welsh Office Agricultural Department (1994) *Lleyn Peninsula Environmentally Sensitive Areas: Guidelines for Farmers,* WOAD, Cardiff.

Westmacott, R and Worthington, T (1974) *New Agricultural Landscapes,* Countryside Commission, Cheltenham.

Westmacott, R and Worthington, T (1984) *Agricultural Landscapes: A Second Look,* Countryside Commission, Cheltenham.